1830
IN FRANCE

Modern Scholarship on
European History

Henry A. Turner, Jr.
General Editor

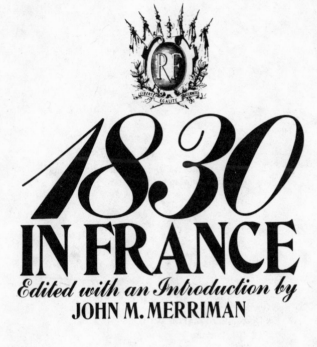

1830
IN FRANCE

Edited with an Introduction by
JOHN M. MERRIMAN

New Viewpoints
A Division of Franklin Watts
New York   London   1975

The author wishes to thank Tim Clifford and Patricia Otto, who helped prepare the index.

New Viewpoints
A Division of Franklin Watts
730 Fifth Avenue
New York, New York 10019

Library of Congress Cataloging in Publication Data

Main entry under title:

1830 in France.

  (Modern scholarship on European history)
  Bibliography: p.
  Includes index.
  1. France—History—July Revolution, 1830–
Addresses, essays, lectures. I. Merriman, John
M.
DC262.E35   944.06′3   75-15796
ISBN 0-531-05373-3
ISBN 0-531-05580-9 pbk.

CONTENTS

INTRODUCTION

It is perhaps not too early to suggest that there are "changing outlines" in the study of the French Revolution of 1830, as Peter Amann's influential bibliographical essay (1963) did for 1848.[1] For some time, the Revolution of 1830 was a historiographical exception in the study of French revolutions. There was little interest in new research, only in the varying interpretations of its political significance. The revolution was considered as a revolution of secondary importance, an echo between the revolutionary period initiated by 1789 and the revolution of 1848, or half-time in the *monarchie censitaire* of 1815–48. Histories written during the Empire and the Third Republic tended to tell more about the politics of those periods than about 1830.[2] Even the essays written on the occasion of the centenary in 1930 were disappointing.[3]

However, in the last ten years, there has been both a noticeable revival of interest in and new approaches to the Revolution of 1830 in France. David Pinkney is largely responsible for underlining the importance of 1830. His several articles have been recently followed by *The French Revolution of 1830* (1972).[4] This work is particularly valuable because it provides the best full narrative of the revolution and takes up the historical problem of what sort of political change took place in 1830.

The most important controversy in the standard interpretations of 1830 has been whether, or to what degree, the revolution was a "bourgeois revolution." The bourgeois revolution hypothesis began with contemporaries of the revolution. Louis Blanc, writing in *The History of Ten Years* (1830–1840), was certain that the bourgeoisie had stolen victory from "the people" in 1830.[5] Alexis de Tocqueville believed that the bourgeoisie's complete victory destroyed the Old Regime forever.[6] For Karl Marx, 1830 brought the wealthiest segment of the bourgeoisie to power, the "bankers, stock exchange kings, railway kings, owners of coal and ironworks and forests, a section of land proprietors that rallied around them—the so-called financial aristocracy. . . . the July Monarchy was nothing other than a joint stock company for the exploitation of French national wealth. . . ."[7] Such strange bedfellows as de Tocqueville and Marx have been joined by most other historians of the period in portraying the revolution as marking a victory of the bourgeoisie, or of its top layer, the *grande* or *haute bourgeoisie*. The descriptions and emphasis have varied. The notion of the "rising bourgeoisie" demanding and finally obtaining political power commensurate with its growing economic and social hegemony has been quite consistent: "One class lost its supremacy. Another replaced it . . . the upper bourgeoisie" (Jean Lhomme); "The Revolution of 1830 was above all the revolt of *commerçants*" (Régine Pérnoud); "Above all . . . the July Revolution was a triumph for the bourgeoisie and for the doctrine of popular sovereignty" (J. P. T. Bury); "The victory of July is not a stolen (*escamotée*) victory, it is indeed the success of the Parisian bourgeoisie. For the first time, the middle class felt the power of its forces. . . ." (Adeline Daumard).[8]

These interpretations therefore tend to view the political crisis of 1827–1830, which culminated with the Ordinances of July 26, as the struggle for power between two factions of France's political elite, one dominated by the nobles, the other by the bourgeoisie, inevitably bursting into revolution. (Félix Ponteil: "It is the struggle of bourgeois interests and feudal interests.")[9] The liberals who formed the majority of the famous "221" deputies, who voted a hostile reply to Charles X's speech opening the Chamber's session in March of 1827, are identified with the bourgeoisie. The Ordinances of July 26, 1830, whether or not they were a *coup d'état*[10] intended to maintain the political hegemony of the nobles, many of whom were more reactionary than even

Charles X against the aspirations of the bourgeoisie. The law indemnifying the émigrés, who left France and their property behind during the revolutionary era, and the statutes making sacrilege a capital offense attempted to turn the clock back to the Old Regime of the nobles and the Church.[11] The bourgeoisie thus found the path to political power blocked and therefore turned to defend the "essential liberties" of the Charter.

The various strains of the bourgeois victory thesis are reinforced by the usual interpretations of the July Monarchy, that regime Alfred Cobban damned as being "so lacking in principle that it could only be named by the month of its founding. . . ."[12] All of the tag-names of the July Monarchy identify it with the bourgeoisie: the *"juste milieu," "enrichissez-vous," "résistance,"* or "middlingness." And who, when thinking of the July Monarchy, does not recall to mind Daumier's marvelous characterizations of the self-satisfied bourgeois?

The bourgeois revolution thesis has been recently challenged by several historians. Guillaume de Bertier de Sauvigny denies that the revolution was the inevitable conclusion of an irreconcilable split in France's *pays légal.* Rather, he argues that the revolution was quite avoidable, the result of the miscalculations and blunders of weak leadership.[13] Bertier de Sauvigny, the foremost historian of the Restoration, is among several historians who suggest that the preoccupation with the causes and the significance of the revolution has obscured the real accomplishments of the Restoration, which restored France to its position of leadership in Europe through a vigorous and skillful foreign policy, provided a working experience in parliamentary government, and was an age of intellectual vitality.[14]

Other historians challenging the bourgeois revolution thesis have begun by questioning the usefulness of the terms "bourgeois" and "middle class" in historical analysis. Alfred Cobban, reacting to the vagueness and imprecision with which these categories are often bandied about, wrote, "The omnibus term 'middle class' is not merely unhelpful but can lead the student sadly into error and confusion." And indeed, most of the historians of 1830 have not been as precise as Adeline Daumard in her description of the Paris bourgeoisie in the first half of the nineteenth century.[15]

David Pinkney has gone further and attacked the whole "myth" of the "bourgeois revolution" of 1830.[16] In an article published in 1963, Pinkney demonstrated that the bourgeoisie did not, for the most part, compose the "crowd" in the Three Glorious Days of July 27–29, 1830.[17] The barricades were manned by artisans and skilled workers who had generalized economic grievances and who rebelled against obvious symbols of the Old Regime. The printers, the workers who would be the most affected by the Ordinances that further restricted freedom of the press, were instrumental in mobilizing early resistance. The appointment of Marshal Marmont, the betrayer of Napoleon, to command of the Paris troops, and the sight of the tricolor, symbol of Imperial glory, roused them to fight.

If the bourgeoisie did not "make" the revolution, was it "theirs" in the sense that they profited from it? Pinkney and some others say no. Pinkney argues that the Chamber of Deputies, elected under the widened franchise in 1831, did not represent the advent of businessmen into political prominence. Both the Chamber of 1829 and 1831 appear to be dominated by the bourgeoisie only if all non-nobles are lumped together.[18] Patrick Higonnet's study of the Chamber of Deputies indicates that there was not any significant change in the social composition of the deputies because of the revolution, even if all non-nobles are grouped together.[19] André-Jean Tudesq's study of *Les grands notables en France, 1840–49* supports Patrick and Trevor Higonnet's contention that the "July Monarchy was not a 'bourgeois' monarchy," at least in that wealth was still very much predominantly noble and in the land.[20] Pinkney further contends that the portrayal of new ministers as of the *haute bourgeoisie* (Laffitte and Périer particularly) is inaccurate. Nor, he says, is it fitting to picture Louis-Philippe as a bourgeois "citizen-King" (*affiche*) in 1830: *"Il n'est pas de distance entre Philippe et moi: il est roi-citoyen, je suis citoyen-roi."*[21] Louis-Philippe was thoroughly royal and aristocratic.[22]

If any social group profited from the revolution, Pinkney suggests that it was a large group of bureaucrats who found jobs because of the revolution, which ended the nobles' control of the administration.[23] Charles Pouthas has indicated the completeness of this turnover in administrative personnel.[24] Pinkney sees no major change in the social composition of the new officials, but stresses their imperial origins. He says, "Indeed the Revolution of 1830 may have come close to being a Bonapartist Revolution."[25]

The debate over the political victors of 1830 may go on, but its value seems exhausted. But this controversy has, at least, forced historians to re-think both the bourgeois revolution thesis and to re-examine what is meant by "bourgeois." However, the preoccupation with this controversy has limited our view of the significance of the French Revolution of 1830. With the Revolution of 1830, France entered its most turbulent period. The Paris-centered, political approaches to the Revolution of 1830 do not tell us about France in this crucial period as wider and more eclectic approaches will. Recent research has suggested a new emphasis in the study of 1830—a social emphasis.

This collection incorporates three central themes of recent scholarship on 1830: (1) the Revolution of 1830 was part of an economic and social crisis that lasted from 1827 to at least 1832; (2) the revolution was more than a Parisian phenomenon and reflected how France was changing economically and socially; and (3) the French Revolution of 1830 had a major impact on French society by dramatically increasing popular awareness of the "social question," that is, the miserable condition of the laboring poor. The revolution directly influenced the emergence of the laboring poor as an increasingly vocal and organized social force in France.

The elections of 1827 initiated a crucial political crisis; 1827 also marked the beginning of a severe economic crisis. Paul Gonnet noted the significance of the years 1827–1832 as a distinct period of economic and social crisis, characterized by the social conflicts lying beneath the surface political issues (which generally concerned only France's political elite).[26] Ernest Labrousse has directly linked economic crisis to the French revolutions, including that of 1830. Other interpretations suggest that "the political crisis of 1830 was bound to, in some way, burst open an abscess which lasted from the end of 1826."[27] Louis Chevalier, in his fascinating but controversial *Labouring and Dangerous Classes in Paris in the First-half of the Nineteenth Century*, has suggested that the demographic and social tension in Paris created a mood of rebellion that exploded in 1830.[28] Louis Girard calls this "a revolutionary climate."[29] Yet we know from David Pinkney's study of the Paris "crowd" that Chevalier's *malsain,* menacing figures which he found in crime statistics and lurking in contemporary novels, did not fight in the Revolution of 1830.[30] The task remains to balance and relate the economic, social, and political crises of 1827–1832. All of the essays in this collection deal, in one way or another, with this theme.

Secondly, one must look beyond Paris to understand the Revolution of 1830. Most studies have been limited to the events in Paris, a tendency that, until quite recently, also hindered our understanding of the Revolution of 1848 and the Second Republic. Studies of provincial France in 1830 have largely been restricted to evaluating the political opposition before and after the revolution, changes in official personnel, and describing the threats of pro-Bourbon uprisings in the south and particularly in the west.[31] Even the centenary essays treat the provinces from only the limited perspective of their reception of the revolution. The contention that "*La province, elle, ne bougea pas*" has been generally accepted.[32]

Yet we now know that provincial France was surging with social conflict in 1830. Several essential studies have related this social conflict to the economic and social transformation of France as a means of describing *how* France was changing. Maurice Agulhon's work on the department of the Var is a good example. His monumental *La République au village* notes that the "violent and collective" rebellions of peasant communities against the whole *fisc,* with its tax assessors and collectors, "reappeared at the time of the political and economic crisis that surrounded the revolution."[33] Agulhon finds the origins of the rural radicalism characteristic of the Second Republic in the collective revolt against the *fisc* and the rural bourgeoisie. Charles Tilly's wide studies of collective violence in nineteenth-century France have related changing patterns of collective violence to major shifts in French economy and society. The proliferation of popular disturbances in provincial France stemmed from increasing pressures against the traditional peasant communal organization exerted by the revenue-hungry state and the developing national economy.[34] We have seen that the hypothesis of a political victory of 1830 of the bourgeoisie can be challenged. Was social con-

6

flict in provincial France in this crucial period of 1830 indicative of the impact, as Albert Soboul has suggested, of rural capitalism and the rural bourgeoisie?[35] If the growing preeminence of the bourgeoisie in France was not evident in the events in Paris in 1830, or in the changes in the governing elite, was the new economy making faster inroads into provincial France than we have previously thought? Events in provincial France indicate that the Revolution of 1830 was not just a political struggle acted out in Paris.

Third, the revolution had a major impact on French society. François Guizot, who was the first Minister of Interior and became a symbol of the *"juste milieu"* of the July Monarchy, was correct when he reflected in 1831 that: "The July Revolution raised only political questions. . . . Society was by no means menaced. . . . What has happened since? Social questions have been raised."[36] Ironically, Bertier de Sauvigny is right when he laments that the revolution meant the end of social unity and peace in France.[37] Certainly the social question did not just magically appear with 1830. But after 1830, politics were never again really the unchallenged domain of the elite. The workers, whose role in 1830 is beyond debate, were thereafter a permanent and increasingly organized force in France. E. J. Hobsbawm describes the impact of 1830 in his *The Age of Revolution*:

> The revolutions of 1830 changed the situation entirely. As we have seen they were the first products of a very general period of acute and widespread economic and social unrest and rapidly quickening social change. Two chief results followed from this. The first was that mass politics and mass revolution on the 1789 model once again became possible. . . . The second result was that, with the progress of capitalism, "the people" and "the laboring poor"—i.e., the men who built the barricades—could be increasingly identified with the new industrial proletariat as "the working class." A proletarian-socialist revolutionary movement therefore came into existence.[38]

The experience of 1830 was an important catalyst for the development of workers' demands and organizations.[39] In addition, what Louis Girard calls a "rapid maturation" of ideas followed the revolution.[40] Utopian socialism, social catholicism, and both democratic and social republicanism developed rapidly after the revolution as workers and intellectuals searched for solutions to the social question. It is no wonder that the July Monarchy has been so often described as the regime of *résistance*. The resistance was real because the upheaval from below was real. The timing was directly related to the Revolution of 1830. This is the third theme of this collection of recent scholarship on 1830.

Included among the authors are several historians who have made major contributions to French social history and a number of younger scholars who have been influenced by their work. All of the authors bring their own particular field of expertise and interest to this collection. The seven essays are original and have been prepared specifically for this volume. We hope that they reflect the enthusiasm of the authors for social history and for current approaches to the study of modern France.

Notes

I would like to thank Henry A. Turner, the editor of the Modern Scholarship on European History series, for his help, and Suzanna Barrows for her invaluable eleventh-hour editorial assistance.

[1] Peter Amann, "The Changing Outlines of 1848," *American Historical Review*, 68, 4 (July 1962), pp. 938–953.

[2] For example, M. Duvergier de Hauranne, *Histoire du gouvernement parlementaire en France*, 10 vols. (Paris: Michel-Lévy Frères, 1857), and Paul Thureau-Dangin, *Histoire de la Monarchie de Juillet*, I (Paris: Plon, 1888).

[3] *Revue d'histoire moderne*, 6 (1831); and Comité Français des Sciences Historiques, *1830: Etudes sur les mouvements libéraux et nationaux de 1830* (Paris: Les Editions Rieder, 1932).

[4] David H. Pinkney, *The French Revolution of 1830* (Princeton, N.J.: Princeton University Press, 1972).

[5] Louis Blanc, *The History of Ten Years* (London: Chapman and Hall, 1844), p. 27.

[6] Alexis de Tocqueville, *Recollections* (Garden City, N.Y.: Doubleday, 1970), p. 4.

[7] Karl Marx, *The Class Struggles in France* (1848–1850) (New York: International Publishers, 1964), pp. 33–34, 36.

[8] Jean Lhomme, *La Grande bourgeoisie au pouvoir, 1830–1880* (Paris: Presses Universitaires de France, 1960), quoted from Lhomme, "Bourgeois Supremacy during the July Monarchy," in James Friguglietti and Emmett Kennedy, *The Shaping of Modern France* (London: Collier-MacMillan Ltd., 1969), p. 231; Régine Pérnoud, *Histoire de la bourgeoisie en France*, II (Les Temps Modernes) (Paris: Editions du Seuil, 1962), p. 417; J. P. T. Bury, *France, 1814–1940* (Philadelphia: University of Pennsylvania, 1949), p. 46; Adeline Daumard, *Les bourgeois de Paris au XIXᵉ siècle* (Paris: Flammarion, 1970), p. 304.

[9] Félix Ponteil, *L'éveil des nationalités et le mouvement libéral (1815–48)* (Paris: Presses Universitaires de France, 1960), p. 258.

[10] Vincent W. Beach, the biographer of Charles X, says that the Ordinances were not intended to be a *coup d'état*, in "Charles X, Polignac, and the Application of Article XIV of the Charter," in Friguglietti and Kennedy, *op. cit.*

[11] See, for example, Mary S. Hartman, "The Sacrilege Law of 1825 in France:

A Study in Anti-clericalism and Myth Making," *Journal of Modern History*, 4, 1 (March 1972), pp. 21–37.

[12] Alfred Cobban, *A History of Modern France*, II (Harmondsworth, England: Penguin Books, Ltd., 1970), p. 131.

[13] Guillaume de Bertier de Sauvigny, *The Bourbon Restoration* (Philadelphia: University of Pennsylvania Press, 1966).

[14] See also Frederick B. Artz, *France under the Bourbon Restoration* (New York: Russell and Russell, Inc., 1963) and Dominique Bagge, *Les Idées politiques en France sous la Restauration* (Paris: Presses Universitaires de France, 1952).

[15] Alfred Cobban, "The Middle Class in France, 1815–48," *French Historical Studies*, 5, 1 (Spring 1967), p. 52. Compare with Lenore O'Boyle, "The Middle Class in Western Europe, 1815–48," *American Historical Review*, 71, 3 (April 1966), pp. 826–845. Daumard, *op. cit.*

[16] David Pinkney, "The Myth of the French Revolution of 1830," in David H. Pinkney and Theodore Ropp, eds., *A Festschrift for Frederick B. Artz* (Durham, N.C.: Duke University Press, 1964), pp. 52–71.

[17] David H. Pinkney, "The Crowd in the French Revolution of 1830," *American Historical Review*, 70, 1 (October 1964), pp. 1–17. There is, however, some evidence of a "lockout" of workers by their bourgeois employers, upon the publication of the ordinances, noted by Paul Mantoux, "Patrons et ouvriers en juillet, 1830," *Revue d'histoire moderne et contemporaine*, III (1901–02), pp. 291–296.

[18] Pinkney, *The French Revolution of 1830, op cit.*, p. 280.

[19] Patrick-Bernard Higonnet, "La Composition de la Chambre des Députés de 1827 à 1831," *Revue Historique*, 239 (1968), pp. 351–379.

[20] André-Jean Tudesq. *Les grands notables en France, 1840–49*, (Paris: Presses Universitaires de France, 1964) 2 vols.; Patrick and Trevor B. Higonnet, "Class, Corruption and Politics in the French Chamber of Deputies, 1846–48," *French Historical Studies*, 5, 2 (Fall 1967), p. 207.

[21] Quoted in Louis Girard, *Le Libéralisme en France de 1814 à 1848: doctrine et mouvement* (Les Cours de Sorbonne) (Paris: Centre de Documentation Universitaire, n.d.), II, 1, p. 26.

[22] Pinkney, *The French Revolution of 1830, op cit.*, pp. 277–278.

[23] Nicholas Richardson, *The French Prefectoral Corps, 1814–30* (Cambridge, England: Cambridge University Press, 1966).

[24] Charles Pouthas, "La Réorganisation du Ministère de I'Intérieur et la reconstitution de l'administration préfectorale par Guizot en 1830," *Revue d'histoire moderne et contemporaine*, IX (Oct.–Dec. 1962), 241–264.

[25] Pinkney, *The French Revolution of 1830, op cit.*, p 293.

[26] Paul Gonnet, "Esquisse de la crise économique et sociale en France de 1827 à 1832," *Revue d'histoire économique et sociale*, 33 (1955), 249–292.

[27] Bertrand Gille, *La Banque et le crédit en France de 1815 à 1848* (Paris: Presses Universitaires de France, 1969), p. 322.

[28] Louis Chevalier, *Laboring Classes and Dangerous Classes in Paris During the First Half of the Nineteenth Century* (New York: Howard Fertig, 1973).

[29] Louis Girard, *Etude comparée des mouvements révolutionnaires en*

France en 1830, 1848 et 1870–71 (Les Cours de Sorbonne) (Paris: Gentre de Documentation Universitaire, 1960), p. 144.

[30] Pinkney, *The French Revolution of 1830, op. cit.,* pp. 252–273.

[31] Jean Vidalenc, "Les troubles de l'Ouest au début de la Monarchie de Juillet," *Actes du 89ᵉ Congrès National des Sociétés de Savantes* (1963), pp. 331–366.

[32] Jean Lucas-Dubreton, *La Restauration et la Monarchie de Juillet* (Paris: Librairie Hachette, 1926), p. 151.

[33] Maurice Agulhon, *La République au village* (Paris: Librairie Plon, 1970), p. 113.

[34] Charles Tilly, "The Changing Place of Collective Violence," in Melvin Richter, ed., *Essays in Theory and History* (Cambridge: Harvard University Press, 1964), pp. 139–164; "How Protest Modernized in France, 1845–55," in W. O. Aydelotte, A. G. Bogue, and R. W. Fogel, eds., *The Dimensions of Quantitative Research in History* (Princeton, N.J.: Princeton University Press, 1972), pp. 210–224; and "Food Supply and Public Order in Modern Europe," working paper of the Center for Research on Social Organization, University of Michigan, to appear as a chapter in Tilly, ed., *The Formation of National States in Western Europe* (forthcoming, 1975).

[35] Albert Soboul, "The French Rural Community in the 18th and 19th Centuries," *Past and Present*, 10 (November 1956), pp. 78–95, and, "La question paysanne en 1848," *La Pensée*, 18, 19, 20 (1948), pp. 55–66, 25–37, and 48–56.

[36] *Le Moniteur Universal*, December 22, 1831.

[37] Bertier de Sauvigny, *op. cit.*

[38] E. J. Hobsbawm, *The Age of Revolution, 1789–1848* (New York: Mentor Books, 1962), pp. 145–146.

[39] For example, Georges Bourgin's important article on the Paris workers after the revolution, "La crise ouvrière à Paris dans la seconde moitié de 1830," *Revue Historique*, 198 (July–September, 1947), pp. 203–214.

[40] Girard, *Etude comparée . . ., op. cit.*, p. 145.

11

CHRONOLOGY

1825

April   Dissolution of the Paris National Guard.
May   Coronation of Charles X at Reims; law makes sacrilege a capital offense.

1827

Beginning of an economic depression following a bad harvest.
Foundation of *Aide-toi, le ciel t'aidera* by Guizot and others.
October   Defeat of Turkish-Egyptian fleet at Navarino by a French-British-Russian naval force.
November   Villèle resigns as chief minister after elections.

1828

January   Ministry of Vicomte de Martignac named.

1829

January 3   *Le National* of Laffitte, Thiers, Mignet, and Carrel appears.
August 9   Ministry of Jules de Polignac named.
September 11   "Breton Association" for resistance to taxes publishes declaration in the *Journal de Commerce* opposing Polignac.

1830

Spring   Series of mysterious fires ravage western France.
March 2   Charles X's intransigent speech opens the Chamber of Deputies' session.

March 17 Chamber of Deputies' reply to King's message approved by vote of 221 to 181.

May 17 Chamber of Deputies dissolved.

July 5 Algiers falls to French forces.

July Elections increased the number of deputies in the opposition to 270.

July 26 Publication of the Ordinances in *Le Moniteur;* Chamber of Deputies dissolved; electorate reduced by about twenty-five thousand voters; new press restrictions; new elections set for September.

July 27 Crowds gather in Paris; Marshall Marmont named to command troops in Paris; meetings and deputies and journalists in Paris.

July 28 Barricades in Paris; fighting.

July 29 Most of Paris falls to the Paris crowd; army leaves city; crowd sacks the Archbishop's palace.

July 30 Poster favoring Louis-Philippe, Duc d'Orléans, appears in Paris; fighting between troops and townspeople in Nantes kills thirteen and wounds at least fifty.

July 31 Louis-Philippe meets with a delegation of deputies and accepts position as "lieutenant-general" of France.

August 2 Charles X abdicates in favor of his nephew, who was to become Henry V.

August 3 Enormous crowd leaves Paris to march on Rambouillet; Charles, his family and intendants leave for England via Cherbourg.

August 6 Bérard calls Louis-Philippe, Duc d'Orléans, to the throne on behalf of the Chamber of Deputies.

August 9 Louis-Philippe becomes "King of the French."

August 11 Ministry of August 11 formed, led by Laffitte, Périer, Guizot, and Dupin.

August and *September* Grain riots, tax rebellions, and forest disturbances in many areas of France; series of wage demands and strikes begin by Paris workers.

August 25 Revolution in Brussels.

October 17–19 Crowds of Parisians call for the death of the ministers of Charles X.

November 3 Chamber of Deputies includes 113 newly elected.

December 15–21 Trial of ministers of Charles X begins in Paris, while crowds call for death sentences.

1831

February 14 Anti-clerical riots last several days.

April 19 Voting qualification lowered from 300 to 200 francs taxes per year, increasing the franchise by about two times, to two hundred thousand.

November Uprising of the Lyon silk workers after strikers are fired upon by the National Guard.

1832

Foundation of the Society of the Rights of Man.

July Insurrection in Paris after funeral of General Lamarque.

1834

April Insurrection of the Lyon silk workers; uprising of the Society of the Rights of Man in Paris and massacre on the Rue Transnonain.

Edgar Leon Newman

What the Crowd Wanted in
the French Revolution of 1830

Primarily because of the work of David Pinkney we know that the Paris crowd of the "Three Glorious Days" of July 27–29, 1830, was dominated by artisans and skilled workers. Independent of the long debate as to who profited from the revolution, the question remains as to what this successful revolutionary crowd hoped to gain for themselves. The answer may perhaps be found in their own statements and in the proliferation of worker demands after the revolution. Edgar Newman finds that their immediate goals were practical. They were not yet republicans or socialists. "Liberty" had a different meaning for them than it had for the liberals of the bourgeoisie.

Edgar Newman teaches at New Mexico State University. He is particularly interested in republicanism during the Restoration. His "The Blouse and the Frock Coat: The Alliance of the Common People of Paris with the Liberal Leadership in the Middle Class during the Last Years of the Bourbon Restoration in France" appeared in the Journal of Modern History, *46, 7 (March 1974). A similar version of this article was presented as a paper at the American Historical Association meeting in New Orleans, 1972.*

About three weeks after the fighting in the French Revolution of 1830 had ended, a new correspondent appeared in the *Tocsin national,* which was described at the time as one of the six democratic newspapers published in Paris.[1] The new correspondent called himself "Pierre Laroze, mason," and he addressed his column "to his comrades, the workers at all levels and in all situations."[2] Using bad French and working-class colloquialisms, "Pierre" scolded his former comrades at the barricades for deserting the revolutionary cause so soon. "The idea of breaking [power]-looms and machinery could not have come to you by itself, it could not have entered into those bowling balls on top of your necks that understood the [Constitutional] Charter well enough so that you risked your lives rather than let it be destroyed. And now what you want to do is against the spirit of the very Charter that you defended so well." Machines, "Pierre" explained to his comrades, had made the clothes on their backs and the cheap copies of Voltaire and Rousseau ("take off your hat") that had taught them to love the Charter. And as for this business of wanting to have the foreign workers expelled, this was contrary to good sense: suppose the foreign countries turned around and expelled the Frenchmen working there! Clearly, agents of the fallen Bourbons must be misleading the people. But they could not mislead "Pierre Laroze," and "Pierre" concluded his column by saying: "I shall always shout, as we all shouted during the Three Days [of the 1830 Revolution] Long Live the Charter! Respect for property! Your friend, LAROZE."[3]

No doubt "Pierre Laroze, mason" was a fraud: he may have been invented by the journal's managing editor, Pierre-Martin Pawlowski, a chasseur in the National Guard who had not yet been disillusioned by the new Orléans Monarchy.[4] In any case, the article written in his name indicates how shocked the middle classes—even those on the political left—were that the workers should behave so badly and make such incomprehensible demands so soon after their great victory. After all, the working classes had been allied with the liberal leadership and the middle class for several years before the 1830 Revolution[5] and had picked up their slogans of Long Live the Charter! and Long Live Liberty! during the 1830 Revolution.[6]

After the revolution was over, about 76 percent of those who told the Commission of National Recompenses why they had fought said that they had fought "for liberty"; about 29 percent said they had fought for "the nation." (There is an overlap because about 12 percent said they had fought for both "liberty" and "the nation."[7]) And these statements, which are all written in the same hand in the archives and thus are subject to doubt, are corroborated by eyewitness reports of the revolution and its aftermath. Godefroy Cavaignac, a young republican who tried to make the people demand a democratic government after their victory, recalled that: "It was too hard to make the people, who had fought shouting *Long Live the Charter*! understand that their first act after their victory should be to take up arms to destroy it."[8] And Amand Bazard, another young republican, wrote that just after the fighting ended "we were going around the city and we assured ourselves that this time again, at least for the moment, the people would be content with fine liberal words."[9] Juste Olivier, a young Swiss student in Paris, recalled that the shout most often heard during the July Revolution was "Long Live the Charter!" (referring to the Constitutional Charter issued by Louis XVIII before his return to Paris in 1814), followed by "Long Live Liberty!" Far less often heard were "Long Live Napoleon II!" and "Long Live the Nation!"[10] Auguste Fabre, editor of the *Tribune*, the leading republican newspaper, noted that the people only shouted "Long Live the Charter! Long Live Liberty!" and seldom shouted "Long Live the Republic!"[11] In fact, on July 31, the crowd turned upon the republicans: they pulled down copies of the *Tribune* from the walls and attacked its offices, shouting that they were going to shoot the republicans.[12] Things were even worse in Lyon, where young Joseph Benoit was menaced by the crowd because he had shouted "Long Live the Republic!" while everyone else was shouting "Long Live the Charter!"[13] Republicans found that their efforts to make the revolution move left were futile;[14] the workers had been indoctrinated with the slogans and, superficially at least, the ideals of the constitutional monarchist liberals.

Thus the Paris crowd in the 1830 Revolution (and the crowds in the provinces as well) were above all else for liberty. But soon after the revolution ended it became apparent that the working-class revolutionaries understood the word "liberty" in a fashion far different from their constitutional liberal leaders. On July 29 a revolutionary crowd of five hundred to seven hundred, led by the printing workers, forced their way into the Royal Printing Workshop in Paris, beat the new mechanical presses with gunstocks and iron bars, and then, after putting the machines out of service, they left without doing any further damage.[15]

On August 14 the new Orléanist government appropriated 1,600 francs to repair the damaged mechanical presses, and the next day the Paris police reported that the printing workers had threatened to break them again.[16] On September 2 the printing workers went on strike,[17] mainly to back up their demand that the government buy up the mechanical presses under Article 10 of the Charter, which said: "The State may require the sacrifice of property on grounds of the legally established public interest, but only upon condition of a previously established indemnity."[18] And a pamphlet defending the workers' position stated, "the mechanical presses . . . [serve] only the interest of a few individuals and are contrary to true liberty."[19] They deprived the workers of their most precious liberty: the freedom to work in the trade for which they had been trained. Another of the printing workers' pamphlets concluded with a description of a crowd attacking and destroying a mechanical press with shouts of "Long live liberty!"[20] But Monsieur Duverger, director of the Royal Printing Workshop, told a delegation of printing workers that his business was entirely free to use labor-saving machines and that one could not attack this freedom of industry without doing considerable damage to society as a whole. The very act of forming a coalition, Duverger continued, was against the law.[21] Consequently, several of the printing workers, appointed by their comrades to their representative commission, were indicted and tried under Articles 415 and 416 of the Penal Code,[22] which forbade coalitions of workers and thus sought to guarantee the liberty of each individual employee to reach an independent agreement with his boss. (This might be called the liberty of the free fox in the free henhouse, with the employer as the fox.)

The month of tensions between the Paris printing workers on one hand and their employers and the government on the other indicated that the two sides were at opposite poles in their understanding of the meaning of the Charter and of "liberty." Meanwhile, other indications were coming in from the provinces of this great and—for the Orléans Monarchy—fatal misunderstanding of the meaning of liberty.

From Louviers (Eure) came the news that the workers had rioted and taken over the Hôtel de Ville on September 3, demanding that the government fix bread prices at a lower level and shouting: "Long live liberty! Long live the Charter! Give us bread!"[23] And in Mont de Marsan (Landes), the crowd had rioted on September 16 shouting, "No more taxes! Long live liberty!"[24]

The crowd, which had been surprisingly docile ever since the suppression of the Vendémaire uprising in October 1795, had suddenly come to life. Victorious in the July 1830 Revolution, they now spoke up for what they wanted and demanded the rights they believed they had won at the barricades. From their behavior in the first two years of the July Monarchy, it is possible to determine the nature of what the crowd wanted in the French Revolution of 1830.

In general, the same groups of people who had been most conspicuous at the barricades of July 27–29, 1830, were also the most vociferous in the years following the 1830 Revolution. During the 1830 Revolution, it was the skilled artisans, especially the building trades workers, who were most strongly represented among the combatants. Professor David Pinkney has calculated that the percentage of masons among the adult dead and wounded was more than double their proportion among the population of employed adult males in Paris, while that of the locksmiths was approximately double and that of the carpenters, joiners, and cabinetmakers at least a third larger.[25] The Comte de Rambuteau, a member of the Chamber of Deputies, was exaggerating only slightly when he wrote in his memoirs that more than half the combatants of July had been building workers.[26]

Professor Pinkney has ascribed the effectiveness of the revolutionary crowds in 1830 to the presence among them of many veterans of Napoleon's wars,[27] and doubtless this is true. But the crowds in the French Revolution of 1789 had been composed of similar groups of respectable artisanal workers,[28] and they had been just as effective against the regular army without the help of Bonaparte's old soldiers. Perhaps one explanation of the combat effectiveness of these skilled workers in 1789 and 1830—and of their forcefulness in voicing their demands after the 1830 Revolution ended—was their membership in the all-powerful *compagnonnages*.

The compagnonnages, those illegal but tolerated[29] nationwide organizations of skilled workers, were excellent schools of brotherhood, teamwork, and fighting. Agricol Perdiguier, a former *Compagnon du devoir de liberté*, recalled in his *Mémoires d'un compagnon* that "in each *compagnonnage*, we learned to handle the cane, the baton, to knock out our man promptly. The strongest, the bravest, the most terrifying were the most celebrated, the best liked of *compagnons. . . . compagnons* were warriors, *compagnonnages* were enemy armies, rival nationalities who dreamed only of crushing one another."[30]

Each compagnonnage held certain jobs for its own members and it defended its territory like a Mafia "family." The police of the Bourbon Restoration had their hands full trying to prevent and to control the frequent brawls between the various orders of compagnons,[31] especially those in the building trades, and, as we have seen, workers from these same trades would be most conspicuous in the 1830 Revolution. No doubt the discipline and pride acquired through the mysteries of the compagnonnages, combined with the skills learned in their street brawls, served the workers well at the barricades in 1830. Then, proud of the victory they had won, the workers began to coalesce: the various compagnonnages, who had once been blood enemies, now began to join hands and put forth demands not just for their own members but rather for their trade as a whole.[32] And since as early as 1823 Paris alone had had 160 artisanal societies, of which 132 could claim 11,143 members,[33] these skilled workers could become a formidable force once they stopped fighting one another.

After the 1830 Revolution, a rash of working-class strikes and demonstrations broke out in August and September as the printing workers,[34] the building trades workers,[35] and workers in other artisanal trades[36] began to demand that their employers and the new government give them what they thought they had won in the revolution. Most of their demands concerned bread-and-butter issues that had also been major demands of the workers during the Restoration. Most popular, of course, was the demand for that cure for all economic ills, higher pay,[37] which had also been the most frequent demand of the working classes during the Bourbon Restoration.[38] Naturally, the demands for higher pay were often accompanied by demands for a shorter workday,[39] just as they had been during the Bourbon Restoration,[40] as the artisans in the skilled trades moved toward the ideal of a ten-hour day. The indirect taxes, especially those which raised the price of wine, were frequent targets of working-class resistance,[41] just as they had been during the Bourbon Restoration[42] and the Empire.[43] Furthermore, the workers continued to insist that the state create more jobs and that employers keep their workshops open;[44] this was nothing new, because the workers had been asking for these things throughout the Bourbon Restoration.[45]

If more jobs were to be made available to Frenchmen, this meant that foreigners working in France would have to be expelled by their employers and by the state.[46] There had been scattered incidents of hostility toward foreign workers during the Bourbon Restoration,[47] especially in Alsace and in Paris, but the reappearance of the tricolored flag in July 1830 seemed to give a new urgency to French xenophobia. Hostility toward foreign workers was not always a sign of French nationalism, for frequently the term "foreign" was applied to workers from another province or district. But in most cases the desire to reserve French jobs for French workers was probably linked to French nationalism and to the workers' desire to avenge the humiliation of Waterloo and to win new glories for the tricolored flag and France.[48]

This issue of expelling foreign workers was one of the principal points of disagreement between the workers and the government during the first months after the July Revolution. On August 15, less than three weeks after the revolution ended, some workers of the faubourg Montmartre, most of them carriagemakers, marched to the Paris prefecture of police to ask that the French be prepared to expel the foreign workers as long as jobs were scarce. The prefect, the noted liberal Girod de l'Ain, replied that their request was inadmissible "not only in the interest of liberty . . . but also in the interest of French workers themselves, who could not renounce without inconvenience a competition that leads to emulation, that favors the spirit of perfection

and has so contributed to fortify French industry." Surely, Girod
de l'Ain continued, such an idea could not be their own, but
must have been "suggested to you by men avid for trouble, jealous of the liberty that you conquered with the price of your
blood, wanting . . . to reestablish the regime you destroyed with
your heroic courage," and he concluded by suggesting that
French workers should try to surpass the foreign workers by the
quality of their work rather than try to get them expelled.[49] The
Constitutionnel, the leading liberal newspaper, commented on
August 29 that requests to expel the foreign workers could only
be coming from "Carlists": that is, from supporters of the
deposed Bourbon monarch Charles X.[50] Similar requests in Paris
and in the provinces during the two months following the July
Revolution met only with the uncomprehending disbelief of the
newly installed officials of the Orléans Monarchý and the newspapers that supported them.

To the skilled workers and small tradesmen, however, the freedom to work at a dignified job was a part of the liberty they had
conquered at the barricades in July 1830. During the 1830 Revolution they had struck out not only at the Bourbons, the nobles,
and the priests, but also at those gathering forces of the
Industrial Revolution that threatened to deprive them of their
dignity and their status. As we have seen, the printing workers
had made it a part of their revolutionary activities to destroy the
steam-operated presses at the Royal Printing Workshops.[51] The
artisans and shopkeepers feared all manifestations of big business,
such as department stores,[52] and omnibuses,[53] but they feared the
new machines worst of all. As Adolphe Boyer, a compositor-
typographer, wrote in 1841: "Now, with the division of labor,
the new processes and the machines . . . workers of all professions
will soon be thrown into the class of unskilled day laborers. . . .
Because of the simplification in the means of production, a man
. . . is no more necessary than a child."[54]

But the artisans were proud men, conscious of their privileged
status as leaders of the working classes: the solemn ceremonies
and the decorum observed in their compagnonnages testified to
their sense of self-worth.[55] Thus, the machine that threatened to
throw the skilled printing worker, thread-spinner, tailor, or
sawyer out of work was seen as an enemy of the entire artisan

class. The protests against the machines, which had been fairly frequent during the Bourbon Restoration,[56] greatly increased in both frequency and intensity as the artisan classes demanded the destruction of machines as a right they had won in the 1830 Revolution.[57] As we have seen, the printing workers even demanded the destruction of machines as a right guaranteed by the Charter.[58]

Needless to say, the workers' efforts to make the Orléans Monarchy a Luddist regime met with only temporary success at best, and working-class Luddism would die down after a couple of years.[59] Nevertheless, even though the sight of the printing workers petitioning the Chamber of Deputies of the "Bourgeois Monarchy" to go out and break machines may seem ridiculous to us, the workers at the time trusted the men they called the "representatives of the nation" to grant their petition as their just reward for fighting in the revolution.[60] Just after the 1830 Revolution, these workers came forward and asked the government to make the changes that they had fought for and won.

In general, they wanted the government to protect their jobs and their standard of living. In addition to expelling the foreign workers and restricting the use of machines, they wanted the state to set fixed wages[61] and hours,[62] or at least to enforce the agreements they had made with their employers through collective bargaining. Similarly, they wanted the government to enforce fair work rules, such as the rules governing fines, job quotas, and job descriptions.[63] Naturally, there was a strong demand, just as there had been during the Bourbon Restoration,[64] for the government to lower the maximum price on bread;[65] with one exception, among the workers only the bakers demonstrated for "freedom of commerce" after the 1830 Revolution.[66] There was even some pressure for the government to reestablish the old Napoleonic "corporations," with their power to regulate the various trades.[67] As J. J. D. ***, a typographer, put it in a letter to the editor of *l'Artisan*, a journal written by and for workers, in October 1830, employers should not be allowed "to lower workers' salaries with impunity" or to fire them at will, nor should they be allowed to hire apprentices to do jobs usually reserved for qualified artisans.[68] Early in November 1833, the cobblers of the Union du Parfait Accord told their employers in a petition that they "no longer want to be the victims of the frightful competition that a great number of you carry on without limits."[69] And on September 9, 1834, an article in *le Peuple souverain* addressed to the barrel makers exclaimed: "Workers, what is killing you is competition!"[70]

The machines, the new methods of production and distribution, and the concentration of capital frightened the artisans. They were proud of their work and willing—even anxious—to compete among themselves,[71] but they looked to the government to protect them from competition that they considered unfair.

The conflicting goals of these artisan workers on the one hand and the officials of the new "Bourgeois Monarchy" on the other produced a strange dialogue of the deaf in which it soon became clear that neither side could understand the other. We have already seen the curious petition of the printing workers asking the Chamber of Deputies to forbid the use of mechanical presses in the name of liberty, the Charter, and the revolution, and we have seen the deputies' reply that the workers' request was contrary to the spirit of liberty, the Charter, and the revolution. Soon, the office of Girod de l'Ain, the prefect of police of Paris and the very incarnation of the spirit of liberalism, became the center of this dialogue of the deaf between the workers and the new regime. On August 22, 1830, at 10:00 A.M. the prefect reported, "four hundred joining workers came before me with a petition to raise their wages. I said that I would give it the greatest attention, even though it seemed contrary to their own interest and to the liberty that should be accorded to industry."[72] The next day, four hundred to five hundred locksmiths came to the Paris prefecture of police to ask for an ordinance reducing their workday from twelve to eleven hours. The bewildered Girod de l'Ain reported: "I said suitable things which they received well. I think," he added, "that they were put in motion by [Carlist] leaders who want disorders."[73] Then on August 24, "the masons, marching with a drum and tricolored flag, came to my prefecture to ask for a raise and a shorter workday. They left after I told them what seemed to satisfy them."[74] The incredulous prefect lamented: "There is real agitation among workers in all industry —they want things that are against their own interests. I am neglecting nothing to convince them." At the same time, he said, he was reinforcing National Guard posts throughout Paris and forming reserve detachments of the National Guard. "This," he said, "should stop the movement led by a few malcontents."[75]

On August 25, Girod de l'Ain posted an ordinance forbidding all meetings, demonstrations, and petitions "which, contrary to the principle of the freedom of industry, ask the government to intervene in fixing salaries or the length of workdays or the choice of workers."[76] General Lafayette, popular hero of the 1830 Revolution and now commandant of the National Guard, issued a similar ordinance that same day asking for an end to all meetings and all "attacks on the freedom of industry."[77]

These ordinances were, needless to say, dead letters—what Girod de l'Ain called the "mania of coalitions"[78] continued unabated, strikes continued to afflict the skilled trades, and petitions continued to flow in to the baffled Paris prefect of police.[79]

For the most part, these strikes and protests were not political in nature[80] for the simple reason that the workers trusted the government they had. The efforts of the democratic republican party to win the people's favor were utterly futile. The republican-organized uprising planned for August 6, 1830, whose purpose was to make the revolution move farther left, was a fiasco,[81] and the republican-backed attempt of five thousand to six thousand students to arouse the people in December 1830, after the announcement of the verdict of the hated ministers of Charles X, was also a failure.[82] The workers, it seems, were irritated by the ravings of these well-dressed young radical intellectuals; far from joining the students, the tanners, hatters, and other workers of the faubourg Saint Marcel complained bitterly about the gatherings of radical students around the Place du Panthéon.[83] Even the crowds at the trial of Sambuc, Danton, and the other young republican leaders in the spring of 1831 were docile, and workers helped the police to arrest troublemakers in the crowd who were trying to arouse the populace.[84] And when on July 14, 1831, one thousand, five hundred students appeared at the Place de la Bastille to plant trees of liberty, "a troup of workers" from the faubourg Saint Antoine armed with sticks, "indignant to see renewed so frequently disorders which deprive them of work," chased the students away and offered their services to the Paris prefect of police.[85] Two days earlier some workers had seen Garigues, a law student, tearing down notices of an official fête; they had grabbed him and brought him to the police post shouting: "He is a republican come to trouble us again; we ought to make an end to that rabble!"[86] And in Lyon on November 23, 1831, after the workers of that city had risen up two days earlier on November 21 and seized control of the Hôtel de Ville, the leaders of the working-class rebels chased out a delegation who had come to the Hôtel de Ville to set up a republican government. The rebel leaders made it clear that they were interested only in getting a fixed wage for themselves, and that they were "entirely devoted to Louis-Philippe and to constitutional liberty."[87] No wonder that in December 1831 the republican Society of the Friends of the People decided not to support the idea of universal suffrage for the time being. A democratic election now, they concluded, would more likely favor a Bonaparte or a Bourbon than themselves, and they decided that a republican dictatorship like that of Robespierre would give them their best chance to seize power.[88]

So the workers had no love for the ideals of republicanism and democracy—or for the men who preached them—at least until 1832.[89] But this did not mean that they were apolitical or that they were concerned only with bread-and-butter issues—they had their political loves and hates. For one thing, like their *sansculotte* fathers of the 1789 Revolution, they hated the priests, the nobles, and the royalists;[90] Girod de l'Ain need never have worried that the workers might be led astray by Carlist agents. For another thing, as we have seen, they loved liberty, even though liberty, which they associated with a good job and national independence, had a different meaning for them than it had for the liberal leaders of the new regime. And furthermore, the workers loved the nation, the army, and the legend of Napoleon—they loved these things more than money and often more than life itself. Many workers had shouted "Long live Napoleon II!" during the 1830 Revolution[91] and most of them would vote for Napoleon's nephew in 1848.[92] They had shouted Napoleon's praises, bought his likenesses, and sung Béranger's Bonapartist songs during the Restoration.[93] After the 1830 Revolution they supported the new regime, but they sang:

> Voilà the tricolor flag
> Europe trembles when it waves
> France took at the Tuileries
> Its revenge for Waterloo.[94]

To the working class, the tricolored flag was a military emblem; as one ex-soldier put it on July 28 during the Three Glorious Days of the 1830 Revolution, the tricolor "is the standard of Fleurus and Austerlitz, it knows the road to victory."[95] The common people hoped that the regime built on their victory in July would lead the *patrie* to glory and avenge Waterloo. By December 1830 the Paris police reported that the Paris workers were talking as if war were certain, "it seems even to be welcomed with pleasure."[96] By 1831, the people were shouting for French military intervention to help the revolutionaries in Belgium[97] and Poland.[98] Henri Gisquet, who showed considerable sensitivity to the sentiments of the common people during his term as Paris prefect of police from November 26, 1831, to September 10, 1836, reported on June 20, 1832, that the working classes wanted war and that the workers were saying that there could be no real peace until the enemies of 1815 had been defeated.[99] Bonapartism was the natural result of working-class nationalism; the people read or had read to them Victor Hugo's "Ode à la Colonne," which appeared and reappeared in the newspapers,[100] and in their *goguettes* they sang the songwriter Emile Debraux's "La Colonne," which thrilled its listeners with the refrain:

> Ah! How one is proud to be French
> When seeing the column.[101]

And they placed flowers, lithographs, and busts of Napoleon at the foot of the Vendome column,[102] where the Emperor's victories were immortalized in bronze, and throughout France they shouted *"Vive Napoléon!"*[103] Even the republicans, as we have seen, foresaw that a democratic election would be won not by them but by a Bonaparte. Like the most rabid football fans, the common people identified with the army and felt that its victories were their own.[104] They believed that a nation, like a compagnonnage, must make its place in the world and win its right to be proud through combat, and they admired military heroes. Robespierre, who had given them bread, was all but forgotten, but Napoleon, who had given them victory, was worshipped like a saint—he had given the people glory and work, and they felt he understood them. The crowd in the French Revolution of 1830 —and before and after that revolution—was, in a word, Bonapartist, with all that that implied. They were nationalists, militarists, and they worshipped military heroes on horseback like Bonaparte and, on a much, much lower level, Lafayette.

In conclusion, we can see that while the crowd in the 1830 Revolution was dependent on others to provide political leadership and to articulate national goals, they showed after the revolution that they had some well-formulated ideals. Proud of their skills and of their privileged position among the working classes, they had fought hard for the two things that set them apart: their status as artisans and their identity as Frenchmen. Thus, all of the things that the crowd wanted in the French Revolution of 1830—jobs, higher pay, a shorter workday, lower taxes, protection from foreign workers, from machines, and from the new large-scale methods of production and distribution, government regulation of prices, wages, and work rules, an end to the reign of the priests and nobles, and a new and aggressive national foreign policy—all of these things can be boiled down to two. What the crowd wanted in the French Revolution of 1830 were these two things: dignity for themselves and glory for France.

Notes

[1] This essay, which is an expanded and annotated version of a paper presented at the 1972 meeting of the American Historical Association, is based on research in France made possible by grants from the U.S. State Department under the Fulbright-Hays Act, from the National Endowment for the Humanities, and from the American Philosophical Society. I would like to thank Professors Charles Ledré, Ernest Labrousse, and David Pinkney for their help, and most of all I would like to express my deep appreciation to Professors Louis Gottschalk and Albert Soboul, who gave unstintingly of their time and advice.

[2] See L********, *Vote populaire, ou plaintes addressées aux quarante signataires de l'acte (de Schonen) du 30 juillet 1830* (Paris: chez l'auteur, August 5, 1830), p. 22. Bibliothèque nationale de Paris, Lb⁵⁰.76. The other five "democratic" newspapers, according to the author, were: *La Révolution, La Tribune des départements, La Voix du peuple, La Patriote, Le Moniteur des faubourgs.*

[3] *Le Tocsin national*, August 18, 1830.

[4] *Ibid.*, masthead.

[5] See Edgar Leon Newman, "The Blouse and the Frock Coat; The Alliance of the Common People of Paris with the Liberal Leadership and the Middle Class during the Last Years of the Bourbon Restoration in France," *Journal of Modern History*, 46, 7 (March 1974), pp. 27–29.

[6] Concerning Paris, see *ibid.* and, for instance, Comte d'Alton Shée, *Mes mémoires, 1826–1848* (Paris: Librairie internationale, 1869), I, p. 266; Lady Aylmer, "Un témoinage anglais sur les journées de juillet: souvenirs de Lady Aylmer," R. Anchel, ed., *Revue d'histoire moderne*, VI (1931), p. 357; Odilon Barrot, ms. papers in the Bibliothèque historique de la ville de Paris (hereafter BHVP), NA 153, Fol. 218, "Un ami de l'ordre" to Lafayette, July 30, 1830; Victor Crochon, "Souvenirs de la révolution de 1830," 3 vol. ms. in the BHVP, II, pp. 34, 87, 88, etc.; Herbert P Gambrell, "Three Letters on the Revolution of 1830," *Journal of Modern History*, I (1929), p. 597; Maréchal Marmont, *Mémoires du maréchal Marmont, duc de Raguse, de 1792 à 1841* (Paris: Perrotin, 1857); Henri Vienne, "Dix jours à Paris du dimanche 25 juillet au mardi 3 août 1830," *Mémoires de la société bourguignonne de géographie et d'histoire*, VIII (1892), p. 91; Guillaume, comte de Villeneuve-Bargemon, "Les journées de juillet 1830, la veille et le lendemain d'une révolution, souvenirs d'un témoin," *Le Correspondant*, Vol. 208 (1902), p. 220; Emmanuel

Viollet-le-duc, "Lettres," *Revue de Paris*, 69ᵉ année (1962), p. 98; Alexandre Dumas, *Mes mémoires*, Pierre Josserand, ed. (Paris: Gallimard, 1966), III, pp. 287, 291, 324, 329.

⁷ Archives Nationales (henceforth, AN), FᴵᴰIII 33–72, Records of the Commission of National Recompensation." The percentages are derived from a survey of 400 individual dossiers of the 3,708 dossiers of persons interviewed before June 10, 1831. Of the 400, 325, or 81%, made no mention of why they had fought. Of the remaining 75, 48 (64%) said they had fought for liberty, 9 (12%) for liberty and the *patrie*, 13 (17%) for the *patrie* alone, 2 (3%) for order, and there were three others.

⁸ Godefroy Cavaignac to Paul-Louis Duvergier de Hauranne, quoted in Paul-Louis Duvergier de Hauranne, *Histoire du gouvernement parlementaire en France 1789–1830*, (Paris: Michael Lévy frères, 1857–71), X, pp. 651–652.

⁹ Quoted in *Oeuvres de Saint-Simon et d'Enfantin* (Paris: Dentu, 1869), III, pp. 7–8.

¹⁰ Juste Olivier, *Paris en 1830, journal* (Paris: Mercure de France, 1951), p. 268. See also note 91 below.

¹¹ Auguste Fabre, *La Révolution de 1830 et le véritable parti republicain* (Paris: Thoisnier-Desplaces, 1833), I, pp. 130–135. But see Comtesse d'Agoult, *Mes souvenirs 1806–1833 par Daniel Stern* (Paris: Calmann-Lévy, 1877), p. 329; Barrès, p. 260; Dumas, III, p. 324; Jacques Laffitte, "Les trois glorieuses," *Revue des deux mondes*, 100ᵉ année (1930), p. 323, for evidence of republican sentiment in the crowd.

¹² Louis Blanc, *Histoire de dix ans* (Paris: Germer Baillière et cie., 1877), I, pp. 357–358; Fabre, I, pp. 153–154, 147; Dr. Adolphe-Robin Morhéry, *Réponse aux outrages et aux calumnies dirigés contre moi* (Paris: Auffray, 1832), pp. 57–58; Vienne, p. 104.

¹³ Joseph Benoit, *Confessions d'un prolétaire (Lyon, 1871)* (Paris: Les Editions sociales, 1968), pp. 33–34.

¹⁴ See also Fabre, I, 153–154, 147; Morhéry, pp. 57–58; Blanc, I, pp. 240, 357–358; Arthur L . . ., *Aux citoyens de la France* (Paris: Chez tous les marchands de nouveautés, August 2, 1830), p. 15; Crochon, II, pp. 695–696, 698; Vienne, p. 104; Viollet-le-duc, p. 101. See also the descriptions of the futile attempt of the republicans to arouse the Paris populace against the constitutional monarchy, such as S. Bérard, *Souvenirs historiques de la révolution de 1830* (Paris: Perrotin, 1834), pp. 264–265; Duvergier de Hauranne, X, pp. 600, 651–652; Francois Guizot, *Mémoires pour servir à l'histoire de mon temps* (Paris: Michel Lévy frères, 1859), II, pp. 30–33; Charles de Rémusat, *Mémoires de ma vie* (Paris: Plon, 1958) II, p. 360.

¹⁵ The best source for the activities of the printing workers in the summer of 1830 is Henry Jador, compositeur et homme de lettres, *Procès de la commission des ouvriers typographes, au bénéfice de la caisse de secours mutuels pour les typographes sans ouvrage* (Paris: Veuve Charles Bechet, 1830). See also *la Gazette des tribunaux*, September 15, 1830; Octave Festy, *Le Mouvement ouvrier au début de la monarchie de juillet (1830–1834)* (Paris: E. Cornély, 1908), pp. 29, 51–55; Jean-Pierre Aguet, *Les Grèves sous la monarchie de juillet (1830–1847)* (Geneva: E. Droz, 1954), pp. 3, 16–22; Paul

Chauvet, *Les Ouvriers du livre en France de 1789 à la constitution de la fédération du livre* (Paris: Marcel Rivière, 1956), pp. 95–101; AN, F⁷3884, Bulletins of police, Prefecture of the Seine, September 1, 2, 4, and 5, 1830.

[16] AN F⁷3884, Bulletins of Police, Prefecture of the Seine, Paris, August 15, 1830. See also *ibid.*, August 17, 1830, and *le Journal des débats*, September 25, 1830, which states that three of the four arrested on August 17 were judged guilty.

[17] AN F⁷3884, September 2, 1830, Paris.

[18] Quoted in John Hall Stewart, *The Restoration Era in France, 1814–1830* (Princeton, N.J.: Van Nostrand, 1968), p. 111.

[19] Un vieux typographe, victime de l'arbitraire, *Les justes alarmes de la classe ouvrière au sujet des mécaniques* (Paris: Chez les marchands des nouveautés, August 20, 1830, Year I of the Restoration of Liberty), p. 6.

[20] Henry Jador, compositeur, *Dialogue entre une presse mécanique et une presse à bras, recueilli et raconté par une vielle presse en bois* (Paris: n.p., 1830).

[21] See Duverger's deposition in *la Gazette des tribunaux*, September 15, 1830.

[22] The articles are quoted in Aguet, p. XIX. The trial is covered in *la Gazette des tribunaux*, September 15, 1830, and in Jador, *Procès de la commission des ouvriers*. The accused were all acquitted.

[23] AN, BB¹⁸1187, report of the procureur général to the Minister of Justice, September 3, 1830.

[24] *Ibid.*, September 16, 1830.

[25] David H. Pinkney, "The Crowd in the French Revolution of 1830," *American Historical Review*, LXX (1964), pp. 3–4; David H. Pinkney, *The French Revolution of 1830* (Princeton, N.J.: Princeton University Press, 1972), pp. 253–254. *Le Constitutionnel*, cited in Crochon, II, pp. 870–877, listed a total of 2,860 killed and wounded, including:

> 185 locksmiths (6.5% of the total; 18% of those whose professions are known)
> 158 cobblers (5.5%; 15.8%)
> 108 joiners and masons (3.8%; 10.8%)
> 70 coachmen (2.4%; 7%)
> 50 tailors (1.8%; 5%)
> 35 domestic servants (1.2%; 3.5%)
> 34 cabinetmakers (1.2%; 3.4%)
> 33 printing workers (1.2%; 3.3%)
> 31 clerks (1.1%; 3.1%)
> 29 carters (1%; 2.9%)
> 29 house painters (1%; 2.9%)
> 28 turners (0.9%; 2.8%)
> 25 day laborers (0.9%; 2.5%)
> 24 hatters (0.8%; 2.4%)
> 24 carpenters (0.8%; 2.4%)
> 22 saddlers (0.8%; 2.2%)

    20 bakers (0.7%; 2.0%)
    20 coiffeurs and wigmakers (0.7%; 2.0%)
    18 concièrges and porters (0.7%; 1.8%)
    17 navvies (0.6%; 1.7%)
    12 founders (0.4%; 1.2%)
    11 roofers (0.4%; 1.1%)
    10 weavers (0.3%; 1.0%)
    10 jewelers (0.3%; 1.0%)

Totals: 1,003   28.5%; 101%

By this account, building trades workers (locksmiths, joiners and masons, house painters, carpenters, and roofers), who made up roughly 10% of the Paris population (see *Recherches statistiques sur la ville de Paris et la département de la Seine,* Vols. V and VI [Paris: Imprimerie administrative de Paul Dupont, 1844–60], V, Tableaux 61 *bis,* 125, and 120, and VI, pp. 628–650), accounted for at least 12.5% of the dead and wounded in the 1830 Revolution in Paris and for more than 32% of the approximately 1,000 Parisian dead and wounded whose trades were known.

[26] Comte de Rambuteau, *Mémoirs,* translated from the French by J. C. Brogan (New York: Putnam, 1908), p. 293. See also Alfred de Vigny, *Journal d'un poète* (Paris: G. Charpentier, 1882), pp. 33, 18.

[27] Pinkney, "The Crowd," pp. 15–16. See also F. B.***, pp. 12, 17–18, 26.

[28] George Rudé, *The Crowd in the French Revolution* (London: Oxford University Press, 1959), pp. 176–190, 246–248.

[29] A note of the Third Bureau of the office of the Minister of the Interior, Paris, February 20, 1829 (AN F⁷9786), indicates government policy toward *compagnonnages.* Strikes or the "damnation" of any workshop by a *compagnonnage* should be prevented under articles 415 and 416 of the Penal Code, as should brawls: "That's all that justice can do." See also Georges Bourgin, "Législation et organisation administrative du travail sous la Restauration," in *Revue politique et parlementaire,* LXVI (October–December, 1910), p. 151.

[30] Agricol Perdguier, *Mémoires d'un compagnon* (Paris: Librairie de compagnonnage, 1964), p. 90. See also pp. 66–67, 73, 84, 89–92, 106, 124–127, 138-142, 149–152, 198, 204–205, 240–243, 282–286, and Jean Briquet, *Agricol Perdiguier, Compagnon du tour de France et représentant du peuple* (Paris: Marcel Rivière et cie., 1955).

[31] A selective sampling of the brawls among the compagnonnages during the latter part of the Restoration is: 1825, Paris (AN, F⁷ 3879, April 4, 1825). 1826, Paris (AN, F⁷ 3879, Gendarmerie, Paris, August 1 and 10, 1826); Lyon (Justin Godart, "Le compagnonnage à Lyon," *Revue d'histoire de Lyon,* II [1903], p. 445). 1827, Paris (AN, F⁷ 3883, Police Bulletins, June 9, 14, 20, 26, July 6, and October 23, 1827); Toulon (AN, F⁷ 9787, Toulon, August 11, 1827); and two brawls in Lyon (Godart, p. 445), 1829. Paris (AN, F⁷ 3883, Police Bulletins, January 5, 1829). 1830, Paris (AN F⁷ 3883, Police Bulletins, May 21 and June 16, 1830).

[32] See, for instance, AN, F⁷ 3884, Bulletin of September 9, 1830, and *La Tribune,* December 23, 1832.

[33] Bourgin, Georges and Hubert, *Les patrons, les ouvriers, et l'état. Le régime de l'industrie en France, de 1814 à 1830* (Paris: Picard, 1912–1941) II, p. IX. See also Anon., *Fédération de tous les ouvriers de France. Règlement de la corporation des ouvriers cordonniers* (Paris: Imprimerie Mie, 1833).

[34] See AN, F^7 3884, August 12, and September 1, 2, 3, and 4, and November 14, 1830, in Paris.

[35] For the AN, F^7 3884, August 22 and 23, September 17, 1830; *le Constitutionnel*, August 23 and September 27, 1830; *le Temps*, September 25, 1830; etc. For the masons and plaster workers, see relevant letters in AN F^7 3884.

[36] For the bakers, butchers, casting workers, chauffeurs of carriages for hire, coachmakers, farriers, leatherdressers, pastry workers, saddlers, tapestry workers, navvies, tinsmiths, tobacco workers, and welders, see AN, F^7 3884.

[37] See, for instance, letters relevant to demonstrations for higher wages which took place in Paris in 1830, by baker boys, masons, locksmiths, farriers, plaster workers, *coupeuses de poils* (the women who cut the rabbit fur to be used in hats), navvies, hatters, and tinsmiths, in AN, F^7 3884. Concerning demonstrations for higher pay in the provinces in 1830, see, for instance: the spinning workers in Roubaix (Nord) (AN, F^7 9787, August 10; AN, BB^{18} 1186, dossier 3957, procureur général, Douai, August 12); and the miners at Anzin, see Ernest Labrousse, *Le mouvement ouvrier et les théories sociales en France de 1815 à 1848* (Paris: Centre de documentation universitaire, "Les cours de Sorbonne" [1947]), p. 101.

[38] Concerning the wage demands of workers during the Bourbon Restoration, see, for instance, 1827, the Paris baker boys (AN, F^7 3881, June 19, 1827); the construction workers on the Pont Neuf, Paris (*ibid.*, August 8, 1827). 1830, the joiners in Lyon (AN, BB^{18} 1185, Lyon, June 30, 1830), and the joiners in Paris (*ibid.*, Paris, June 30, 1830).

[39] Some of the working-class movements in favor of a shorter workday that took place between August 1 and December 31, 1830, were: the Paris masons (AN, F^7 3884, Police Bulletins, Paris Prefect of Police, August 24, 1830); the Paris locksmiths and mechanics (*ibid.*, August 25 and 26; *le Globe*, August 26; *l'Artisan*, August 26; etc.; the plaster workers of Bagnolet and Montreuil, Paris (BHVP, Paris, Sept. 8; AN, F^7 3884, Sept. 8); and the Paris hatters (AN, F^7 3884, Oct. 1 and Nov. 3, 4, and 5, 1830).

[40] Some of the movements in favor of a shorter workday during the Bourbon Restoration were: 1821, the stoneworkers on the château of St. Ouen near Paris (AN, F^7 9787, Paris, February 11 and 14, 1821). 1822, the joiners in St. Denis near Paris (AN, F^7 3876, June 7, 1821). 1828, the workers in the department of the Rhône (AN, F^7 3797, no. 21, November 15, 1828).

[41] See Roger Price, "Popular Disturbances in the French Provinces after the July Revolution of 1830." *European Studies Review*, 1, 4 (1971), pp. 323–355; and, for example, AN, BB^{18} 1187 for disturbances in Mont de Marsan (Landes) and Brudes (Pyrénées Orientales), letters of September 13 and 18, 1830. See also Paul Gonnet, "Esquisse de la crise économique et sociale en France de 1827 à 1832," *Revue d'histoire économique et sociale*, 33 (1955), pp. 279–280.

[42] During the Bourbon Restoration the strongest resistance to indirect taxes

came during the period immediately following a change of regimes. For instance: 1814, Limoges (AN, F⁷ 3733, Bulletins of the General Police, April 14 and 28, 1814) and Bordeaux (*ibid.*, October 12). During the First Restoration of the Bourbons, 1814–1815, more than 60 percent of the people brought before justice were accused of violations related to the *droits réunis* (see AN, BB¹⁸ 943–50).

[43] See Bertier de Sauvigny, pp. 82–83.

[44] Some of the incidents in which the workers demanded work after the 1830 Revolution were: 1830, the women who marched on Rambouillet (Vienne, p. 116); the Paris saddlers and carriage workers, house painters, locksmiths, and some unemployed workers (AN, F⁷ 3884, August 15, 23, 25, and November 29, 1830). 1831, several hundred workers in Lyon on January 19 (Gonnet, p. 283); about two hundred tailors in Paris on January 20 (*le Moniteur*, January 21, 1831); several demonstrations on March 1, 2 and 8 in Paris (AN, F⁷ 12329, March 2 and 8, 1831); and many Paris workers on March 2 (AN, F⁷ 3885, March 2, 1831).

[45] Some of the incidents in which the workers demanded work in the latter years of the Bourbon Restoration were: 1828, a demonstration by eight hundred masons in Paris in January (Gonnet, p. 282). 1829, workers in the faubourg St. Antoine, Paris (AN, F⁷ 3883, January 7, 1829).

[46] Some incidents of French workers demanding that foreign workers be expelled, in addition to those mentioned in the text, are: about four hundred carriage and saddle workers in Paris (AN, F⁷ 12329, August 15, 1830); about sixty Paris workers, mostly saddlers (AN, F⁷ 3884, August 25, 1830; *la Tribune*, August 24, 1830); and the Paris smelting workers (AN, F⁷ 3884, August 25, 1830).

[47] A sampling of incidents of hostility toward foreign workers during the latter years of the Restoration: 1825, the Paris building trades workers tried to drive out Alsatian workers willing to work cheaper than the French (AN, F⁷ 3879, March 2, 10, 17, and 19, 1825); 1829, the masons of Montmorillon (Vienne) asked the mayor to forbid the employment of foreigners (Gonnet, p. 257).

[48] See below, pp. 28–30 and Courtheoux, pp. 130–131.

[49] AN, F⁷ 3884, Paris, August 15, 1830. See also *ibid.*, August 24, 1830, *le Constitutionnel*, August 16 and 17, 1830, and *le Journal des débats*, August 17, 1830.

[50] *Le Constitutionnel*, August 29, 1830.

[51] See above, p. 20.

[52] See *le Peuple*, January 25, 1829: "the competition of banker-retailers with their immense bazars is mortal for the shopkeeper."

[53] See, for instance, AN, F⁷ 3884, August 17, 1830, and *le Constitutionnel*, August 17, 1830; AN, F⁷ 12329, October 25, 1830; *ibid.*, January 7, 1831; Festy, p. 389.

[54] Quoted in Edouard Dolléans, *Histoire du mouvement ouvrier* 1830–1871 (Paris: Armand Colin, 1957), I, p. 14.

[55] See Perdiguier, pp. 97–98, 107–109, 139–141, 143–145, 159–167, 176–179, 228–235, 255–279, 288–291, 296–302, 310–312, 318–322, and also, for instance,

"Règle des compagnons chapeliers formant la Société de Paris," 1828, ms. in the Musée du compagnonnage, Tours.

[56] The following incidents are samples of working-class opposition to machines during the latter years of the Bourbon Restoration: 1828, there were protests against machines by the Paris women who cut rabbit fur (AN, F⁷ 3882, April 12, 1828), and the Carcassonne linen workers (Gonnet, p. 283). 1829, the Paris printing workers went on strike to protest the use of mechanical presses (AN, F⁷ 3883, January 12, 1829), and the steam-operated mills of Carcassonne were set on fire (Contamine, "La Révolution de 1830 à Metz," p. 116).

[57] Some instances of working-class opposition to the use of labor-saving machines after the 1830 Revolution, in addition to those given in the text, are: 1830, the Paris printing workers (BHVP, NA 153, Fol. 103, Duverger, commissioner at the Government Press to Lafayette, July 30; F⁷ 12329, August 15 and September 1; AN, F⁷ 3884, September 2, 4, 5, and 6, etc.); the Paris weavers and others broke looms August 17 (Villeneuve-Bargemon, pp. 228–229); the Paris tobacco workers destroyed the steam engines at the Royal Tobacco Works (ibid., September 15), and threatened them again on February 22, 1831 (AN, F⁷ 3885, February 22, 1831); on August 20, 1830, the Paris workers went to the Quai de l'horloge to destroy the bateau broyeur, a rock-smashing machine mounted on a boat (AN, F⁷ 12329, September 7, 1830).

[58] See above, p. 20.

[59] See Aguet, pp. 13 and 374.

[60] See le Constitutionnel, August 19, 1830 and le Globe, September 6, 1830.

[61] Some of the workers who asked that the government set fixed wages after the 1830 Revolution were: 400 Paris carpenters (AN, F⁷ 3884, August 22 and 23, 1830; le Constitutionnel, August 23); the carriage and bakery workers in the faubourg Montmartre and the Paris stonemasons and locksmiths (AN, F⁷ 12339, August 23–26, and September 17, 23, and 24, 1830); the Paris drapers (le Globe, September 12); the Paris blacksmiths (AN, F⁷ 12329, September 9, 10, etc.).

[62] Some instances in which the workers asked the government to set fixed hours after the 1830 Revolution were: on August 23, 400–500 Paris locksmiths and mechanics asked the Paris Prefect of Police to issue an ordinance reducing their workday by an hour (AN, F⁷ 3884, August 23); on August 27, about 300 Rouen workers involved in the spinning of thread asked the authorities to reduce their workday to 12 hours from 16–17 hours (AN, BB¹⁸ 1189, Rouen, September 7; BHVP, NA 154, Fols. 29–31); in August the Paris locksmiths petitioned the Prefect of the Seine for a one-hour reduction in their workday (BHVP, NA 154, Fols. 11–12, 62 and 64; AN, F⁷ 12329, September 17, 23, and 24, 1830); in September the Paris mason unsuccessfully petitioned the king to limit the number of hours in their workday (le Globe, September 14, 1830).

[63] Some of the occasions in which the workers asked that the government intervene to help establish fair work rules were: the textile workers in Rouen, August 27, 1830 (BHVP, NA 154, Fol. 29–31, Duhamel to Vinaigan, September 6, 1830); in October, the workers in the Paris piano and furniture shops

petitioned the Prefect of the Seine and asked him to stop the manufacturers from charging rent for tools that they once had given free to their workers (BHVP, NA 154, Fol. 107, Petition to the Prefect of the Seine, Paris, October 12, 1830).

[64] Some incidents in which the workers demanded that the government of the Bourbon Restoration fix a lower price for bread are cited in Gonnet, p. 250. See also James Rule and Charles Tilly, "Political Process in Revolutionary France 1830–32," in this volume, pp. 41–85.

[65] Some incidents in which the workers demanded that the government fix a lower price for bread after the 1830 Revolution were: August 17, the Paris National Guard had to be called out to stop a demonstration by 300–400 workers, who were trying to force the government to reduce the price of bread (AN, F^7 6777, August 17, 1830); on September 3, in Louviers (Eure), the crowd invaded the Hôtel de Ville and successfully demanded that the government lower the fixed price on bread to 24 sous for eight pounds (AN, BB^{18} 1187, September 3, 1830); for other incidents, see Roger Price, op. cit.; Gonnet, p. 250; see also Charles Tilly, "How Protest Modernized in France," in The Dimensions of Quantitative Research in History, William O. Aydelotte, Allan G. Bogue, and Robert William Fogel, eds. (Princeton: Princeton University Press, 1972), pp. 210–225.

[66] Le Journal des débats, August 17, 1830. (The butchers also asked for "freedom of commerce" [le Journal des débats, August 17, 1830]).

[67] Project de pétition des petits commerçants, des chefs d'atelier et des ouvriers de Nantes, quoted in Festy, pp. 140–141.

[68] J. J. D.***, Typographer, to l'Artisan in l'Artisan, October 10, 1830.

[69] Adresse de l'Union du parfait accord des ouvriers cordonniers et bottiers de la ville de Chalon-sur-Saône à leurs maîtres, in la Tribune, November 20 and December 4, 1833.

[70] Le Peuple souverain, September 9, 1834.

[71] See, for instance, Perdiguier, pp. 107–108 and 228–235.

[72] AN, F^7 3884, August 22, 1830.

[73] AN, F^7 3884, August 23, 1830.

[74] AN, F^7 3884, August 24, 1830.

[75] AN, F^7 3884, August 24, 1830.

[76] A copy of this poster may be found in AN, F^7 9787. See also la Gazette des tribunaux, August 28, 1830.

[77] Quoted in Festy, pp. 44–45.

[78] AN, F^7 3884, September 8, 1830.

[79] See, for instance, AN, F^7 3884, September 1, 2, 3, 4, 7, etc.

[80] See Girod de l'Ains's comment, AN, F^7 3884, October 25, 1830.

[81] See Edgar Leon Newman, "Republicanism During the Bourbon Restoration in France, 1814–1830," (Unpublished Ph.D. dissertation, University of Chicago, 1969) pp. 308–310; Louis Blanc, I, pp. 414–417, 428–430; Duvergier de Hauranne, X, p. 600, 654–655; and Duc d'Audiffret Pasquier, ed., Mémoires du chancelier Pasquier (Paris: Plon, 1894), VI, pp. 335–336, etc.

[82] AN, F^7 3884, December 26, 1830, Paris. See also BHVP, NA 154, Fols. 112–113, 117–134, etc.; AN, F^7 12329, September 13, October 1, 5, etc., and

especially December 19; *Moniteur*, December 21; Pasquier, VI, pp. 438–442; Broglie, IV, p. 84; and Castellane, II, pp. 384–388, 400.

[83] AN, F⁷ 3885, March 11–13, 1831, Paris; Castellane, II, 422 (March 15, 1831). No doubt some masters were lumped in with the workers by police, who called them all *"ouvriers."*

[84] AN, F⁷ 3884, April 14–16, 1831; Castellane, II, pp. 436–437 (April 15–17, 1831).

[85] See Henri Gisquet, *Mémoires de M. Gisquet, ancien préfet de police, écrits par lui-même* (Paris: Marchant, 1840), I, pp. 223–224, and Castellane, II, pp. 434–435 (July 14, 1831). The next day, the *National* and the *Tribune* accused the workers of being paid agents of the police.

[86] AN, F⁷ 3885, July 12, 1831.

[87] *Le Moniteur*, November 24, 1831.

[88] AN, F⁷ 3885, December 22, 1831.

[89] See Labrousse, p. 110, and Vienne, p. 104.

[90] A small sampling of the crowd's anticlerical activities: 1830, on July 29, the last of the Three Glorious Days of the 1830 Revolution, the Paris crowd sacked the archbishop's palace (BHVP, NA 153, Fol. 107, Paris, July 30, 1830. Gambrell, p. 602); in the afternoon of July 29, the Paris crown invaded the Jesuit house in Montrouge (Pinkney, *The French Revolution of 1830,* pp. 268–269); during the 1830 Revolution the Cardinal de Rohan was attacked by the Paris crowd at the Barrière de Vaugirard and had to be extricated by the mayor of Vaugirard (Duchesse de Gontaut, *Mémoires*, 1773–1836 [Paris: Plon, 1909], p. 361); on August 31, a large hostile crowd gathered at the Place Notre Dame in Paris when they heard a rumor that the Sisters of Charity were poisoning the wounded in the Hôtel Dieu hospital (AN, F⁷ 12329, September 1, 1830; AN, BB¹⁸ 1186, September 1, 1830).

Some incidents of anti-royalist sentiments were: 1830, during the July Revolution there were frequent shouts of "No more Bourbons!" (Dumas, III, pp. 301, 353) and some resistance to the Orléans family because they were Bourbons (*ibid.*, pp. 358–359, 402, 423); Barrot, I, p. 104; Castellane, II, p. 359; Pinkney, *The French Revolution of 1830,* pp. 267–268, and after the revolution some combatants said that they had fought because of their hostility to the Bourbons (AN, F¹ᴰ III 33–72; Pinkney, *The French Revolution of 1830,* p. 268).

[91] Comtesse d'Agoult, p. 329; Comte d'Alton-Shée, I, p. 53; Odilon Barrot, Mémoires (Paris: Perrotin, 1834), I, p. 114; Blanc, I, pp. 188 and 327; Hippolyte Bonnelier, *Mémorial de l'Hôtel de ville de Paris* (Paris: Houdaille, 1835), p. 75; Etienne Cabet, *La Révolution de 1830* (Paris: Deville, Cavelin et Pagnerre, 1833), pp. 120 and 143, etc.

[92] See Roger Price, *The Second French Republic, A Social History* (Ithaca, N.Y.: Cornell University Press, 1972), p. 222. See also A. Corbin, "Migrations temporaires et société rurale au XIXᵉ siècle: le cas du Limousin," *Revue historique*, No. 500 (October–December, 1971), pp. 331–333.

[93] The evidence of the workers' continuing devotion to Bonaparte during the Bourbon Restoration is overwhelming. A random survey of persons arrested for "seditious shouts" during the First Restoration shows that 100

percent of those shouts were Bonapartist in nature. (AN, BB[18] 943–950). See also the bulletins of the General Police (AN, F[7] 3733–3745, 3794–3796) and of the Paris Prefecture of Police (F[7] 3874–3884), and the reports of the Criminal Division of the Ministry of Justice (AN, BB[18] 943–1187). The Ministry of Justice noted 282 "seditious incidents" between 1825 and July 1830, of which 81 were pro-Napoleonic and two pro-republican, and the rest of indeterminable loyalty (Pinkney, *The French Revolution of 1830.* p. 49).

[94] Barthélemy and Méry, "La Tricolore," in *Chansons populaires* (Paris: Pagnère, 1834), pp. 27–29.

[95] Crochon, II, p. 229.

[96] AN, F[7] 12329, December 7, 1830.

[97] AN, F[7] 12329, June 8, 1831; AN, F[7] 3886, September 1, December 24, 25, 1832. See also the demands of the citizens of Metz that France march to the Rhine, made in September 1830 (Contamine, *Metz et la Moselle*, p. 364) and in 1831 (*ibid.*, pp. 372–374), and see *l'Atelier*, September, 1840.

[98] AN, F[7] 12329, March 9, 10, 11, June 8, 1831; AN, F[7] 3885, July 4, 1831; Castellane, p. 420.

[99] AN, F[7] 3886, June 20, 1832. See also Pasquier de Montesquoiu, late October 1814, quoted in Duc d'Audiffret-Pasquier, *Mémoires du Chancelier Pasquier* (Paris: Plon, 1894), III, pp. 46–47. Also see Vaulabelle's comment (VII, p. 325) that the people wanted an aggressive foreign policy.

[100] See, for instance, *l'Artisan* of October 17, 1830, which reprinted the poem from *le Globe* for the benefit of its working-class readership.

[101] Emile Debraux, "Le Colonne," quoted in Albert Cim, *Le Chansonnier Emile Debraux, roi de la goguette (1796–1831)*, (Paris: Flammarion, 1910), p. 68.

[102] AN, F[7] 3885, May 5, 10, 11, 12, 1831; AN, F[7] 6783, Commandant of the First Legion of Gendarmerie to the President of the Council of Ministers, Paris, May 6, 1832. May 5, 1831, was the tenth anniversary of Napoleon's death.

[103] The strong Bonapartist feelings expressed during the 1830 revolution have been cited above in note 93. An incident of Bonapartist activity after the 1830 revolution is: The police reported evidence of some Bonapartist sentiment during the disturbances in Paris that occurred during the trial of the former ministers of Charles X (AN, F[7] 12329, December 24, 1830).

[104] See, for instance, Richard Cobb, *The Police and the People, French Popular Protest, 1789–1820* (Oxford: Clarendon Press, 1970), pp. 118–171; Elizabeth L. Eisenstein, "The Evolution of the Jacobin Tradition in France, The Survival and Revival of the Ethos of 1793 Under the Bourbon and Orléanist Regimes," (Unpublished Ph.D. dissertation, Radcliffe College, 1952); and Newman, "Republicanism During the Bourbon Restoration in France."

James Rule and Charles Tilly

Political Process in Revolutionary France, 1830–1832

*The study of a particular revolution raises questions about the
revolutionary process in general. Crane Brinton's* The Anatomy
of Revolution *was an early comparative study of the phases of
revolution. Others boldly followed. James Rule and Charles Tilly
break with these various "natural history theories" of revolution
and offer a convincing and useful alternate model. The application of their model to the French Revolution of 1830 helps us
understand the full significance of the spread of collective conflict
in France after the Three Glorious Days. They suggest that this
change of power in Paris was not the culmination of the revolution, as the natural history theories would tell us, but rather that
it was the beginning of a larger conflict that was not ended until
1832.*

*James B. Rule teaches sociology at the State University of New
York, Stony Brook. He is the author of* Private Lives and Public
Surveillance *(London, 1973) and, with Charles Tilly,* Measuring
Political Upheaval *(Princeton, 1964). Charles Tilly teaches sociol-
ogy and history at the University of Michigan. E. H. Carr said,
"The more sociological history becomes, and the more historical
sociology becomes, the better for both." Charles Tilly's work has
influenced and indeed been "better for both." His numerous books
and articles range from* The Vendée *(New York, 1964) to* An
Urban World *(Boston, 1974),* The Formation of National States
in Western Europe *(Princeton, 1975), and, with Louise and
Richard Tilly,* The Rebellious Century *(Cambridge, Mass., 1975).*

*This is a revised, extended version of "1830 and the Unnatural
History of Revolution" (*Journal of Social Issues, *28 [1972], 49–76);
material from the earlier article is used by permission of the
Society for the Psychological Study of Social Issues.*

Every way of seeing the world, wrote Kenneth Burke, is also a way of not seeing it. By this he meant that no scholar could ever hope to glimpse the magnificent outlines of a historical landscape without first clearing away the tangled undergrowth of irrelevant, trivial, and tangential facts.

But how do we choose what to cull and what to save? More important, how can we reckon the effects of such decisions upon our own and others' views of historical events? When we think of 1830, for example, our memories ordinarily present us with some key images epitomizing what was significant in the revolutionary events. For most of us, the key image might be an event like the one at the Hôtel de Ville in Paris on July 31:

> Orléans, Lafayette, the municipal commissioners, and the deputies formed a semicircle facing the others, and Jean Viennet, deputy of the Hérault . . . read the proclamation of the Deputies. The promise of the "public liberties" at the end won applause and bravos, and when the Duke reaffirmed his commitment to them, Lafayette advanced and shook his hand warmly. . . . Someone produced a large tricolor flag, and, taking it, Lafayette and Orléans advanced together . . . to a balcony overlooking the Place de Grève. On seeing the pair, the crowd shouted, *"Vive Lafayette!"* but ignored his companion. The two men dramatically embraced, and from the crowd below came a thunderous response, *"Vive le Duc d'Orléans! Vive Lafayette!"*
>
> "The republican kiss of Lafayette," wrote Lamartine long after the event, "had made a king." (Pinkney 1972, pp. 161–162)

No one would doubt the importance of the event described here —the alliance between monarchy and republicanism, the enshrining of "public liberties," the popular acclaim of the new monarch. But seeing dramatic events as *the* essence of the revolution automatically diverts attention from other events and processes of great importance.

Like all moments at which national power hangs in the balance, the July Days have an intrinsic interest for historians. For analytic purposes, however, we want to push these outstanding events back into the crowd of conflicts that surrounded them. Let us consider all violent events of any size that occurred from 1830 to 1832. We have drawn accounts of these events from newspapers, archives, and historical works without regard to the historical importance subsequently ascribed to them—which in most cases has been negligible. Seen in the company of these poorly known conflicts, the street fighting in Paris during the period of July 27 to July 29 appears as one phase in a long succession of violent encounters. The following *précis* suggest the range:

March 24, 1830: In Merdrignac (Côtes-du-Nord), the Bishop tries to remove the sacred ornaments from a discontinued church, but is met by a crowd of 200, including many women. The curé has to flee the church, as the crowd throws back the gendarmes and seizes the keys to the church from the mayor. (*Journal des Débats,* 3/25/1830)

July 29–31, 1830: In Amiens (Somme), "the emotion of the events in Paris begins to spread in Amiens. The crowd fills the streets, alive with rumors. . . . Impromptu orators urge the people to revolt. In the evening, crowds of rioters break street lamps, tear down and trample the *fleur-de-lys* signs of the royal ministers, shouting 'Down with Charles X!' " (Calonne 1906: p. 180) A crowd breaks into a seminary, but decamps when troops arrive with the mayor at 2 A.M. On the 30th and 31st come demonstrations and public meetings, but substantial detachments of cavalry, gendarmes, and National Guards keep things under control. (Calonne 1906; *Le Moniteur,* 8/2/1830)

September 15, 1830: At Moissac (Tarn-et-Garonne), a "gang of subversives" including wine merchants and workers of all sorts marches on the house of the tax collector shouting, "Down with the excise taxes!" The official hands over all his papers and registers, which the crowd burns at once. From there, the "subversives" go to the official in charge of tobacco taxes, and burn *his* files. The crowd marches on two tax offices, breaks up some of the furniture, and burns files. National Guards, reinforced by "good citizens," make arrests and disperse the crowd. (Archives Nationales, BB[18] 1188)

May 2, 1831: In Bordeaux (Gironde), a crowd of longsawyers and other workers go to the Helfenberger sawmill and destroy the steam engine that supplies power there. After the National Guard clears them out, the workers assemble in a nearby square and warn other mill owners to dismantle their machines. Later, other groups of workers demonstrate elsewhere, chase employed workers off the job, and demand both the destruction of steam engines and the expulsion of outside workers from Bordeaux. National Guards and regular troops disperse them and make arrests. (*Le Constitutionnel,* 5/7/1831)

June 2, 1832: At the Saturday market of Auch (Gers), a crowd threatens certain merchants who "had the weakness to give in to that violence and sold their grain at 25 francs per hectoliter, instead of the 27 and 28 francs which was its true price and which they had asked at first." The day before, at nearby Fleurance, a similar crowd had roughed up merchants, dumped grain wagons, and split open sacks of grain. (*Le Constitutionnel,* 6/11/1832)

Most of these events are far removed from the dramatic actions the word "revolution" usually evokes. Except for the response to the July Days in Amiens, none of them is obviously connected to the national transfer of power. Yet in complex and indirect ways they were all connected to the revolutionary process and the changing structure of power. The whole pattern of these apparently trivial and non-revolutionary events changed as the revolution moved on. The change in pattern reflected and affected the development of the national struggle for power.

What we ordinarily identify as "the revolution" marked but one part of a process that took years to unfold. The process was by no means strictly violent. The actions involved ran the whole gamut from street fighting to solemn parliamentary debates and querulous back-room bargaining. But the acting out of these conflicts brought about changes in the character of violent political events over the period from 1830 to 1832. The revolutionary days represented a high-water mark of collective violence in France during this period, but by no means the only such peak. And the settings and parties accounting for these fluctuations shifted with the moving configurations of power in France during this time. How that happened is the central problem of this paper.

Natural Histories of Revolution

Nor were these changing power relationships in themselves extraordinary, in the sense of being atypical of French political life in other periods. Of course, 1830 is typically seen as extraordinary *eo ipso*—a revolutionary year, a clear-cut break in political continuity. But the fact of institutional discontinuity has often blinded analysts of revolution—and especially sociologists—to the fact that the contests, interests, and alignments in which the transfer is embedded are the stuff of "normal" political life.

Here we break with most versions of what sociologists have

termed "natural history theories" of revolution. The intuitive charm of viewing revolution as radically different from normal social process, as a unique species following a coherent, characteristic life history, has encouraged writer after writer to play Audubon to revolution, first outlining the life cycle and then offering a number of colorful illustrations. Few have thought to criticize the natural historical analogy itself, and no one has assembled the sort of systematic evidence it would actually take to test those few portions of the available natural histories of revolution that will survive logical scrutiny.

Sometimes the sense of revolution as a departure from normality appears frankly in the language of pathology. Crane Brinton's urbane *Anatomy of Revolution*, for example, likens the development of revolution to that of a fever:

> In the society during the generation or so before the outbreak of revolution, in the old regime, there will be found signs of the coming disturbances. . . . Then comes the time when the full symptoms disclose themselves, and when we can say the fever of revolution has begun. This works up . . . to a crisis, frequently accompanied by delirium, the rule of the most violent revolutionists, the Reign of Terror. After the crisis comes a period of convalescence, usually marked by a relapse or two. Finally, the fever is over, and the patient is himself again. (1952, pp. 17–18)

We do not propose to join the old game of Improving Brinton. (Simple rules, for those as yet uninitiated: *Inning One*: Scold Brinton for his prejudices; show no quarter. *Inning Two*: Promulgate a revised version of Brinton's stages of revolution. *Inning Three*: Congratulate yourself on your achievement.) Nor do we intend to argue with Briton's historical judgments about the specific revolutions he took up, although we disagree with a number of them. We hope instead (1) to identify some of the general reasons why natural historical models of revolution have worked badly and are not likely to work well, (2) to block out an alternative model of revolution emphasizing its continuities with routine contention for power, and (3) to check some of the implications of that model against a series of events for which an unusual store of information is available: the French Revolution of 1830.

The turmoils of the 1960s in Europe and America have stimulated a great deal of new work, some of it excellent, on revolution, political conflict, collective violence, and related processes. Among others, Bienen (1968), Gurr (1970), and Russell (1974) have recently provided wide-ranging reviews of the literature. We have ourselves turned our hands to criticism and synthesis elsewhere (e.g., Tilly and Rule 1965, Tilly 1964, 1974a). As a consequence, there is no need to review the literature as a whole here.

Two or three comments will suffice. First, almost all recent quantitative work on political conflict, including revolution, has consisted of comparisons of numerous countries at approximately the same point in time rather than of the analyses of change over time which would be appropriate for the direct testing of natural history hypotheses (e.g., Feierabend and Feierabend 1966, Gurr 1968 and 1970, and Rummel 1966; among the rare exceptions are Kirkham, Levy and Crotty 1970, and Russell 1974). Second, social historians have recently been doing rich, systematic work on the forms and personnel of revolution in Europe and America (e.g., Cobb 1961–63, C. S. L. Davies 1969, Hofstadter 1970, Rudé 1970, and Williams 1968); that work, which often does treat change over time, is more directly relevant to the verification of natural historical models, but has not so far been employed in that way. Third, recent social scientific investigations have tended to lump revolutions together with other forms of political conflict under such headings as "internal war," "instability," "civil violence," "aggressive behavior," or, simply, "violence." As a result, the proposal of distinct natural histories for revolution itself has become rarer than it used to be.

Natural history theorists differ from other students of the subject in that they depict revolution as the culmination of a series of qualitatively distinct developmental stages. The stages form a standard sequence; one stage cannot manifest itself until the preceding one is complete. In some cases the revolutionary change represents the end of the cycle, the final stage of revolutionary development. Elsewhere, there are stages subsequent to the revolution, through which the society moves from chaos back to normality. In general, the appearance of the first stages is a warning or a promise, but not a certain sign that the process will run its full course. What marks this variety of theorizing as natural history are the assertions (a) that the "late" developmental stages do not appear unless the "early" ones have already occurred and (b) that some sort of inner logic propels the process, so that in the absence of major obstacles it will work out a standard sequence. Revolutions, like butterflies, have natural histories.

The number and content of the stages varies widely from one natural historical scheme to another. In Brinton's analysis, the first stages are characterized by widespread governmental inefficiency in times of relative prosperity, followed by the desertion of the government by the intellectuals. Next comes an increasing popular revolutionary excitement leading to the overthrow of the old regime, followed by a period of rule by moderate revolutionary elements. Finally comes the "rule of terror and violence," followed by a return to something like the *status quo ante*.

Rex Hopper (1950), another natural history theorist, sees four stages:

—Preliminary Stage of Mass Excitement and Unrest
—Popular Stage of Crowd Excitement and Unrest
—Formal Stage of Formulation of Issues and the Formation of Publics
—Institutional Stage of Legalization and Societal Organization

Far more than Brinton's, Hopper's stages refer to the states of mind of the revolutionary and proto-revolutionary population, and thus sum up a social psychology of revolution.

These stage schemes have many variants, most of them interesting—and all of them inconclusive. We could review Sorokin's two stages, Meadows' three, or Edwards' five and gain insight from each one. But how would we choose among the bewildering array? Presumably by examining their internal consistency, their openness to verification or falsification, their value in reducing complex phenomena to their essentials, their fruitfulness as guides to empirical investigation, and the fit between the results of that investigation and the propositions derivable from the scheme.

On these grounds (as opposed to the moral, aesthetic, or heuristic grounds one might also invoke for the judgment of such schemes), the natural historical analyses of revolution stand up poorly. Their logic is peculiar, their vulnerability to proof slight, their reduction of complexity undoubted but misdirected, their fruitfulness for further investigation strikingly limited, and their fit with other facts than those from which they were originally inferred quite bad. Most of these shortcomings spring from the very *modus operandi* of natural history and are therefore unlikely to disappear. In particular, the practice of working backward from outcome to antecedent conditions provides little means (and no incentive) to determine how frequently, and under what circumstances, those same antecedent conditions exist without the development of revolution. That having reasoned backward we should present our conclusions forward, and in a dramaturgic framework, only aggravates the difficulty.

Let us concretize our complaints by scrutinizing three recent sophisticated statements, the first by James Davies, the second by Neil Smelser, the third by Chalmers Johnson. The first is marginal to natural history, the second contains a very special version of natural history in application to a wide range of phenomena which happen to include revolution, and the third belongs squarely in the great tradition of natural histories of revolution.

Davies on the J-Curve

Davies (1962) does not present a scheme of "stages" as such; he does argue that a set of qualitative developmental changes leads to revolutionary outbreaks and that the full manifestation of all these changes is necessary before a revolution can take place. The crux is that revolutions "are most likely to occur when a prolonged period of economic or social development is followed by a short period of sharp reversal" (1962, p. 4). "Economic or social development," in turn, is "opportunity to satisfy basic needs, which may range from merely physical . . . to social . . ." (1962, p. 8). Davies considers three successful revolutions—Dorr's Rebellion in early nineteenth-century Rhode Island, the Russian Revolution of 1917, and the Egyptian Revolutions of 1952—and finds evidence of such a pattern in each case. He refers to the pattern as the "J-curve" of need-satisfaction, with the progressive period of increasing satisfaction representing the shaft of the J and the sharp downturn its crook.

Davies' scheme requires some sort of weighting and summing of the satisfaction of "human needs" in a population. Unless that assessment of needs is both reasonably accurate and logically independent of the behavior it is supposed to explain, the scheme will provide no means of distinguishing situations with a high likelihood of revolution from other situations. In practice, Davies reads back from the fact of revolution to the presumably frustrated needs, and shifts the weights assigned to various needs along the way. The discussion of Dorr's Rebellion, for example, derives the long upward slope of the J-curve in terms of the increasing prosperity of the textile industry, on which a large segment of the population depended. But the final "sharp reversal" precipitating the violent outbreak turns out to be the frustration of demands for popular suffrage in the state. Davies employs similar mixtures of needs in the development of J-curves for other revolutions. The mixing and shifting of needs makes it easier to fashion a plausible fit of the theory to any particular revolution, but makes it correspondingly more difficult to draw any reliable inference to the cases of revolution (or, for that matter, of nonrevolution) not yet inspected.

The point is no quibble. On the contrary, it is crucial to the viability of Davies' argument. Davies appears to start with the accomplished fact of revolution, then cast about in the period immediately preceding it for evidence of the sharp reversal of some need within some part of the population, then look farther back for needs that have undergone increasing satisfaction for some length of time. Given that different groups in any population experience the satisfaction and frustration of various needs at various times, such a search has a high probability of success. It also has a high probability of identifying as crucial for revolution circumstances that are in fact commonplace outside of revolutions—as with the famed methodologist who achieved a hangover with bourbon and water, Scotch and water, not to mention rye and water, and therefore stopped drinking the offending substance: water.

So what of frustrations that do not result in revolution? Frustration is as endemic in social life as need-satisfactions are various. Needs, as Davies himself points out, are always elastic, expanding to encompass more than the individual enjoys at present; this disparity presumably always entails its degree of frustration. For Davies, the crucial difference is between what one might think of as routine frustration and a "sudden, sharp reversal" of need satisfaction. How one could actually hope to measure the degree of difference between these two states at any one point in time, let alone over a series of points for, say, the entire population of a country, is not clear. Davies suggests a public opinion poll but neglects to mention what kind of poll would do the job. Is there any way to determine that the "gap between what people want and what they get" (to use Davies' words) is "intolerable" other than by the fact that they refuse to tolerate it?

This desultory picking at the scabs of Davies' scheme finally uncovers the real wound underneath. The actor has absconded! *Who* endures the frustrations in question, *who* makes revolutions, and what connection do the two actors have with each other? The J-curve formulation offers us two equally absurd alternatives:

> (a) regardless of who experiences the frustration of crucial needs, the "society" as a whole responds to them, and beyond some threshold the response takes the form of revolution;
> (b) the individual's propensity to foment or join revolutionary action is directly proportional to his degree of frustration, hence revolutions occur when more than some critical number of individuals are performing revolutionary actions and hence revolutionaries come from the most frustrated segments of the population—frustrated, to be sure, by the special up-then-down process Davies describes.

On the surface, the second alternative will appear more plausible to those who do not find the reification of society attractive. Unfortunately, closer scrutiny reveals that the second alternative not only compounds the practical difficulties already discussed by requiring the weighting and summing of frustrations for each individual, or at least each group, within the population in question, but also treats as automatic precisely what is most problematic about the development of revolutions: the transition from uncoordinated individual dissatisfactions to collective assaults on the holders of power. Nor is it a simple matter of filling in the blanks. The fillings for these particular blanks will cause the essential structure of the J-curve hypothesis to explode through contradiction or to decay through qualification.

Smelser on Collective Behavior

Smelser's system (1963) is richer and more consistent than Davies'. It is thus more likely to survive quick criticism. Collective behavior, of course, includes the whole range of non-normative behavior carried on by groups of men; revolution constitutes a subtype of a more general case. Nevertheless, Smelser takes pains to show that all the various species of collective behavior exhibit the developmental stages that he posits.

The scheme specifies six conditions that must be met, or "activated," before an episode of collective behavior can take place (1962, pp. 15–17). They are (1) *structural conduciveness* or "permissiveness" of the social structure to a given form of collective behavior; (2) *structural strain*; (3) growth and spread of a *generalized belief*; (4) *precipitating factors*; (5) *mobilization* of participants for action; (6) the operation of *social control*. While all these elements may exist for varying lengths of time before the episode of collective behavior even begins, they enter the process itself in precisely that order. Hence the description of the scheme as a "value-added" analysis.

Smelser's is the most systematic and helpful discussion of the defining features of collective behavior we have. The natural historical portion of the work, however, rests on propositions that are obvious or that represent explications of the initial definition of collective behavior. This becomes apparent when one attempts to derive predictions of the form, locus, and intensity of collective behavior in different social settings from those propositions.

Structural conduciveness, for example, means simply that collective behavior, like any other behavior, is circumscribed by its social context. The occurrence of a financial panic, Smelser points out, presupposes the existence of a money economy. Structural strain, the second determinant, seems to mean any sort of shared dissatisfaction with the way the world works (although at times it shifts to the structural conditions—e.g., role-conflict—under which such shared dissatisfactions arise). Since collective behavior means some collective attempt to make the world work differently, Smelser has simply called our attention to the fact that people do not act together to contravene existing social patterns unless motivated to do so.

The same sort of observations applies to the third determinant, "growth and spread of a generalized belief," which appears to mean that people do not act concertedly unless they share some common perceptions of their social world. (Smelser's suggestion that such generalized beliefs include a symbolic representation of the strains to which the actors are responding, on the other hand, is more intriguing, less obvious, and more open to empirical verification.) The effect of any particular set of "precipitating factors" again appears only to lend itself to establishment after the fact and therefore to have no predictive value. The fifth determinant, "mobilization of participants for action," states the truism that only mobilized men act collectively. Like Davies' leap from dissatisfaction to rebellion, it leaves the essential questions untouched: where, when, and how does the mobilization actually occur?

The last determinant, the "operation of social control," does not run parallel to the first five. It is unclear why the workings of social control should affect collective behavior only after people are mobilized for action; Smelser himself seems to include the effects of social control among the conditions of structural conduciveness, his first determinant. If we drop the idea of sequence, however, we are left with the observation that others resist collective behavior and the assertion that the interaction between the resistance and the collective behavior produces a new equilibrium. The first enters into the practical definition of collective behavior, since without resistance we would never detect its occurrence; the second is merely a conceptual convenience not open to proof, an artifact of the observer's willingness to mark a beginning and an end to any particular instance of collective deviation from expected behavior.

In short, Smelser's scheme of stages turns out to be the careful explication of a definition—quite a useful definition, but a definition nonetheless. This disappointing result comes from the characteristic *modus operandi* of sociological natural history: starting with the identification of the "species" and working backward to identify its necessary antecedents. The result is the identification of stages in the development of the species that are either present by definition or common in situations that do not produce the species. The actual work of explanation only begins at that point.

Johnson on Revolutionary Change

Chalmers Johnson's *Revolutionary Change* (1968) exhibits most of the same difficulties. Like Davies and Smelser, Johnson views the life cycle of revolution as a homeostatic process, in which the early stages of growing disequilibration lead to the climactic events of the change of regime itself, to be followed by re-equilibrating processes which bring the society back to its accustomed balance. Like Smelser, Johnson defines the main condition of normality in terms of value-integration and portrays the first condition of susceptibility to revolution as the failure of synchronization between values and realities. In particular, Johnson sees that failure as manifesting itself in the population's withdrawal of moral authority from the government. He sees three clusters of causes of revolution:

> First, there are the pressures created by a disequilibrated social system—a society which is changing and which is in need of further change if it is to continue to exist. Of all the characteristics of the disequilibrated system, the one that contributes most directly to a revolution is *power deflation*—the fact that during a period of change the integration of a system depends increasingly upon the maintenance and deployment of force by the occupants of the formal authority statuses. The second cluster of necessary causes revolves around the quality of the purposeful change being undertaken while a system is disequilibrated. This quality depends upon the abilities of the legitimate leaders. If they are unable to develop policies which will maintain the confidence of nondeviant actors in the system and its capacity to move toward resynchronization, a *loss of authority* will ensue. Such a loss means that the use of force by the elite is no longer considered legitimate, although it does not necessarily mean a revolution will occur at once. . . .
>
> The final, or sufficient, cause of a revolution is some ingredient, usually contributed by fortune, which deprives the elite of its chief weapon for enforcing social behavior (e.g., an army mutiny), or which leads a group of revolutionaries to *believe* that they have the means to deprive the elite of its weapons of coercion. (1968, p. 91)

Johnson then attempts to link these very general phenomena to individual behavior through the sequence: rapid change, systematic disequilibrium, overtaxing of existing means of homeostatic and purposive response to change, panic-anxiety-shame-guilt-depression, etc., formation of movements of protest. True to his predecessors, he proposes the suicide rate as a prime index of disequilibrium.

The resemblances to Davies' and, especially, to Smelser's arguments are striking. The drawbacks are similar. To the extent that "failed synchronization between values and realities" can be identified at all independently of the revolutionary behavior it is supposed to predict, the evidence that it differentiates revolutionary settings from others is in extremely short supply. That failure is the general condition of mankind. Similarly, it is true by definition that power deflates and legitimate leaders lose authority during revolutions, but nothing in the evidence known to us indicates that the deflations and loss necessarily *precede* revolutions or, conversely, that their occurrence predicts to revolution. (One could, if willing to work within this conceptual framework, manufacture a plausible case that despite the disagreeable resistance of Parliament, Charles I's power was *in*flating up to shortly before the outbreak of the Civil War in 1642; it is even easier to point out how regularly terror quells dissent.) Only the process of moving backward from the fact of revolution to its presumed standard features makes it so easy to arrive at such helpless propositions.

Again we face the Case of the Absconded Actor. The ideas of power deflation and loss of authority treat generalized inabilities of a regime to make its dictates felt and widespread opposition to the exercise of governmental power. That the inability should be generalized and the opposition widespread gain credibility from their connection with the underlying assumption that "a whole society" somehow expresses itself in revolution. We would be inclined to deny the existence of any such actor as a "Whole Society" as well as the utility of His invention. But even leaving aside doubts on that score for some other polemical occasion, it is not clear that the assumption helps in solving the problem at hand. The nub of revolution is a seizure of power over a governmental apparatus by one group from another. If we want to limit the portentous word "revolution" to those cases in which the groups are social classes and/or the seizure of power produces extensive changes in social life, sobeit. It remains that the bare requirements of such a change are the involvement of only a small portion of the population. Nor does it seem at all likely that a relatively uniform state of mind on the part of the remainder of the population is a necessary condition for such a change. Yet except for the important point concerning the control of the military and other repressive forces, Johnson's argument provides us with no reliable way of anticipating either the nature of the conflict or the identity of the participants. Smelser's scheme, Davies', and, indeed, the whole range of natural historical theorizing leaves those central explanatory questions virtually untouched.

In their present condition, natural history theories of revolution are nearly irrefutable—not because they are manifestly correct, but because they consist mainly of ways of rationalizing events after the fact. Even Crane Brinton, who provides us with the most concrete characterizations of the stages of revolution, offers them as no more than preliminary empirical generalizations, restricted to the few great revolutions he takes up. Any effort to apply systematic evidence to the available natural historical analyses will therefore require recasting the arguments into testable propositions. The model that we propose below aims in that direction. It is a kind of natural history theory in that it views revolutionary violence as a stage in the development of broader political changes. But it differs from the theories discussed above in that it identifies these changes not as "abnormal," but as the stuff of normal political life.

A Political Process Model

For any population, we may ask whether there exist one or more organizations controlling the principal concentrated means of coercion within the population. Such organizations are *governments*. We may then enumerate all groups within the population which, during some particular span of time, collectively apply resources to the influence of a certain government. They are *contenders* for power with respect to that government. To the extent that a contender can routinely lay claim to the generation of action or yielding of resources by agents of the government, the contender is a member of the *polity*, which therefore consists of all contenders successfully exercising routine claims to government response. Some groups are not contenders, and some contenders (which we call *challengers*) are not members of the polity; the members of the polity differ among themselves in the amount and type of response their application of resources to the government produces.

So much for definitions. We imagine the general operation of polities in the following way: Every polity establishes tests of membership, and all polities include among such tests the ability to mobilize or coerce significant numbers of people. Furthermore, within the polity, members continually test one another: repeated failures of partial tests lead to fuller tests that lead, if failed, to exclusion from the polity. Each new entry or exit redefines the criteria of membership in a direction favorable to the characteristics of the present set of members; the members tend to become attached to those criteria as a matter of principle. The life of the polity therefore consists of (a) the routine application of resources to the influence of the government by members of the polity; (b) attempts by non-members (ordinarily resisted by members in collaboration with agents of the government) to influence the government, including attempts to gain membership; (c) an ongoing series of contests, ranging from parliamentary maneuvering to street fighting, among members of the polity. (Actually *a* will frequently lead to *c*, as when one member lays claim to resources already committed to another, and *b* will frequently coincide with *c*, since members often form coalitions with non-members in order to increase the resources available for application to their common ends.)

Because of the testing process by which contenders acquire or lose membership, collective violence tends to increase when the membership of the polity is changing rapidly. Collective violence will pit members against members, and agents of the government (especially repressive forces like troops and police) against non-members, but rarely non-members against non-members, agents of the government against members, or agents against each other. In the event of revolution, however, all these regularities change.

Revolution, in this political model, consists of the fragmentation of a single polity. The case in which the fragmentation turns out to be permanent greatly resembles the revolution—indeed, the two cases are often indistinguishable at the start—but the term "revolt" or "civil war" applies more easily in that case. Leon Trotsky (1932, pp. 222–230) stated the essentials of the fragmentation years ago under the heading of "dual sovereignty." We differ from Trotsky in three ways: (1) in claiming that in many revolutions sovereignty is actually multiple, rather than dual; (2) in considering it more likely that the alternative polities will be composed of *coalitions* of classes than that they will be single classes; (3) in recognizing that the coalitions sometimes include groupings which are based on language, religion, region, or some other form of solidarity than class.

The fragmentation of the polity can occur in several different ways. The most likely is for some new coalition of contenders (at the extreme, a single non-member of the polity) to lay claim to exclusive control over the government while the remaining established members of the polity continue to press *their* exclusive claims, while some portion of the population honors the claims of each of the fragment polities. These circumstances may well produce a temporary fragmentation of the government (as when insurrectionary armies administer part of a country) in addition to the fragmentation of the polity. In any case, a revolution begins when previously acquiescent citizens faced with strictly incompatible demands from the government and an alternative authority obey the alternative authority. It continues until only one central authority remains.

So far we have merely set up a conceptual scheme, embedded in a strongly political view of conflict, which contains a few propositions so general as not to be amenable to verification in their present form. The scheme, nevertheless, narrows the search for the causes of revolution from the detection of anomie, strain, dysfunction, or frustration to the specification of the conditions producing the following outcomes:

(a) appearance of contenders (or coalition of contenders) advancing exclusive alternative claims to the control over the government currently exerted by members of the polity;
(b) acceptance of those claims by a significant segment of the population;

(c) formation of coalitions between members of the polity and the contenders advancing the alternative claims;

(d) unwillingness or incapacity of the government to suppress the alternative coalition and/or the acceptance of its claims (historically, the unreliability of armed forces has been crucial in this regard).

If these are indeed the constituent elements of a revolutionary situation, they have some interesting implications for the natural history of revolution. They give us no particular reason for expecting a gradual crescendo of conflict up to the point of revolution, followed by a rapid readjustment, which is the sequence a tension-release model implies.

On the contrary. A more reasonable sequence would run:

(1) the gradual mobilization of contenders, unacceptable to the members of the polity and/or making exclusive claims to governmental control;

(2) a rapid increase in the number of people accepting those claims and/or a rapid expansion of the coalition including the unacceptable or exclusive contenders;

(3) an unsuccessful effort by the government, acting on behalf of the members of the polity, to suppress the alternative coalition and/or the acceptance of its claims;

(4) establishment by the alternative coalition of effective control over some portion of the government;

(5) struggle of the alternative coalition to maintain or extend that control;

(6) reconstruction of a single polity through the victory of the alternative coalition, through its defeat, or through the establishment of a *modus vivendi* between the alternative coalition and some or all of the old members.

It is a matter of pure convenience whether we say dual sovereignty—and therefore revolution—commences at stage 2, stage 3, or stage 4. It ends, obviously, at stage 6.

Some Inferences from the Model

This "natural history" of revolution, like those reviewed earlier, contains little more than the explication of a definition. It leads, however, to some intriguing observations on the sequence of violent conflicts in revolutions. First, the level of conflict is likely to be much higher *after* the first major actions of the revolution than before, because the emergence of dual sovereignty challenges the position of every member of the polity, and thus begins a major round of testing.

Second, the struggle between the two polities is itself likely to produce a polarized form of conflict, activating an exceptional proportion of the population on one side or another.

Third, the successful revolutionary coalition—whichever combination of the original contenders it contains—is likely to face considerable resistance as it attempts to *reestablish* routine governmental control over the population as a whole after seizing the governmental apparatus. To the extent that the revolutionary action begins with the seizure of a crucial but narrow geographical and/or organizational part of the apparatus, the struggle is likely to shift away from that locus after the revolutionaries consolidate their control there. In geographically and organizationally centralized states like those of the modern West, revolutionary conflicts are most likely to originate at the center and then shift to the periphery if the center is won.

Fourth, the initial revolutionary coalition is likely to fragment, leaving a few contenders exceptionally powerful, for several reasons: (a) the initial seizure of control requires a larger coalition than does the maintenance of control; (b) the divergence of the longer-run objectives of the coalesced contenders is likely to become more salient and serious after the initial effort of dislodging the previous polity from control is past; (c) those contenders that have mobilized rapidly in response to short-run crises but remain relatively underorganized are also likely to *de*mobilize more rapidly than other contenders, and thus to lose position in the testing that immediately follows the initial seizure of power. On these matters, coalition theorists (e.g., Coleman 1973, Gamson 1968a, Schelling 1973) have already suggested some promising hypotheses.

Testing the Model

Though easy to state, these ideas are difficult to test—for they require a form of data much harder to assemble than the bald recitation of events that fuels the natural history arguments.

Needed for this "political process" model of revolutionary change are data which relate the manifest conflicts of the revolution to different segments of the base population before, during, and after the revolutionary events, via an analysis of the changing actions and relations of the principal contenders for power. These materials must be gathered in such a way as to view events transpiring before, during, and after the revolution with the same analytical lens, so as to avoid the natural history fallacy of "working backward" from the accomplished fact of revolutionary change in order to identify stages that "had" to lead to revolution. Such data are a thousand times more difficult to assemble than are straightforward accounts of the principal events. The collection of the information on which we shall draw in the following analysis took seven years of the time of good-sized research teams at Harvard, Toronto, and Michigan. Even that information fails to represent directly several crucial parts of the processes of mobilization, contention, and transfer of power that we have been discussing. Despite a number of trials, we have not so far been able to develop a reliable procedure for enumerating contenders, measuring their mobilization, and characterizing their relationship to the existing structure of power, which is truly independent of the conflicts we are attempting to explain. The portions of the argument we are in the best position to test directly are therefore those dealing with the timing and personnel of violent conflicts.

The data consist chiefly of coded, machine-readable accounts of every violent conflict above a certain scale occurring in France noted by trained readers scanning two national daily newspapers for each day over the periods from 1830 through 1860 and 1930 through 1960, plus a random three months per year over the period from 1861 through 1929. Information on these events is drawn not only from the original newspaper accounts, but also from archival sources and secondary historical materials. In addition, further data consist of machine-readable descriptions of a wide variety of social indicators year by year for the eighty-six to ninety French *départements* and for France as a whole.

A "violent event," for these purposes, is a continuous interaction between two or more formations, or between one formation and the property of another, in which at least one formation has fifty or more participants and in the course of which at least one formation seizes or damages persons or objects. (Acts of war between states, however, are excluded.) The following report, illustrates the sort of information being analyzed. It describes events that took place in the southern French city of Carcassonne in March 1832.

> The disturbance which afflicted this commune on the eighth of this month broke out again yesterday (Sunday), with even greater violence. The insistence of the Bishop on supporting the interdiction of Father Bataillé, the parish priest, and the presence of other priests sent to Saint-Vincent parish to conduct the Sunday services, brought forth a large crowd in the church, and the priests were chased from the premises. The Prefect, who on the eighth had refused to call in the National Guard to disperse the crowd, took recourse to the Guard on this occasion, declining to call in the regular army for fear of creating additional antagonism.
>
> Thus the National Guard assembled at Canal Square. The Guard would have succeeded in calming the disturbance, except for the presence of the Prefect, the General, and several municipal officials. The sight of these brought the crowd to new excesses. The crowd jeered the Prefect, threatening to throw him in the canal, and forced him to flee to the side of the General. A hail of stones thrown at the officials by the crowd struck the General on the head and the deputy mayor on the face. The latter later submitted his resignation. The crowd then became still more threatening. Four officers of the Guard left their troops to harangue the crowd, with some effect. "We'll obey you," cried some of the principal residents of the Carcassonne, "for you are good patriots." The crowd dispersed. Calm returned, and the night passed quietly. Now that these deplorable events have occurred, the Bishop and the Prefect can no longer do us any good; their presence alone creates general antagonism and ferment. The most peaceable and respectable citizens are hurrying to sign a petition to the legislature seeking the removal of the Prefect and the transfer of the Bishop.
>
> The authorities have been astonished at the moral authority over the crowds shown by the National Guard. . . . (*Le Constitutionnel*, 3/19/1832)

Some of the available accounts are more detailed than this one, and a majority of them are sketchier.* Taken together, the approximately one thousand and four hundred disturbance reports from 1830 through 1960 constitute a comprehensive sample of events in which people were sufficiently committed to their objectives to take violent action, plus information on the contexts of the events.

Our procedure yields, so far as we can tell, a more representative sample of violent conflicts than would reliance on standard histories or on any combination of major series of documents available to French historians for the period in question. Yet it tends to underrepresent areas and segments of the population that are either less accessible or less interesting to journalists. This bias is probably greater in times of crisis at the center, which draws attention away from the rest of the world.

Yet the general bias is endemic and probably constant over short periods. The method appears to capture the general fluctuation of conflict over time fairly well. A comparison between the number of violent events in the sample and those mentioned in the inventories of two of the standard archival series on the internal policing of France (Archives Nationales BB[18] and BB[30]) yields the following numbers of disturbances by quarter from 1830 through 1832:

| | 1830 | | | | 1831 | | | | 1832 | | | | |
	1	2	3	4	1	2	3	4	1	2	3	4	Total
sample	2	5	25	18	9	4	7	3	17	42	7	2	141
archive	5	1	47	17	15	4	4	4	9	12	10	7	135

The comparison is weakened somewhat by the inventories' imprecision concerning the number of participants and the extent of violence in the smaller conflicts and by their tendency to lump together a number of related events (notably the multiple counter-revolutionary movements in the West during the second quarter of 1832) into a single item. But in general the swings in frequencies correspond to those of our sample ($r = .52$). For

---

*On the basis of this report and two others, all drawn from *Le Constitutionnel,* our coders estimated the total number of participants at four hundred to six hundred, and broke them into two formations: one a "crowd of common ideology" and the other the National Guard plus public officials.

that reason, it may be useful to extend the series back a few years in time via the archival materials:

	1826	1827	1828	1829	1830	1831	1832
sample	—	—	—	—	50	23	68
archive	13	11	13	22	70	27	38

The counts show a much higher frequency of collective violence immediately *after* the revolution than in the years before, despite the accumulation of a certain number of food riots in 1829. The observation, which is reinforced by the quarterly count presented above, will take on some importance later.

As we completed our enumeration of violent events meeting our criteria, we coded them extensively in a uniform manner. That involved breaking the participants in each event into "formations"—sets of persons acting together—and describing each formation's characteristics and actions separately, as well as characterizing the setting and the event as a whole. The items coded ranged from multiple measures of the scale of the event to detailed sequences of action for individual formations to manifest objectives of the participants. In this report, however, we draw only on our classifications of formations and our estimates of the number of participants in each event.

Here we analyze only one small segment of the sample: The violent events recorded from the years 1830, 1831, 1832. Those events include all the larger violent encounters that were part of the Revolution of 1830, but they also include a number of small incidents to which historians have not attributed any particular political significance. Inclusiveness is a virtue, for it permits us to study how the occurrence of revolution affects the whole pattern of violent conflict.

The Revolution of 1830

The Three Glorious Days of July 1830, brought about a popular overthrow of entrenched power, one which spelled the definitive end of the Bourbon monarchy in France and led to a sweeping change in the personnel of the government's upper echelons. (In our general analysis of the context we rely especially on the following accounts: Aguet (1954), Dolléans (1967), Chevalier (1958), Labrousse (n.d.), Mantoux (1901), Girard (1961), Lhomme (1960), and Pinkney (1964 and 1972).) In place of the

Bourbon Charles X, the revolution elevated Louis-Philippe of Orléans to the throne—not as King of France, but as "King of the French." The revolution changed the cast of French political life, bringing France one step closer to parliamentary democracy. Nor did these changes come without bloodshed. In the course of the Three Glorious Days of fighting between insurgents and the army in the streets of Paris, some two thousand Frenchmen lost their lives.

The Revolution of 1830 did not excite the popular involvement of 1848. It did not accomplish the sweeping rearrangements of 1789. Its rank and file did not share the single-minded commitment to a revolutionary program of the Communards of 1871. It was no less a revolution for all that. In our view, the effort to single out a class of "true" revolutions through the extensiveness of popular participation, the depth of the structural changes resulting from the transfer of power or the radicalism of the intentions of the participants defeats itself. It makes crucial to the definition of the phenomenon to be examined just those features that are hardest to detect, and which ought to be treated as variables. It makes virtually impossible what is already a very difficult task: analyzing what distinguishes those transfers of control over governments that *do* involve massive popular participation and widespread structural change from those that do not. Employing the more strictly political criterion of multiple sovereignty makes it clear that 1830 brought France a genuine revolution. Once we examine 1830 outside the shadows of 1789 and 1848, moreover, we can see well enough that the transfer of power was far more extensive than appears at first glance.*

Who took part? Who were the members of the polity on the eve of the revolution, who the contenders testing one another in the revolutionary and post-revolutionary power struggles? Jean Lhomme's summary is convenient: First, the backers of Charles X, the most powerful group up to the revolution; Lhomme sees them as representatives of the landed aristocracy. Second, poised against this group, another privileged element: a counter-elite composed of the upper bourgeoisie, with activist representatives in the Chamber of Deputies, the press, and other key positions.

---

*For a fuller discussion on this point, see Pinkney (1972, Chapter IX).

In terms of the conceptual scheme we are employing, both these groups count as *members* of the polity; there are, of course, others, but they matter less for the present analysis. Two other groups identified by Lhomme as active in the political contests of this period were the numerous urban working classes—poor, inarticulate, and badly organized, but still capable of some degree of collective action—and the rural poor, as destitute as their urban counterparts but different in political orientation. These latter groups were active *contenders* in the power struggle during the years under study, but were excluded by the first two from *membership* in the national polity.

These rough categories simplify enormously a rich, complex class structure. For most purposes, a class analyst of this period would want to distinguish the expanding class of small manufacturers from the world of small craftsmen and shopkeepers that supplied so many of the revolutionary activists from 1789 to 1848, the true peasants from the agricultural proletariat, the factory workers from the unskilled laborers, and so on. These distinctions matter a great deal to our more refined treatments of nineteenth-century conflicts. For present purposes, they would simply obscure the general argument.

Our categories, for all their crudeness, take us a giant step toward a more subtle understanding of the revolutionary events themselves; although representatives of the first three groups all had their roles to play in the Three Glorious Days, they were different roles indeed. The revolution came after a period of smoldering if unspirited conflict between the government and the bourgeois counter-elite. The immediate spur to action came on July 25 when the government, facing a defeat from its antagonists in the Chamber of Deputies, promulgated a series of measures suspending freedom of the press, dissolving the recently elected Chamber, and restricting the franchise. The parliamentary opposition—the bourgeois counter-elite—called on the nation to resist, posting placards to this effect throughout Paris. Perhaps more important, the opposition press closed down in response to the government's measures, sending the printers and other workers into the streets. News and agitation spread through the existing networks of neighborhood, work, and local political organization. By July 27 barricades had appeared in the city—especially in the old working-class neighborhoods—and fighting between insurgents and the army had begun. By the 29th, the challengers had won the day. The king abdicated and fled the country; the Duke of Orléans was installed in his place. Three short days sufficed to depose the last of the Bourbons and shift the reins of power.

We recount the events partly to emphasize the nature of the coalition that effected the overthrow. The bases for action on the part of the working-class *challengers* and the bourgeois *members* of the polity were quite different. David Pinkney's work on the Paris Revolution of 1830 has shown that the disparities were so great that unanimity (however one might reckon it) was impossible. Pinkney argues, for example, that the working-class crowd was uninvolved in the quarrel between the government and its elite antagonists:

> . . . thousands of Paris workingmen during the depression years of the late 1820s and early 1830s had specific grievances—lack of work, low wages, the high price of bread—that had nothing to do with the dispute over censorship that alienated the printers and journalists from the Polignac ministry. (1964, p. 2)

The conventional way to deal with this discrepancy has been to treat the workers as impelled, rather blindly, by hardship; Pinkney's analysis, however, makes it easier to see that a genuine coalition of groups with rather different objectives was at work in the early revolution. The nature of the coalition adds irony to the fact that although few bourgeois died in the Parisian events in comparison to the terrible toll of workers, the upper bourgeois picked up the pieces, set the cast of the new government, and occupied the stations of power within it.

This account of the Paris days also provides another ground for skepticism about those natural history theories of revolution that implicitly posit a single state of mind or shared tension through entire populations. For the actual change in government was accomplished both in a remarkably short time and through the participation of a small segment of the French populace: perhaps twenty thousand participants—less than a hundredth of one percent—of a nation of twenty-five million. Certainly these twenty thousand people were in a strategic location. Certainly many other noncombatant Frenchmen shared at least some of their outlook. But only the rashest observer could automatically ascribe the perceptions, grievances, and desires of those who fought to the rest of the populace. A minority of a specific class in a single city were able to dislodge the Bourbon regime from its position of power. To stake one's explanation of the change of government on what the rest of the French nation was thinking or feeling seems to us unwarranted and risky.

Instead, the model of revolution already presented directs attention to shifts in the form, locus, and intensity of conflict as the struggle for power continues. If the model is correct, we should expect to find:

(1) a significant rise in the level of conflict *after* the inception of the revolution, as (a) the struggle for power over the central governmental apparatus generalizes; (b) all contenders find their positions within the polity open to test and change; (c) the coalition which acquires control over the center attempts to reimpose control over the peripheral segments of the population as a whole;

(2) a movement of conflict toward the centers of power as the revolution begins, and toward the periphery as it proceeds to reimposition of central control over the remainder of the population;

(3) an increased use of specialized repressive forces as the revolutionary coalition consolidates its control over the center, demobilizes some of the contenders that took an active part in the initial seizure of power, and extends its control to the periphery;

(4) a general "politicization" of conflict with and after the revolution, as the existence of the revolutionary situation encourages all contenders to test each other in order to maintain or aggrandize their positions, and as every conflict comes to have some significance for the structure of the polity to emerge from the revolution;

(5) a general tendency for both the politicization and the intensity of conflicts to vary as a direct function of the proximity of different segments of the population to the center.

Now, these inferences from our general scheme obviously assume a highly centralized government; they very likely draw some of their plausibility from their fit with what we already know to be the common run of modern European experience. The peasant wars so powerfully analyzed by Eric Wolf (1969), on the other hand, will only fit these statements after some tugging and squeezing. We claim only that these are reasonable inferences from our argument to the sorts of centralized governments modern Europe *did* produce, and therefore to the polities that have supplied theorists of revolution with most of their classic cases, and that "natural history" schemes either provide no inferences regarding these matters or suggest contrary ones.

The Timing of Collective Violence

As preliminary tests of these assertions, let us examine data concerning the timing, locus, and participants in violent conflicts within France from 1830 through 1832. First, timing. Figure 1 displays the fluctuation in collective violence by quarter from January 1830 to December 1832, in terms of numbers of violent events and estimated participants in them. (The estimating procedure (a) gives precedence to specific numbers reported in the accounts used, (b) permits the coder to draw inferences from the territory occupied by the violent event, the number of arrests and casualties and the descriptive words used by witnesses, (c) assigns to those violent events for which there is too little information to make even that sort of judgment—in this case 8 of the 141 disturbances—the mean value of the estimates for other disturbances in the same quarter.) On the whole, the curves of violent events and of participants move together. The largest exception in the three years is the third quarter of 1831, during which the number of violent events declined to three, but the famous November insurrection in Lyon brought the participants up to over seventeen thousand. The graph also displays the general tendency for the average size of violent events to rise in times of widespread conflict like July 1830 and June 1832.

Perhaps the most remarkable thing shown in these curves is the relative quiescence of France during the six-month period immediately prior to the revolution. From the first of January to the end of June 1830, we discover a total of seven violent events. During the five months from the beginning of August to the end of the year, however, there are a total of thirty-five. This accords badly with those natural history theories that posit a gradual buildup of excitement or tension during the pre-revolutionary period, followed by a downturn and general subsidence once the

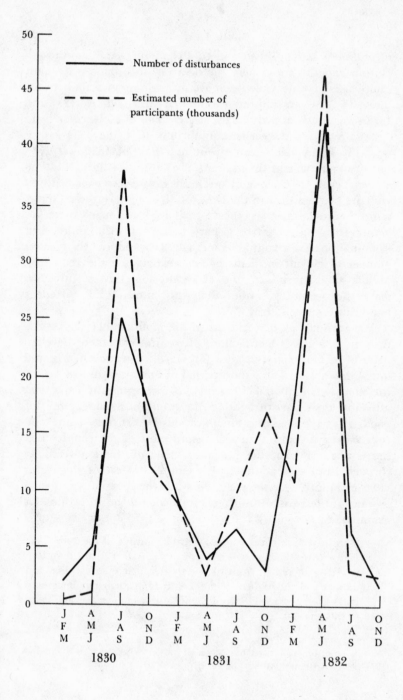

revolution is accomplished. Indeed, Paris itself, the site of the revolution and the area where the data on disturbances are most complete, shows no violence above our minimum scale between the first of the year and the revolutionary days. Nor do 1831 and 1832 show much of a systematic *decrescendo* of violence or homeostatic return to the earlier equilibrium. It is true, 1831 is considerably less violent than the second half of 1830, yet 1831 remains more violent than the first six months of the revolutionary year. And 1832, though likewise showing a lower incidence of violence per month than the last half of 1830, nevertheless shows more than twice as many incidents as 1831 and many more per month than the pre-revolutionary period of 1830. Indeed, an examination of our sample shows that 1832 produced the greatest number of violent incidents of any year during the 1830–1860 period. By any reckoning, the Three Glorious Days of July 1830 mark the beginning, rather than the climax, of a turbulent period in French history.

A closer look at the incidents in the months after the revolution in 1830 shows a still more interesting pattern of development of revolutionary violence. The revolution itself had played out within a remarkably short period of time. Within five days of the first signs of popular hostility to the regime in Paris, and after just three days of fighting, the Bourbon monarchy fell for good; given the state of communications at that time, the revolution was an accomplished fact before most of the country had heard about it. Yet the reestablishment of single sovereignty through France as a whole took months.* Most of the major cities of France were the scenes of sympathetic responses as soon as news of the Parisian insurrection reached them. In Nantes, for example:

> The July Ordinances were known the morning of the 29th. They had a powerful impact. Feelings ran high all day and disorderly crowds gathered in front of the theater that evening. The gendarmes and the soldiers of the Tenth Line Regiment intervened and restored order. Fifteen demonstrators were arrested and taken to the Château.

---

*At this point our discussion has benefited particularly from David Pinkney (1971, personal communication; and 1972).

The next morning, there was great agitation, and it spread to the masses. The merchants and the upper bourgeoisie did not hide their fears. They asked for the reestablishment of the National Guard, but the authorities did not seem inclined to listen to them.

The mayor was strongly urged ... to free the demonstrators who had been imprisoned in the Château the night before. He said all he could do was speak to the military commander. After that reply, a group formed and headed for the headquarters of the military division, grew along the way, and included a hundred-odd persons when it got to the Place Louis XVI. There it found a detachment of the Tenth in battle formation before the headquarters. In the midst of the shouts and imprecations of the crowd, someone fired a gun. The soldiers responded with a volley. The demonstrators fled, with seven of them shot to death and some forty of them more or less seriously wounded.

The populace invaded the guard house and disarmed the soldiers on duty there. The military authorities limited their action to securing the Château and the Place Louis XVI, and the city was abandoned to itself. Some citizens who had met at the Bourse during the day organized patrols which walked the city that night and maintained order.

The members of the court and the Chamber of Commerce took the initiative in reestablishing the National Guard and appealed to the loyalty of their fellow citizens in a notice posted Saturday, July 31. Because of a delay in the mails, only on the night of August 1 did people learn of the departure of Charles X and the establishment of a provisional government. The Prefect and the mayor, considering the game lost, left the city on the 2nd; that night General Despinois, taking part of his garrison with him, headed for the Vendée, hoping to raise an insurrection there. The National Guard organized. Lt. General Dumoutier, who lived near the city, took command.

Mayet, senior member of the prefectoral council, took over direction of departmental affairs on the 3rd. On the 4th, the official news finally came. The tricolor flag went up. On the 6th, Dumoutier took command of the Twelfth Division. (Libaudière 1905, pp. 81–83; a far superior account, too long to quote here, appears in Giraud-Mangin)

Between the time of the revolution in Paris and August 4, similar events broke out in Toulouse, Bordeaux, Lille, Amiens, and Dijon. All of these incidents represented assertions of strength by local representatives of the forces who had seized power in Paris. In terms of our political process model of revolution, these events represented the first of a series of tests among various members of the polity and contenders for political power to determine the concrete power relations that would result from the revolutionary change at the center.

These essentially urban events played themselves out almost immediately after the revolution, even though the overall level of violence hit another peak before the end of the year. Inflating the rates during the remainder of 1830 was another kind of violent confrontation, one pitting a different combination of parties against one another in a different kind of mutual testing. These were outbreaks of attacks against the agents and symbols of central control. Particularly favored for such attacks were the taxation offices by which Paris collected its much-detested internal taxes and which cut the income of local farmers while rasing the level of food prices in the cities and towns. For example, an account of a tax riot in the Champagne city of Epernay in December 1830 begins:

> Six hundred wine growers descended on the house of the collector of excise, sacked his offices, seized his record books, and burned them in the square by the city hall. (Archives Nationales BB[18] 1191)

and then goes on to give details: The presence of women and children in the crowd, the refusal of part of the National Guard (themselves recruited from the winegrowers) to act against their brothers, the request for troops from outside, the dispersal of the rioters. Another account of the same incident from a newspaper source notes that the mayor of the town and other "good citizens" tried to prevent the invasion, but to no avail. An equally typical example came from Villeneuve (Landes). On September 8, 1830, after an apparent agreement among peasants and merchants not to pay tolls or excise taxes, the mayor (assisted by gendarmes and National Guards) sought to enforce the collection of taxes at the local fair. A crowd beat the mayor and drove a herd of steers into him. The National Guards of Villeneuve and adjacent communes eventually made eighty arrests. (Archives Nationales BB[18] 1187; *Gazette des Tribunaux*, 11/25/1830; *Journal des Débats*,

10/13/1830) Again, the same pattern: rural interests seize the occasion of the post-revolutionary period to challenge the ability of the local representatives of the central authorities to make good their customary demands.

Attacks like these, endemic during this period, were no mere symbolic gestures. One of the main political issues of the time—both before and after the revolution—was the ability of the central government to squeeze taxes out of the rural populace. These events in the fall of 1830 represent another process of testing, as those in control of the central government struggled to consolidate its power and to exclude the rural poor from participation in the polity. The fact of a change of power at the top had resulted in a scramble for position among the other contenders within the polity, with each group seeking to establish its claim for what it saw as most crucial to it. The rural contenders simply responded to the new power arrangement at the center as an opportunity to press harder than ever for the same interests that they had been pursuing all along.

Nor were the rural poor the only groups whose representatives asserted their claims against the new government immediately after the revolution. Paris itself was the scene of a number of protests from its poorer citizens; the events of the fall demonstrated that the critical role of workers during the revolution had not led to working-class support for the middle-class government. Finally, in December of 1830, the trial of the ministers of deposed Charles X brought about a massive riot that rocked the new government. It showed plainly that the situation had not "re-equilibrated" itself during the months since the revolution.

Urbanity and Collective Violence

Another significant comparison in the nature of participation in violent collective conflict during this period lies in the urbanity of their settings. Table 1 shows the estimated number of participants in violent events during each period by the urbanity of the departments in which the events occurred. (At the time, France was divided into 86 administrative units, or departments, averaging about 375,000 in population.) The entries in each cell are rates per 100,000 population, corrected to an annual basis. Of course, the fact that an event took place in a department with more than 15 percent of its population in urban places does not necessarily mean the event itself was urban; a violent event in an urban department can still take place outside the confines of the city.

The comparisons are striking. The urban departments show consistently higher rates of participation in violent events throughout. Nevertheless, the geographic pattern varies considerably from one period to the next. The correlation coefficients at the bottom of each column in Table 1 conveniently summarize the varying strength of the relationship between the urbanity of a department and the volume of participation in its violent events. The coefficients display both the general tendency of participants in violence to concentrate in the more urban departments and the sharp fluctuation of the pattern from period to period. The rapid geographic fluctuation in itself is a finding of some importance, for it suggests two interesting conclusions: (a) the locus and character of the issues about which Frenchmen were fighting shifted dramatically as the revolution moved from phase to phase; (b) other studies that have found strong relations between levels of conflict and structural variables at a single point in time may well have mistaken historically contingent relationships for general effects of structure.

How did the pattern change as the revolution proceeded? During the pre-revolutionary period we find low rates throughout France; they do not differ greatly among the groups of departments. The picture changes drastically, however, once the revolution gets under way. During the revolutionary period, the extent of violence rose sharply for all classes of departments except the most rural ones: the change produced a strong relationship between urbanity and violent conflict. In the months following the change of government, the disparity between the most and the least urban departments narrowed; the rates in the less urban departments rose, registering the shift of focus of conflict from the largest urban centers toward the provincial towns and the countryside. Concretely, the swelling of rates in the less urban departments during the closing months of 1830 represented the spread of tax rebellions and similar forms of resistance to central control. During 1831 and 1832 the differentials between the most and least urban departments widened again, although in 1831 the

TABLE 1

Estimated Participants in Collective Violence per 100,000 Population by Urbanity of Department, 1830–32 (corrected to annual basis)

Percent of population in cities of 10,000+	Jan.–June 1830	July–Aug. 1830	Sept.–Dec. 1830	1831	1832	1830–1832	Total Participants (Thousands)	Total Population (Millions)
0	23	19	54	5	22	20	3.8	6.4
0.1–5.0	7	42	84	0	64	34	6.7	6.5
5.1–10.0	0	92	218	34	75	66	19.8	10.0
10.0–15.0	18	720	136	19	213	135	19.5	4.8
15.1+	28	2904	413	719	823	727	104.4	4.8
TOTAL	13	573	175	120	193	158	154.2	32.5
Total Participants (Thousands)	2.1	31.1	19.0	39.2	62.8	154.2		
r, participants x urban population	.01	.91	.66	.43	.89	.91		

persistence of tax conflicts in the moderately rural departments, while struggles among the members of the revolutionary coalition accelerated in Paris and other large cities, reduced the correlation between urbanity and rates of participation. The largest single conflict of 1831 was the bloody revolt of the Lyon silk workers. In 1832 levels of involvement in collective violence rose in all classes of departments; in April, May, and June they approached the heights of July and August 1830, as repeated street-fighting in Paris coincided with widespread guerrilla in the counterrevolutionary West.

Statistics like these, showing the prominent place of urban settings in political violence, have convinced many observers that violence stems directly from migration or specifically urbanization. It is true, of course, that both Paris and most of the other cities where extensive collective conflict took place during this period had undergone considerable relatively rapid growth in preceding years. But further analysis of our data shows that it was urbanity itself, rather than the process of urbanization, which was most strongly associated with collective violence.

Table 2 presents regression coefficients for four departmental variables—total population, urban population, net migration, and increase of urban population—as predictors of man-days expended in disturbances. Urban population itself is the most durable predictor of level of collective conflict over the five periods shown here. Extent of urban increase is probably the next strongest predictor. Net migration itself is a relatively weak influence compared to these two.

None of the four indicators is particularly strong for the pre-revolutionary period; the coefficients, which are much greater for the year 1831, are only somewhat stronger. These are, in fact, the periods with the least collective violence. During these two periods urban increase shows some importance as a predictor of levels of collective violence. But during the revolutionary and immediate post-revolutionary periods of 1830 and throughout 1832—in short, during the most turbulent periods—urbanity itself is much the strongest predictor. It is true that these figures do not in themselves show that violent events during this time occurred *within* towns and cities. Table 2 simply shows that urban *departments* were the scenes of collective violence, though an examina-

TABLE 2

Standardized Regression Coefficients for Man-Days Expended in Violent Incidents in France, 1830–1832, by period.

Period	Total Population 1831	Urban Population 1831	Net Migration 1826–1831	Urban Increase 1821–1831	Multiple R
January–June, 1830	.0734	−.2407	−.1423	.3458	.1964
July–August, 1830	−.4410	.9949	−.1615	.2206	.9421
Sept.–December, 1830	−.3844	.8570	−.0432	.0641	.7474
1831	−.0925	.3650	.4045	.6350	.7228
1832	−.4689	.7798	−.1556	.2384	.9244

tion of the incidents themselves shows that they took place largely in towns and cities rather than the nearby countryside.

There are some special points worth noting in the rates for France as a whole. These figures should make it clear that, however modest the final rearrangements in French social structure brought about by the revolution, the events of the revolutionary period did activate the French populace. The number of participants during the two-month revolutionary period, especially in the most urban departments, shows a remarkably high level of involvement in relation to the total population. The Revolution of 1830 may have lacked the long-term social implication of the Great Revolution of 1789, but it was certainly no palace coup, no matter of indifference to the bulk of the French population.

The Participants

A still further comparison of the different contributions to the process of revolution of different groups within the French polity comes from an analysis of the *formations* taking part in violent events. A formation is a group taking an independent role in a disturbance, as reckoned by its apparent autonomy or organization, distinctness of objectives, etc. In some instances, like the destruction of government taxation facilities during the immediate post-revolutionary period, the sample records only a single formation, since the insurgents had no antagonists present in person on the scene. The more common case is two formations contesting with each other. Some instances contain three or more formations, in different combinations of alliance with or antagonism against one another. For every incident we have attempted to gather as much information as possible about the identity of the formations taking part and the nature of their participation. This makes it possible to compare, in Table 2, the proportionate involvement of various kinds of formations throughout the revolutionary period.

The shifts in participation during this period are worth noting in detail, for they demonstrate a number of changes suggested by our model. Overall, Table 3 shows a broad trend toward the *politicization* of violent collective conflict. The "simple crowd"—any group recruited simply by virtue of its members having been in one particular place at a particular time—decreases in propor-

TABLE 3
Types of Formations Participating in Collective Violence, 1830–1832
(percent of total in specified period)

Formation Type	Period					
	Jan.–June 1830	July–Aug. 1830	Sept.–Dec. 1830	1831	1832	Total
Simple crowd	30.8	22.2	23.5	12.0	15.1	17.4
Ideological group	0.0	29.6	5.9	24.0	28.8	22.6
Occupational group	23.1	11.1	21.6	12.0	6.2	11.1
Repressive force	7.7	25.9	33.3	42.0	41.8	37.3
Other	38.5	11.1	15.7	10.0	8.2	11.5
Total	100.1	99.9	100.0	100.0	100.1	99.9
Number of Formations	13	27	51	50	146	287

Chi-square, 16 d.f. $= 39.1$, $p < .01$

tionate participation from its pre-revolutionary high to a mark-edly lower level during 1831 and 1832. In general, the proportion of occupational groups also decreases, except during the immedi-ate post-revolutionary period, when the protests of winegrowers and certain urban working-class groups apparently swells the rate. Growing over time, however, are the rates of participation by repressive forces—police, army, National Guard, etc.—and "ide-ological groups." The latter are formations which, in our judg-ment, were recruited and defined in terms of allegiance to some specific political position or grouping. The increase in participa-tion by these two groups suggests that, with the revolution, the business of acting out violent conflicts became very much a matter for specialists—the agents of the government, on the one hand, and activist representatives of various political tendencies, on the other.

To some extent, certain of these differences may stem from the limitations of our knowledge of this period. The readers and coders may, in some cases, have interpreted the presence of formations in a more ideological light simply by virtue of the fact that the revolution had occurred. Nevertheless, the broad outlines of changing participation, which we have derived from Table 2, are probably accurate. The participation of repressive forces, for example, rose as the new government strove to fix its control over the polity. The frequencies of participation by repressive formations for 1830–1832 were as follows:

Period	Percent of Violent Events in which Repressive Forces Were Present
Jan.–June 1830	17
July–Aug. 1830	43
Sept.–Dec. 1830	59
1831	78
1832	82
1830–32	70

Since repressive formations—troops, police, National Guards, and other armed forces employed by governments—are relatively easy to identify in our records, there seems little doubt that a major change in the character of violent encounters occurred as the revolution moved on. As the survivors of the revolutionary coalition sought to consolidate their control over the government, they increasingly used organized force against their enemies.

Although they have rarely been documented as systematically as they are here, the politicization of collective violence and the rise of repressive formations after the transfer of power are well known to historians of revolution. The promulgators of natural historical schemes for revolution ought to consider those two phenomena carefully, for they identify some serious difficulties in the schemes available to us so far. First, the strong variation in participation from group to group and time to time renders implausible (or at least inadequate) those theories that trace revolution back to a generalized state of tension or frustration. We have not undertaken the demonstration here, but it does not appear, in any reasonable sense of the words, that the participants were drawn from the tensest or most frustrated segments of the population, or that the change in the structure of disturbances corresponded to a shift in the distribution of tension or frustration in the population at large. Changes in the power relationships of politically active groups at the local and national levels lay behind the variations we have detected.

Second, the rising prominence of repressive forces in these violent conflicts bespeaks the heavy involvement of governments in the struggles behind them. It is therefore improper to attribute the successive phases of a revolution to changes in the orientation of the population at large or even to changes in the position of some single group of "rebels." An adequate theory has to deal with relations among contenders and governments.

Third, both the politicization and the rise of repression grow from two large processes that are central to revolution but have little place in natural historical theories of revolution: (1) the struggle of those who have seized power to reimpose control over the rest of the population, which often produces a wider and fiercer conflict than the initial transfer of power; (2) the breaking up of the revolutionary coalition and the effort of some members of that coalition to exclude others from power. These are the processes that tend to produce far higher levels of collective violence *after* the initial revolutionary transfer of power than before it. Among natural history theorists, Crane Brinton (an expert historian of the French Revolution) and Pitirim Sorokin (an active participant in the Russian Revolution) were well aware of these processes; in general terms, however, both of them attributed these processes to the confrontation between a tendency of the most ruthless, extreme revolutionaries to succeed their moderate brethren and to the intolerability of extremism to ordinary people. Neither of these principles explains much of 1830's natural history.

Nor is 1830 a special case, except in the sense that all revolutions are special cases. The parallel data we have assembled for the French revolution of 1848 (see Tilly 1970, 1972) fall into similar patterns: widespread resistance to the reimposition of central control, violent post-revolutionary struggles among the members of the revolutionary coalition, important shifts in the geographic pattern of violence corresponding to the oscillating struggle for power, far higher levels of involvement after the initial transfer of power, and so on. We do not have the same sort of systematic data for the great revolution that began in 1789; we recognize, moreover, that the events of that revolution had a far wider impact than did those of 1830 and 1848. Within the limits of the generalizations we have offered, nevertheless, the 1789 Revolution also appears to exemplify the pattern. That should hardly be surprising, since it was our reflection on 1789 and its aftermath that first led us toward the rejection of the natural historical models and to the formulation of our alternative model.

There are, of course, some difficulties in our argument and in the evidence we have offered for it. We have not provided reliable criteria for identifying contenders or for indexing their relative position independently of the revolutionary struggles we propose to explain; instead, we have relied on scholarly consensus concerning the main blocs involved in the revolution of 1830. Such a consensus often does not exist. Even where it does, it can hardly form a reliable basis for the sort of comparable measurement over many cases which the verification of our argument would require.

Again, our scheme yields only rather weak inferences concerning the kinds of countries and/or periods in which revolution is likely. It does little more than redirect the search away from general tempos of structural change or broad levels of tension toward the formation of political coalitions successfully making certain kinds of claims.

Finally, the evidence presented in this paper raises doubts about conventional natural historical analyses, but it is insufficient to rule out a number of alternative interpretations of revolutionary processes. The alternatives include the more sophisticated frustration-aggression formulations, which have been appearing in recent years. We are inclined to believe that the frustration-aggression road, too, turns into a blind alley, if not the same one to which natural history leads. But there we may be proved wrong. However the search among the intellectual avenues now open to the student of revolution finally turns out, it will surely take us to a much more explicit theory of the political process itself than modern sociologists and psychologists of revolution have been willing to employ.

References

Aguet, J.-P. *Les grèves sous la Monarchie de Juillet.* Geneva: Droz, 1954.

Amann, P. "Revolution: A Redefinition." *Political Science Quarterly,* 77 (1962), pp. 36–53.

de Bertier de Sauvigny, G. *La révolution de 1830 en France.* Paris: Armand Colin, 1970.

Bienen, H. *Violence and Social Change.* Chicago: Adlai Stevenson Institute of International Affairs, 1968.

Brinton, C. *The Anatomy of Revolution.* New York: Norton, 1938.

Calhoun, D. "Studying American Violence." *Journal of Interdisciplinary History,* 1 (1970), pp. 163–185.

de Calonne, A. *Amiens au XIXe siècle.* Paris: Picard, 1906. Vol. 3 of *Histoire de la ville d'Amiens.*

Chevalier, L. *Classes laborieuses et classes dangereuses à Paris pendant la première moitié du XIXe siècle.* Paris: Plon, 1958.

Cobb, R. *Les armées révolutionnaires, instrument de la Terreur dans les départements.* Paris: Mouton, 1961–63. 2 vols.

———. *The Police and the People.* Oxford: Clarendon Press, 1970.

Coleman, J. S. *The Mathematics of Collective Action.* Chicago: Aldine, 1973.

Davies, C. S. L. "Révoltes populaires en Angleterre (1500-1700)." *Annales; Economies, Sociétés, Civilisations,* 24 (1969), pp. 24–60.

Davies, J. "Toward a Theory of Revolution." *American Sociological Review,* 27 (1962), pp. 5–19.

———. "The J-curve of Rising and Declining Satisfactions as a Cause of Some Great Revolutions and a Contained Rebellion," in H. D. Graham and T. R. Gurr, eds., *Violence in America: Historical and Comparative Perspectives* (Washington: U.S. Government Printing Office, 1969), pp. 547–576.

Dolléans, E. *Histoire du mouvement ouvrier, 1830–1871.* Paris: Armand Colin, 1967.

Edwards, L. *The Natural History of Revolutions.* Chicago: University of Chicago Press, 1927.

Feierabend, I., and Feierabend, R. "Aggressive Behaviors within Polities, 1948–1962: A Cross-national Study." *Journal of Conflict Resolution,* 10 (1966), pp. 249–271.

Gamson, W. *Power and Discontent.* Homewood, Ill.: Dorsey, 1968a.

———. "Stable Unrepresentation in American Society." *American Behavioral Scientist,* 12 (1968b), pp. 15–21.

Gillis, J. "Political Decay and the European Revolutions, 1789–1848." *World Politics,* 22 (1970), pp. 344–370.

Girard, L. *Etude comparée des mouvements révolutionnaires en France en 1830, 1848 et 1870–71.* Paris: Centre de Documentation Universitaire, 1961.

Giraud-Mangin, H. "Nantes en 1830 et les journées de juillet." *Revue d'histoire moderne,* 6 (1931), pp. 461–465.

Gurr, T. "A Causal Model of Civil Strife: A Comparative Analysis Using New Indices." *American Political Science Review,* 62 (1968), pp. 1104–1124.

———. *Why Men Rebel.* Princeton: Princeton University Press, 1970.

Hofstadter, R. "Reflections on Violence in the United States," in R. Hofstadter and M. Wallace, eds., *American Violence: a Documentary History* (New York: Knopf, 1970).

Hopper, R. "The Revolutionary Process: a Frame of Reference for the Study of Revolutionary Movements." *Social Forces,* 28 (1950), pp. 270–279.

Huntington, S. *Political Order in Changing Societies.* New Haven: Yale University Press, 1968.

Johnson, C. *Revolutionary Change.* Boston: Little, Brown, 1968.

Kirkham, J., Levy, S., Crotty, W. *Assassination and Political Violence.* Washington: U.S. Government Printing Office, 1970.

Labrousse, E. *Le mouvement ouvrier et les idées sociales en France de 1815 à la fin du XIXe siècle.* Paris: Centre de Documentation Universitaire, n.d.

Lhomme, J. *La grande bourgeoisie au pouvoir.* Paris: Presses Universitaires de France, 1960.

Libaudière, F. "Précis des événements de 1830 à Nantes." *Annales de la Société Académique de Nantes,* 1905, 8th s., no. 6, pp. 81–83.

Mantoux, P. "Patrons et ouvriers en juillet 1830." *Revue d'histoire moderne et contemporaine,* 111 (1901), pp. 291–296.

Meadows, P. "Sequence in Revolution." *American Sociological Review,* 6 (1941), pp. 702–709.

Moore, B. *Social Origins of Dictatorship and Democracy.* Boston: Beacon, 1966.

———. "Revolution in America?" *New York Review of Books,* January 30, 1969, pp. 6–12.

Oberschall, A. *Social Conflict and Social Movements.* Englewood Cliffs, N.J.: Prentice-Hall, 1973.

Pinkney, D. "The Crowd in the French Revolution of 1830." *American Historical Review,* 70 (1964), pp. 1–17.

———. *The French Revolution of 1830.* Princeton, N.J.: Princeton University Press, 1972.

Rudé, G. *Paris and London in the 18th Century.* London: Collins, 1970.

Rummel, R. "Dimensions of Conflict Behavior within Nations." *Journal of Conflict Resolution,* 10 (1966), pp. 65–74.

Russell, D. *Rebellion and Armed Force.* New York: Seminar Press, 1974.

Schelling, T. C. "Hockey Helmets, Concealed Weapons, and Daylight Saving: A Study of Binary Choices with Externalities." *Journal of Conflict Resolution,* 17 (1973), pp. 381–428.

References

Smelser, N. *Theory of Collective Behavior*. New York: Free Press, 1963.

Sorokin, P. *The Sociology of Revolution*. New York: Lippincott, 1925.

———. *Social and Cultural Dynamics. III. Fluctuation of Social Relationships, War and Revolution*. New York: Bedminster, 1962.

Stone, L. *The Causes of the English Revolution, 1529–1642*. London: Routledge & Kegan Paul, 1972.

Tilly, C., and Rule, J. *Measuring Political Upheaval*. Princeton: Center of International Studies, Princeton University, 1965.

Tilly, C. "Reflections on the Revolutions of Paris: A Review of Recent Historical Writing." *Social Problems*, 12 (1964), pp. 99–121.

———. "Methods for the Study of Collective Violence," in M. A. Levine and R. W. Conant, eds., *Problems in the Study of Community Violence* (New York: Praeger, 1969a), pp. 15–43.

———. "Collective Violence in European Perspective," in H. D. Graham and T. R. Gurr, eds., *Violence in America: Historical and Comparative Perspectives* (Washington: U.S. Government Printing Office, 1969b), pp. 5–34.

———. "The Changing Place of Collective Violence," in M. Richter, ed., *Essays in Social and Political History* (Cambridge: Harvard University Press, 1970), pp. 139–164.

———. "How Protest Modernized in France, 1845–1855," in W. Aydelotte, A. Bogue, and R. Fogel, eds., *The Dimensions of Quantitative Research in History* (Princeton: Princeton University Press, 1972).

———. "Revolutions and Collective Violence," in F. I. Greenstein and N. Polsby, eds., *Handbook of Political Science* (Reading, Mass.: Addison-Wesley, 1974a).

———. "Town and Country in Revolution," in John Wilson Lewis, ed., *Communism, Revolution, and the Asian Peasant* (Stanford: Stanford University Press, 1974b).

Trotsky, L. *The History of the Russian Revolution*. London: Victor Gollancz, 1932.

Williams, G. *Artisans and Sans-culottes*. London: Edward Arnold, 1968.

Wolf, E. *Peasant Wars of the Twentieth Century*. New York: Harper, 1969.

John M. Merriman

The *Demoiselles* of the Ariège, 1829–1831

The department of the Ariège, in the Pyrénées, seemed far from the political issues that dominated Paris in the spring of 1830. In the department's forests, another kind of struggle was going on. Bands of peasants disguised as women and known as the demoiselles were chasing forest guards and charbonniers (charcoal-burners) out of the forests. They were defending their traditional rights of pasture and gleaning against the government and local notables.

John Merriman examines the intersection of social crisis and the Revolution of 1830 in the Ariège and suggests that the events there were indicative of the impact of the revolution and of rural capitalism on the traditional peasantry.

The author teaches history at Yale University. His major interest is social change and revolution in nineteenth-century France. He is the author of "Social Conflict in France and the Limoges Revolution of April 27, 1848," Societas—A Review of Social History, IV, 1 (Winter, 1974), is finishing a book on the radicalization and subsequent repression in France during the Second Republic, 1848–1851, and is currently studying the working class of Limoges from 1815 to 1914.

The Revolution of 1830 was part of a significant social, economic, and political crisis in France that lasted from 1827 to 1832. The popular protest of this economic depression included numerous grain riots, tax rebellions, forest disturbances, and possibly the mysterious series of fires in western France that still have not been adequately explained.[1] Such violence reflected more than just this particular economic crisis.[2] France was changing: the combination of a developing rural capitalism and a centralized, bureaucratic state, which protected and sponsored it, was winning its struggle with the French peasantry. The forcible integration of the peasantry into the national state and economy was not easy. The social and economic transformation of modern France in the nineteenth century came only at the expense of traditional peasant rights, local control over food supply and natural resources, and even the solidarity of the community itself.[3] In the spring of 1830, while the famous "221" deputies were opposing the intransigent Bourbon, Charles X, and his minister Polignac in the name of what they believed were their essential political liberties, peasant communities and the urban poor were resisting tax collectors, grain merchants, gendarmes, and forest guards.

The Revolution of July 1830 was precipitated by political issues that were of concern to only a small proportion of the population. Nevertheless, the revolution was not finished when Charles X had fled, the tricolor was flying, and a new administration began to carry out its duties to a new king. As the victors of the "Three Glorious Days" tried to consolidate their power won in the name of "liberty," the common people seized the opportunity afforded by the events in Paris and renewed their own struggle with vigor. They attacked customs barriers, ripped apart tax registers, rioted against the high price of grain, and devastated royal and privately owned forests.[4] This protest sometimes included an additional dimension, learned from the revolutionaries in Paris and seemingly legitimized by the tricolor and the official proclamations announcing the new regime—they often protested in the name of "liberty." The events of 1830 are an important indication of how France was changing economically and socially.

Far from Paris, in the mountainous department of the Ariège on the Spanish border, the struggle between the peasant communities and their antagonists, the revenue-hungry state and the local beneficiaries of a new economy, was waged in the forests. The most significant years of the peasants' organized resistance to these powerful "outsiders" were from 1829 to 1831, appropriately peaking in 1830. The "War of the *Demoiselles*," as it became known for reasons that will soon be apparent, lasted from 1828 until 1872. It has only recently been described in its entirety.[5] If we look closely at the two most important years of this "war," we will see a good example of how the traditional peasantry was affected by the impact of rural capitalism, which gradually transformed French society. We will also see that the Revolution of 1830 was part of this interrelated social, economic, and political transformation.

The Ariège is extremely heavily forested. In 1830 there were 175,000 hectares of forest in the department, often making up a considerable percentage of the area of communes. On the edges of the forests and in the valleys, a very poor subsistence agriculture was possible, particularly at the lower elevations. But many communities in the *arrondissements* of St. Girons and Foix were completely dependent upon access to the forests for survival. In these communes the peasants pastured cattle and sheep as a "cash crop" and sold them in the markets below the mountain elevations. But these peasants also depended on wood from the forests for use as fuel and for repairing their houses in order to survive the harsh Ariège winters. Until about the middle of the eighteenth century, the *seigneurs*, and the Crown, who owned most of the forests, had always freely granted rights of pasturage and of gleaning to the peasants. In some areas there was a traditional yearly allotment of wood for fuel and repairs of houses. But generally the peasants just took as much wood as they needed and pastured their flocks freely. There was certainly enough forest and wood plentiful enough so that there does not seem to have been any speculation. The forests were valuable only to the peasants. Ownership and use were two different things, and use was by far the most important. Collective peasant rights of usage had only been infrequently challenged, even if the actual deeds or the

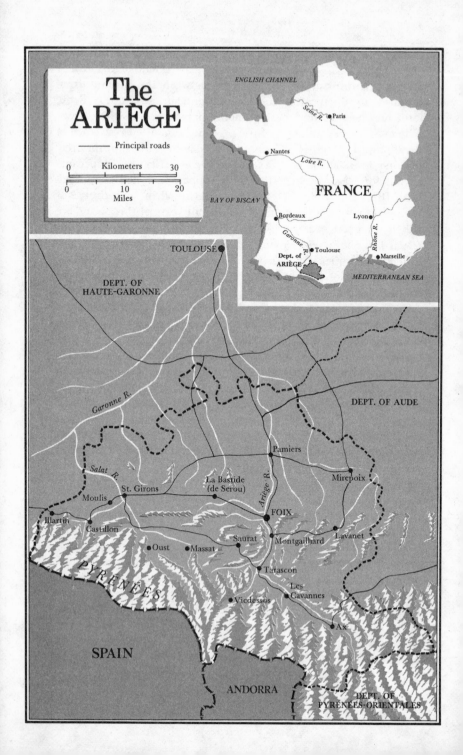

grants themselves often no longer existed. The conflict of interest between the owners, the Crown and the seigneurs, and the users, the peasants, was only latent.[6]

Beginning in the second half of the eighteenth century, this situation began to change. As France's metallurgical industry slowly developed, the number of forges increased in the department. The wealthy landowners could profit by using the wood from their forests to supply the forges. The price of wood soared, particularly in the 1820s. The departmental notables, whose number included many bourgeois who had purchased "*biens nationaux*" during the revolution (by 1830 only twelve of the forty-three forges in the Ariège still belonged to the seigneurial families—the others were owned by bourgeois), began to challenge and oppose the peasants' use of their forests. Many contestations between the "owners" and the "users" ended up in the courts, where the local notables usually won.[7]

And for the first time, the Ariège began to be overpopulated.[8] There were now more peasants depending upon access to the forests for survival. Complaints of the devastation of the forests were frequent. As the price of wood rose, the local notables and the forest administration became more determined to keep the peasants and their meager flocks out of the forests. During the bad winter of 1816–1817, the peasants had difficulty finding enough wood for fuel and were put in the position, in the words of one mayor, of "dying from the cold and hunger or breaking the laws."[9]

In 1827 a new forest code of 225 articles was implemented in France. This code was both an attempt to prevent the diminution of France's forest resources and a major concession to commercial and industrial interests. The code put under the strict control of the forest administration all woods and forests belonging to the state, and Crown, *and* "the woods and forests of the communes and of sections of communes." It created a complex and complete series of regulations covering all types of usage of the forests by peasant communes, even in forests that were communally owned, to be enforced by the forest administration, civil authorities, and the courts. From the point of view of the Ariège peasants, the most important articles forbade the pasturing of any "*bêtes à laine*," goats, lambs, or sheep, which the forest administration believed were eating their way through France's forest resources; established strict rules about the registration, marking, and pasturing of other animals; carefully regulated all other rights in the forests, such as, in the Ariège, the right to a yearly cut of wood for fuel and for repairing houses in each commune concerned; put one-fourth of the communal forest into reserve if the commune owned at least ten hectares as well as certain categories of fully grown and underwood areas; prevented any division of the communally owned forests among the inhabitants; and barred any clearing of forested land without specific authorization.[10]

The forest code also gave the sub-prefects the power to authorize the *propriétaires* of forested areas to hire private forest guards, who took an oath of service before the local court. They were to do the same thing as the royal forest guards did in the state, crown, and communal forests, that is, search the woods for peasants taking wood or grazing animals in violation of the forest code.

The tribunals were busy with an enormous number of prosecutions for violation of the forest code or of the private property of the notables. The latter were particularly vindictive. Even the local administration officials sometimes spoke of the "rapaciousness" of these fortunate few. Some peasants desperately searched for old deeds granting them rights of usage, checking the basements of deserted churches, and going as far to look as Montauban.[11] Many communes, already staggering under the onerous taxes that victimized the poor throughout France, were now faced with the loss of their most important, and in some cases only, resource. General Laffite, the department's leading citizen, later aptly described the situation of "an indignant people and several oppressive families of this department; here as elsewhere everything was organized for the domination of some and the suffering of others."[12]

The peasants had no alternative but to resist. In February 1829 the Prefect, the Baron de Mortarieu, reported to the Minister of Interior that "for some time now, forest offenses have multiplied in a very alarming progression; there exists . . . principally in the arrondissement of St. Girons a spirit of resistance against the execution of the new code."[13] In May there were reports of "groups of armed men, disguised as women, and masked" in the royal forest of St. Lary, southwest of St. Girons.[14] Throughout the late spring and the summer violations of the forest code increased. Forest guards and *charbonniers* were attacked in what appeared to be an increasingly systematic fashion. A strange disguise was sometimes reported, even in the arrondissement of St. Gaudens in the neighboring department of Haute Garonne. Some of the incidents, which began to spread into new regions of the department after beginning in the canton of Castillon in 1829, are particularly revealing. They will serve as an introduction to a discussion of the nature of peasant resistance, in the months preceding the Revolution of 1830, to the loss of traditional rights in the forests.

In October 1829, Marrot, a wealthy property-owner and lawyer who lived in St. Girons, complained that the peasants were taking wood from his forest every day and even selling it publicly in St. Girons, while local authorities looked the other way. On October 14 he went into the woods with one of his guards. They came upon a number of peasants taking wood. When the peasants saw them, they sounded the alarm. The guard later reported that "suddenly all of the fields of the gorge were filled with peasants making the most menacing yells!" Marrot and his guard were assailed with rocks. "My master fired at an individual dressed as a woman!" Marrot filed a formal complaint for damages against the commune of Moulis.[15]

In Illartein, in the valley of Ballongue near St. Lary, a band of peasants threatened an innkeeper suspected of lodging forest guards, shot into his house, warned him that they would return in greater numbers, and continued their search for forest guards in other houses and inns.[16] All of the peasants were disguised as women. In Aleu the mayor received notice "that if he should present the slightest charge [against any forest offender], his house and barns would be burned."[17] In the royal forest of Buzan, the forest inspector and his guards found animals grazing illegally. When they attempted to seize the animals, they were fired upon by peasants and driven away.[18]

Beginning in 1830, the incidents spread into the cantons southeast of St. Girons. Several wealthy landowners, principally M. Laffont-Sentenac and M. Trinqué, dominated this area. On January 26, 1830, forty peasants disarmed and threatened one of Laffont-Sentenac's forest guards. The next day an imposing crowd of between two hundred and four hundred peasants came to Massat, the *chef-lieu* of the canton of that name, and chanted, "Long live the King, Down with the Forest Administration!"[19] A month later, nearly eight hundred came to Massat, armed with hatchets, scythes, and guns, and warned that as many as three thousand would return. The next day sixty peasants in nearby Boussenac burned down the house of a forest guard.[20] On March 13 armed peasants devastated land belonging to Laffont-Sentenac and threatened to kill his sharecroppers if they did not leave within eight days. The inhabitants of Boussenac were suspected of this attack.[21]

The difficulties of M. Trinqué are even more illustrative of the situation in the arrondissement of St. Girons. Trinqué bought the rights to the wood cut of 1829 in the forest forming part of the commune of Ustou, high in the mountains, quite close to Andorra. He paid four thousand francs, and his total investment would be twelve thousand francs, a considerable sum but easily returned with profit. On July 8, 1829, his charbonniers spent the day working in the forest. M. Trinqué tells us:

> At the moment of the completion of this work, when the *charbonniers* were to return to my forge toward two in the morning [!], a band of armed and disguised madmen appeared before my *charbonniers* and made them promise to abandon their work under the threat of death. Nevertheless, I was able to persuade them to stay in the forest, with the promise to obtain the protection of the authorities. Last Sunday, the 12th, toward four in the afternoon, a crowd of masked and armed men, who were without doubt the same who had appeared before, entered the work area, and, firing rifle shots, chased away fourteen *charbonniers*. The people of Ustou, joyous spectators to this horrible scene, offered no help to the unfortunate *charbonniers*. The mayor of Ustou was sick in bed, and could not find anyone to represent and support him, not even the deputy mayor, who said that he could not go to the scene because he had to be away . . . everyone agrees, the justice of the peace, the mayor and the *charbonniers*, that the inhabitants of the commune themselves are the authors of similar attacks.[22]

The next spring, 1830, Trinqué again complained that the peasants were devastating his forests. On April 2 several armed and disguised peasants came to the nearby commune Rivèrenert, led by a "Monsieur Laporte, captain of the Demoiselles." They gave the mayor a letter for Trinqué and announced that if Trinqué did not grant "to the inhabitants of the commune and to those of Massat the free exercise of pasturage, his forest would be ravaged on a daily basis and himself and his guards exposed to the most horrible treatment."[23] The mayor urged concession. Trinqué therefore went to the commune of Massat, where the peasants had gathered for an official function, and told the assembled villagers that he would give them pasturage for two years with the exception of certain areas of underwood, if they would guarantee no further destruction by the demoiselles. In nearby Rivèrenert, after unsuccessfully trying to persuade the mayor to call an assembly, Trinqué offered the peasants the same conditions offered in Massat. But when he said, "with the exception of the underbrush," the villagers cried out, "All or nothing." Trinqué's troubles were therefore not over; following this event, he "no longer dared to make any act of ownership in his own forest."[24]

By the end of 1829 there had been more than thirty separate incidents in the arrondissement of St. Girons, such as those described above. These incidents involved the participation of armed and disguised bands. These bands became known as the "demoiselles," because the peasants were disguised as women.

The disguise was first mentioned in St. Lary, in May 1829, when, as we have seen, "groups of armed men, disguised as women" were noted.[25] By July reports specifically mentioned the sighting of these "demoiselles."[26] One forest inspector described the disguise as leaving the "shirt out and darkening the face with red and black."[27] The disguise generally consisted of a white linen-cloth shirt, always left out and giving the impression of a woman's skirt or gown, some darkening of the face, and often some form of headwear. There were variations to the disguise, which seem to have corresponded to the extreme cultural, linguistic, and geographic compartmentalization of communes in the Ariège. Thus in one case, peasants from one commune were easily distinguished from others by local authorities because their disguise included a twig attached to their shirts, long a symbol of that particular commune.[28]

The similarity of the disguises contributed to the establishment of a collective identity of the demoiselles. A proclamation of the prefect of the Ariège on February 22, 1830, stated that:

> Any person who, beginning the 24th of February, is found masked, face darkened, any sort of weapon in hand, shirt left hanging out, or dressed in any sort of disguise, will be immediately arrested and handed over to the Prosecuting Attorney of the *arrondissement*.[29]

This collective identity was fostered by the peasants themselves in order to give the impression of a well-organized, para-military structure that could not be defeated. Warnings, which threatened or preceded appearances of the demoiselles, were frequently signed by a "captain" or "chief" of the demoiselles. The warnings themselves were quite similar to the "Swing" letters at the same time in England, which usually preceded attacks upon threshing machines ("Revenge for thee is on the wing, from thy determined Captain Swing").[30] One warning in Massat, scene of numerous appearances of the demoiselles, read:

> By order of the *superieur Demoiselles,* we advise the public of the town of Massat that the first person who furnishes lodging [to a forest guard will have] his house demolished [and], the penalty below [here was drawn a cross with the words 'A Mort'] . . . We warn the *clercs* of Massat that when the guards go into the forest, it will begin their own agony.[31]

The disguise served two important functions. First, it made each peasant anonymous while violating the forest code—taking wood from privately owned forests—or chasing away the "outsiders" from the forests, the forest guards and the charbonniers. Secondly, it expressed, and thereby reinforced, the solidarity of the communes involved in the struggle. The disguise, associated with the carnival in peasant communities, was an integral factor in communal behavior related to the community sense of justice and of traditional collective rights.[32]

The particular disguise of the demoiselles was neither unique nor novel to French peasants. As Natalie Zemon Davis has suggested, the link between the carnival and charivari forms of festivity and modes of collective communal protest is essential.

Peasant carnivals and festivities "help explain how the peasant community defended its identity against the outside world."[33] It was quite logical that communities used traditional modes of group behavior, and particularly those festival modes expressing popular definitions of justice, when struggling to assert and defend those beliefs and values against those of "outsiders."[34]

In his recent study of the "War of the demoiselles," François Baby has even gone as far as to characterize this "war" as a *"révolte carnavalesque."* Placing what he calls a *"jacquerie"* into the context of the region's traditional folklore, Baby sees the struggle as a "drama of social vengeance," a psychodrama mystic enough to be a "social exorcism," complete with the sexual overtones of the peasants, invariably male when disguised, attempting, as a cuckhold, to retake possession of the forest, to which is ascribed feminine characteristics, from the "outsiders," the forest guards and charbonniers who have violated it.[35] What is at least clear is that the peasant community found in the carnival-like disguises the solidarity against the powerful "outsider" who had disturbed and threatened the local sense of justice. Just as peasants often donned masks during festivals in early modern Europe to mock any inversion of the traditional, popular definition of justice or "misrule," so the Ariège peasants appropriately donned masks in seriousness to "do justice" to the outsiders impinging on their collective rights and customs.[36]

The outsiders were the representatives of the state and the forge owners and their guards and charbonniers. The guards and charbonniers were associated with the loss of traditional rights. They were strangers to the regions in which they worked, intruders who spoke and dressed differently. The forest guards were notoriously underpaid, uneducated, not above taking bribes, and, as a result, rather choosy about whom to turn in for violations of the forest code.[37] As outsiders, the guards and charbonniers were threatened by clumsily scrawled placards (*"Charbonniers*, if you work any more in this forest, your hours are numbered"), shot at, chased away, and often their worksheds were burned. It was virtually impossible for them to find lodging, because of the demoiselles' warnings to anyone who would give them a place to stay. For example, "fifty masked and armed" peasants completely burned down a barn where charbonniers had been sleeping. Both the forest guards and the charbonniers were effectively prevented from doing their assigned tasks.[38]

Departmental authorities were faced with the extremely difficult task of repression. The communes stood solidly against the administration, which had few allies within any Ariège commune. Government usually came to the patois-speaking communities only when it wanted taxes or conscripts. When the gendarmes, forest officials, administrative officials, and troops came in search of information on the demoiselles, they found that, in the prefect's words, "Be it through fear, be it because of personal interest, be it through agreement, the inhabitants all maintain an obstinate silence."[39]

Most mayors were of little help to the administration. They were not just representatives of the government but members of the communities. At best they were deliberately or naturally inefficient. More often, they were silent observers or even themselves participants in the "illegal" pasturing and wood-gathering. But if the mayors were revoked from their positions, who would replace them?[40] Furthermore, there was not an elite of citizens to be trusted as allies of the government. Calling out the National Guard of the insurrectionary communes was hardly a solution—many of its members were also "members" of the demoiselles. If there were members of the involved communes who sympathized with the notables and the administration, they dared not speak out. We have seen that measures were taken by the demoiselles to intimidate those who might be interested in lodging forest guards or charbonniers. Finally, the possible death penalty for any convicted demoiselle was probably an important deterrent against turning anyone in to the administration.[41]

Various normative appeals, such as proclamations by the prefect and Sunday morning pulpit denunciations of the demoiselles, only intensified community hostility against the guards, forest administration, notables, and curés. When the Bishop of Pamiers ordered his curés to preach against the demoiselles, he received a letter, dated Masset, February 1, 1830, signed, "Jeanne Grané, *le chef des Demoiselles*":

> We insurgents, under the mask of the women called *Demoiselles;*
> Garchal, curé of Biert, and Séres, of Soulan, have had the impru-

dence to preach against us. The said parishes have written you several times. You are unrelenting, but we will know how to teach them . . . the lesson which was given to the clergy and to the nobility in 1793. Their residences will be torn down and burned, their properties pillaged and burned, their bodies torn to pieces, their limbs will be sent by the parishes of the *arrondissement* to better set an example.[42]

Whether these dire predictions would have come to pass is purely speculative, but there were no more reports of priests preaching against the demoiselles.[43]

Temporary concessions to the peasants in August of 1829 failed to halt the resistance to the new forest code. Despite the prefect's own hard-line stand that perhaps the best solution would be to eliminate all peasant rights of usage in royal forests, a royal decree of August 12, 1829, temporarily restored the right to pasture sheep in certain areas for a period of one year and allowed for possible appeals by communes for future extensions of these rights. But the incidents did not stop. The insurrectionary communes still perceived their rights as traditional and full rights of usage.[44]

Force was the only alternative to complete capitulation by both the forest administration and the local notables. In July of 1829, the Minister of War began to send troops into the department to support the harassed and undermanned gendarmes and forest guards. By August 21, 1829, there were 750 additional troops in the Ariège; by April 1830 there were more than 1200.[45] But the troops were ineffective, especially during the long winter, which took its toll in reduced efficiency and even deaths. The peasants, who knew the woods so very well, could appear and disperse with astonishing ease. Many incidents occurred in communes with relatively large concentrations of troops. Furthermore, the quartering of troops in the communes, particularly in those only marginally involved in the struggle, only served to exacerbate local hostility against the administration.[46] And so, for all of the troops and forest guards, there were few warrants for arrest and even fewer actual arrests. For example, of eight warrants from an incident at Augirein, seven of the accused were listed as being "in flight."[47] There were two major trials, which were given the widest possible publicity throughout the department in order to intimidate the peasants.[48] But, in general, the demoiselles were not inhibited by the show of force by the Bourbon administration.

Finally, on March 15, 1830, the prefect announced that each commune would be made collectively responsible for violations of the forest code committed on its property, by virtue of a law that dated from the Empire. The twenty leading taxpayers, hardly an impressive fortune in many communes in the poor arrondissements of St. Girons and Foix, were to advance the sum to the commune in order to pay damages to the state or to the notables. It was clear that the demoiselles were the peasants from the communes struggling to maintain their rights of usage in the forests. This participation and responsibility was now legally acknowledged. The law itself was utilized by the courts several times, beginning with the assessment of 5875 francs in damages against the commune of Rivèrenert, to be paid to M. Trinqué, the state, and a small sum to two forest guards. Shortly thereafter, Boussenac was assessed the incredible sum of 20,000 francs.[49]

Throughout the spring, the demoiselles appeared frequently and over an increasingly wider area. The frequent appearances of the demoiselles in the commune of Saurat, who were easily recognizable as local people, led the mayor to write that "the people of Saurat only long for the moment when they can bring themselves justice and be assured of their rights of pasturage in the mountains."[50] But when July came, the demoiselles were not to be seen. The peasants needed less wood in the summer climate and, probably more important, many left the department to work the harvests at the lower elevations.[51]

During this same spring of 1830, a major political crisis mounted in Paris. But the confrontation between Charles X and the determined Chamber of Deputies had little noticeable impact in the Ariège. There was no organized political opposition or resistance against taxes, nor were there electoral associations.[52] It was only on August 3 that the prefect, the Baron de Montarieu, issued a proclamation that "Grave disorders trouble the capital of the Kingdom; the authority of the King has been ignored there —it will not be such in the department of the Ariège." By the fifth, as in numerous departmental *chef-lieux* in France, a provisional committee of administration had been formed. The prefect's announcement attributed this measure to "the request of several inhabitants of the Ariège for the creation of a commission with the powers to maintain order, public security, and law enforcement."[53] The next day the provisional committee of administration appointed the retired General Laffite, a popular and influential native of the department, to command the department, with the power to reorganize the National Guard.[54] A few local officials resigned. One regime passed to another. On August 9 it was reported that "the flag of liberty is flying in all of the communes of our department."[55]

At this point, so conventional histories would tell us, the revolution was over. But this sort of interpretation overlooks an essential point: the poor in France seized the opportunity provided by the events in Paris and asserted their economic grievances in renewing the struggle for power at the local level with determination.[56] This sustained the revolutionary situation in France, and the timing of the widespread social protest is indicative of the revolutionary process in general, as has been demonstrated earlier in this volume by James Rule and Charles Tilly.[57] The new administration was confronted with a widely based challenge to its authority.

In examining the role of the peasants in the Revolution of 1830 in the Ariège, we will note two important aspects of their participation: Many communes became involved, and their collective protest covered a wider geographical area and had several objects. While the peasants' collective action maintained the sense of "doing justice" to the outsiders impinging upon traditional rights, a new dimension could be found—the poor began to claim to act and even petition in the name of "liberty" and this "legitimization" of protest made disguise unnecessary. The demoiselles temporarily disappeared.

If there was ever a moment for peasants to recapture ground they had lost, it was during the period immediately following the revolution. The local administration was disorganized; gendarmes, forest guards, tax collectors, and even soldiers were uncertain as to whom they were serving. In this first wave of violence, peasants attacked the châteaux and property of their antagonists, seigneurs and the bourgeoisie alike. They rebelled against the onerous taxes that made them even poorer, burned down a large forge, and, as we would suspect, renewed their struggle for the forests with collective enthusiasm. They saw themselves as "doing justice" to their antagonists, the outsiders. Generally, they were not disguised.

In early August, within days after the first sketchy news from Paris, the château of the unpopular Astrié de Gudanes was attacked by peasants who believed that he had usurped their forests. He had recently intensified the hate of the poor by taking to court numerous peasants for violations of the forest code, including some who were fined two francs for each animal they pastured even in "defensible" or permitted areas without attaching a small bell.[58] The population of the commune of Miglos, where the demoiselles had previously appeared in the bitterly contested forests, stormed to the home of a local notable and held him prisoner for four days.[59] Three communes assembled at the sound of the tocsin early in the morning and went together to pillage the château of Bélesta in the arrondissement of Foix.[60] The mayor of Rabat wrote the provisional administration in Foix that he believed that a leading property-owner would be harmed by the commune because "he represents for some of the people the former *seigneurs*."[61]

Forests in all three arrondissements were pillaged. Two hundred to three hundred people went into the previously tranquil forest of Camarade in the arrondissement of Pamiers. In the royal forest of Pradières, the mayor watched passively as two forest guards were threatened and driven away (possibly by demoiselles) while the local population cut down trees. Marrot, the lawyer from St. Girons, again wrote that his forests were being pillaged. In the commune of Prayols, all but five or six families participated as the guards were driven away and peasants took as much wood with them as they could carry.[62]

The most spectacular and perhaps most significant example of peasant revindication came on August 21. In the commune of Luzenac, near Ax, high in the arrondissement of St. Girons, four hundred to five hundred peasants announced that they were "doing justice" and burned the three buildings of the forge to the ground while fifty soldiers stood by helplessly. The peasants, who were not disguised, believed that the wood supplying the forge was in the domain of their traditional rights of usage. At the same time, an anonymous letter written to the mayor of Saurat said:

> The chief of the regiment of *Demoiselles* has the honor to tell you that the forges which are near the forests will be completely destroyed, and yours is in that number. Long live Liberty![63]

Popular revindications were not just limited to the battle for the forests, nor even to the forest communes. In the town of Pamiers, which was the chef-lieu of the arrondissement, townspeople participated in the type of tax "disturbance" that swept France after the revolution. A crowd knocked on the door of the customs-barrier tax office and demanded that the official hand over to the crowd the registration of the *boissons* tax. Knowing the burdensome tax structure all too well, they had an agenda, making three or four stops in town that afternoon and taking five tax registers with them. In the mountains, resistance against the taxes began almost immediately following the first news from Paris. A proclamation of the provisional committee of administration urged the people of the department to pay. But in Vicdessos, a warning from the demoiselles was followed by the arrival of people from the neighboring communes to "do justice" to the tax collectors there.[64]

However, the impact of the revolution on the peasants of the Ariège was more complex than simply creating the opportunity for the poor to "do justice" to their antagonists. First, some communes collectively attempted to wrest concessions from the notables who owned forests and often forges. Second, the peasants sometimes claimed to act in the name of "liberty," which, after all, was what the revolution in Paris was supposed to have been about. Third, they paused at that crucial stage when the new regime might have proven to be conciliatory. Temporarily, the demoiselles virtually disappeared and the peasant communites appeared as petitioners to the new administration for concessions. The response of the new government would be crucial in influencing the outcome of the struggle in the Ariège between the new economy and the new seigneurs and the peasant community and its sense of traditional rights.

Some communes took advantage of the confusion that followed the news of the revolution to the Ariège and attempted to wrest concessions from the property-holders. The inhabitants of Mongailhard, a commune adjacent to Foix, "assembled on the public place. . . . everyone manifested the firm resolution to claim the lands which were usurped from the commune." Only with "the greatest difficulty" was the mayor able to persuade the commune to refer the claim to the administration.[65] But further away from Foix, in the regions where the forests had recently been hotly contested, the peasants moved on their own. In at least ten cases, they were able to obtain concessions. One hundred peasants of the commune of Mirepoix went to the home of the Marquise de Portes, the mother of a member of the Chamber of Deputies, in order to force her "to give back to the inhabitants the rights of usage that they claim to have in the woods."[66] On August 26, "a great part" of the people of Freychenet went with the mayor and his deputy to neighboring St. Paul where they joined peasants from nearby Mercus. Together, they forced the "agents" of a property-owner to give them the right "to pasture in all of the woods of the said *Mademoiselle*, except those held in reserve by law." A number of communes were able to force concessions from Astrié de Gudanes after attacking his château. The peasants were reported as being satisfied with these concessions. "*Voilà la paix*," wrote General Laffite. News of the burning of the forge at Luzenac and of the concessions spread quickly and without doubt encouraged other communes to act.[67]

Before the revolution, cries of "Long live the King, down with the forest administration!" could be heard in the Ariège ("If the Czar only knew . . ."). After the events in Paris, popular protest became associated with the slogan "liberty." The peasants learned from the proclamation in each commune announcing the change in regime that "liberty" had been won in Paris. So the letter that warned the mayor of Saurat that the forge there would be burned was marked, "Long live liberty!" A cry of "Long live liberty" was heard in Luzenac as the forge went up in flames. The mayor of Ax noted that peasant demands for concessions had been part of "the outburst under the word, 'liberty.' " The mayor of Prayols, where the peasants from several communes were freely taking wood in the forests, wrote:

> The liberty which His Majesty Philippe I [sic] has just given the French nation has been misinterpreted by our mountain peasants, who now believe themselves authorized to violate the laws, in

delivering themselves, without any limit, to all the disorders that they can commit against the forest administration.

The commander of the gendarmerie for the troubled arrondissement of St. Girons complained that "The public says resolutely that it has conquered liberty and that it wants to gain from its conquest; woe to him who would want to prevent it."[68] A good example of the convergence of social protest and the impact of the advent of political liberty occurred in the small town of Ax, almost literally as far as one could go from Paris and still be in continental France. In the words of the mayor, on August 22,

> . . . at three in the afternoon, I was with the deputy mayor and the secretary of the *mairie,* occupied with administrative affairs, when a numerous group invaded the town hall and demanded in the name of liberty that M. the Marquis d'Orgeix give them the use of his forests which they had fifty years ago; that the Monsieurs Astrié de Castellet give up their project of establishing the boundaries of the royal forests [which would be] prejudicial to their usage; that there be no more forest guards and that the taxes on beverages no longer be collected, all under the threat of death and fire. In this position, being unable to be supported by the National Guard, of which two-thirds participated in this uprising, having only twenty-five soldiers at my disposition, I did not think that I had any other choice than to be prudent.

After promising that "justice" would be done, the mayor sent a deputation to the Astrié family and the Marquis d'Orgeix. He then promised the peasants that the forest guards and the tax collectors would cease their functions, in return for a guarantee of their safety. The satisfied peasants left the Town Hall well after midnight.[69]

At the same time, the mayor of Engomer, where there was a forge that the peasants particularly resented, wrote the new administration in Foix that the best way of calming the peasants would be to end the hated salt tax and to revise the forest code.[70] Of course, he was right. Liberty in the Ariège did not mean the "essential political liberties," the *Charte,* or an extended electoral franchise. While it encompassed the general resistance to the burdensome indirect taxes that weighed so heavily on the poor in France, it primarily meant the return of traditional rights of usage in the forests.

The change in regime temporarily altered the response of both the peasants and the administration to the forest question. Once the initial wave of peasant violence subsided, the communes involved in the forest struggle became virtual petitioners to the new administration. And while the communes appealed to the new administration for "justice," the demoiselles were only rarely seen. The new administration seemed to offer some hope of conciliation.

The new government in Paris, faced with waves of disturbances across the country, increased militance among the Paris workers, the threat of a major counterrevolution in the west, and the difficulties inherent in reorganizing the judicial, administrative, and military hierarchies, sometimes showed surprising conciliatory efforts in the early months of its rule because the discontent of the poor was so widespread and intense.[71] The fourteen hundred troops in the department of the Ariège in September 1830 were probably not any more likely to be able to put an end to the disorders in the department than the troops before the revolution.[72]

The appointment of the local hero General Laffite as commander of the department made conciliation seem possible. Laffite, who remained extremely influential even after the new prefect assumed authority, understood the situation clearly and tended to sympathize with the communes against the greedy local notables. He publicly expressed hope in the new government, urging the peasants to remain calm. His numerous reports to the Minister of War in Paris explained the local situation and indicated that conciliation would be advisable, particularly in that the previous "administration, tribunals and Gendarmerie had only one feeling, that of a brutal partiality" against the peasants.[73] Even the Minister of War agreed that the rights in the forests were necessary for the existence of the "mountain people" and that perhaps the Forest Code of 1827 should be reconsidered because it did not take into consideration "immemorial usage and perhaps some misunderstood rights." The military commander in Toulouse hoped that the "great propertyholders" would "relent a little in their egotism" and that even the government, for the sake of peace in the Pyrénées region, would renounce some profit from the forests.[74]

In September small commissions were established for each department in the Pyrénées to check the validity of titles of ownership and usage in the forests and to see where additional concessions were needed. In the Ariège, where the difficulties were most extreme, a larger special commission was created to consider the claims of the property-holders and of the communes. This commission included six notables representing the large property holders and the forges, five representatives of the communes (four were mayors, the other a member of the Municipal Council of Foix), and eleven property-owners "representing the general interest of the department."[75]

A number of communes did formally petition the administration and this commission. The communes of the canton of Cabannes wrote that "rights of usage should be represented as the rights of property are represented." This petition noted that the reason for the somewhat deteriorating state of the commune's forests was not, as the owners alleged, because of use by the commune. Rather it was because "several of them [the *maîtres de forges*] have doubled their revenues. . . . all have indeed become extremely rich, and the *communes usagères* are in misery, their conduct has even made the seigneurial despotism be missed." The tiny (326 inhabitants) and impoverished commune of Montoulieu, surrounded by royal forests "in which it is rigorously forbidden to the inhabitants to cut a single branch," begged concessions, particularly for wood necessary for fuel as the winter approached.[76] The commune of Montgailhard, as we have seen, was persuaded by its mayor to forsake pillaging the wood and to turn their claim over to the new administration. The mayor petitioned on behalf of the commune.[77]

At the same time, two other conciliatory gestures were intended to limit disorders in the Ariège. A general amnesty was granted for those accused or convicted of violations of the forest code before the revolution. And, upon the recommendation of Laffite and others, an attempt was made to upgrade the personnel of the forest administration, especially the forest guards.[78]

The revolution had an important impact on the nature of the peasant's battle for the forests. The opportunity that the events in Paris gave the peasants, particularly by seeming to legitimize protest in the name of "liberty," and the first moves toward conciliation temporarily changed the form of peasant protest. Although the incidents of peasant mobilization increased in the two months following the change in administration, the disguise seemed virtually to disappear. The revolution legitimized protest and peasant action. Then, once the special commission had been organized in September as the most important of the conciliatory gestures, the Ariège was relatively calm.

Ultimately the new administration changed very little. The situation in the Ariège was not altered in any fundamental way. The commission, which reported in December 1830, offered only partial concessions. Although there was some modification of the forest code, such as the reestablishment of the right to pasture sheep, the forest administration still determined what were the "defensible" or permitted areas of pasturage.[79] The erosion of traditional communal rights continued. The forest administration itself was no more sympathetic to the peasants than before. A special report of the Forest Commissioner in Toulouse said that the peasants' claims were "without foundation." He recommended the confiscation of wood and the maintenance of garrisons of soldiers in communes where the peasants continued to resist in order to "stop the pretension that they should become the masters of the forests."[80] The "mountain bourgeoisie," which was being reorganized into an elite National Guard, had clearly won a decisive battle in the struggle for the forests.[81]

Some of the peasants saw this quite early. At the end of August 1830 a letter from a "captain" of the demoiselles warned the new officials and the clergy of an insurrection that would follow the example of Paris and conquer liberty: "This three colored flag is the only hope of our liberties, our beautiful hopes have been betrayed." A women in Illartein said that if the forest guards returned at all, "it will be necessary for the white robes to return."[82] The forest guards did, of course, soon return, even to Ax, despite the mayor's proclaimed hiatus in that commune. The commune of Montgailhard found that it had waited in vain, after presenting their claim to the administration as their mayor suggested, and went back into the forest to take wood and dodge the forest guards of the July monarchy. The mayor of one commune, elected after the revolution because he had led the peasants into the forest to take wood, was revoked by the prefect, and his successor was only installed with the help of troops. When gendarmes came to a hamlet to search houses for wood, a crowd of peasants drove them away.[83]

The next spring the demoiselles were back in the forests in full disguise.[84] They appeared in the forests as late as 1872, but never again as frequently or in such large numbers. The squeeze on the peasants of the Ariège continued; the great depopulation of the Ariège began. Many peasants simply left, moving out of the mountains to find a livelihood elsewhere.[85]

The battle for the forests was very much a part of the Revolution of 1830. The revolution not only came during an important stage of the confrontation between rural capitalism and the peasant community, it widened and intensified the struggle. The peasants challenged the new administration; their claims were often formulated in the name of "liberty." The revolutionary situation, as James Rule and Charles Tilly have suggested, was perpetuated. The Revolution of 1830 did not end with the resumption of political power in the department by the new administration. It continued, involving the local issue—the forests, and who had rights to them. When the new administration demonstrated that it would perpetuate the policies of the forest administration and stood solidly with the local notables, peasant resistance continued.

The Revolution of 1830 marked a stage in the Ariège peasant community's losing fight for its traditional rights. The demoiselles represented the solidarity of the community against the powerful outsiders who were usurping the use of the forests. They were a colorful but tragic vestige of an old world and a different set of economic relations—in which use was communal and far more important than ownership. But the experience of the Ariège peasants was certainly not unique. In many regions of France the impact of rural capitalism was already apparent.[86] A fundamental conflict of interest divided the peasant community from the state and local notables—noble and bourgeois. The grain riots and forest disturbances of the 1827–1832 period illustrated the way in which this conflict was being resolved—against the peasants.

The communal solidarity of resisting the impingement of outside control over local resources, against both the bourgeois and the *fisc*, may go a long way toward explaining the evolution of rural radicalism during the Second Republic, as Maurice Agulhon has described for the Var.[87] The Revolution of 1830 was also an anticipation of the appearance of the common Frenchman as a contender for political power. The "liberty" of 1830, even if only the myth of a political elite, was a strong heritage, especially when it became rooted in the solidarity of the peasant community of equals. The era of "Long live the King, Down with the Forest Administration!" was just about over in France. The reaction of the poor, including those who remained in the Ariège and those who moved into the less mountainous regions of southern France, to the impact of state-protected capitalism would become more articulate, more organized. The communal solidarity of peasants fighting the fisc and the advance guard of rural capitalism soon gave way to a more modern age of protest.[88]

Notes

The research for this study was made possible by a faculty summer grant from the History Department of Yale University. I would like to thank Charles Tilly, Rod Aya, Susanna Barrows, and Anne Locksley for suggestions on an earlier draft.

[1] Paul Gonnet, "Esquisse de la crise économique en France de 1827 à 1832," *Revue d'histoire économique et sociale*, 33, 3 (1955), pp. 249–292.

[2] On the significance of popular protest, see Charles Tilly, "The Changing Place of Collective Violence," in Melvin Richter, ed., *Essays in Theory and History* (Cambridge: Harvard University Press, 1970), pp. 139–164; Charles Tilly, "How Protest Modernized in France, 1845–55," in W. O. Aydelotte, A. G. Bogue, and R. W. Fogel, eds., *The Dimensions of Quantitative Research in History* (Princeton: Princeton University Press, 1972), pp. 210–224; and Louise Tilly, "La révolte frumentaire, forme du conflit politique en France," *Annales*, 27 (May–June, 1972), pp. 731–757.

[3] Particularly relevant approaches include, Charles Tilly, "Food Supply and Public Order in Modern Europe," a working paper of the Center for Research on Social Organization, the University of Michigan, forthcoming as a chapter in Charles Tilly, ed., *The Formation of National States in Western Europe*; Albert Soboul, "The French Rural Community in the 18th and 19th Centuries," *Past and Present*, 10 (November 1956), pp. 78–95; and E. P. Thompson, "The Moral Economy of the Crowd in the 18th Century," *Past and Present*, 50 (February 1971), pp. 76–136.

[4] Gonnet, *op. cit.*; Roger Price, "Popular Disturbances in the French Provinces After the July Revolution of 1830," *European Studies Review*, 1, 4, (1971), 323–55; James Rule and Charles Tilly, "Political Process in Revolutionary France, 1830–32," in this volume, pp. 42–85.

[5] François Baby, *La Guerre des Demoiselles en Ariège (1829–1872)* (Montbel, Ariège, 1972). Maurice Agulhon's discussion of the forest problem in the Var and its impact on the creation of rural radicalism during the Second Republic is invaluable, in *La République au Village* (Paris: Plon, 1972), pp. 42–92. Baby figures the separate "appearances" of the *demoiselles* at 114 between 1829 and 1872, including 36 in 1829 and a peak 53 in 1820 (page 93). See also Louis Clarenc, "Le code de 1827 et les troubles forestiers dans les Pyrénées centrales au milieu de XIX° siècle," *Annales du Midi*, 77, 73 (July 1965), pp. 293–317.

[6] Baby, *op. cit.* and Clarenc, *op. cit.* give a good picture of the importance

of the forests and the general economic and social situation. See also Archives Départementales de l'Ariège (henceforth, ADA), Pe 45, "Aperçu sur le service forestier de l'*arrondissement* de St. Girons" (September 29, 1830) and the reports of General Laffite to the Minister of War (henceforth, MG), in the D³ series of the Archives of the Ministry of War at Vincennes (henceforth, AG). The prefect estimated that two-thirds of the population of the mountainous regions depended upon raising cattle or sheep for survival (Pe 45, Prefect of Ariège [henceforth, PA] to Minister of the Interior [henceforth, Int.], March 2, 1830). The state owned the vast majority of the forests in some cantons (Clarenc, p. 294).

⁷ Note Agulhon's chart of forest litigation in the Var, *op. cit.*, pp. 50–73. The petitions of the communes of Unac, July 5, 1829, and "Observations presented by the mayor of Massat," n.d. (ADA, Pe 45) are particularly revealing. Baby, *op. cit.*, p. 31, noted the changing class of the forge-owners.

⁸ André Armengaud, *Les populations de l'Est-Acquitain au début de l'époque contemporaine* (Paris, 1961), p. 165. Baby, *op. cit.*, p. 30, says that three of the most insurrectionary cantons were becoming rapidly overpopulated between 1804 and 1841 (Massat, 21 percent growth in population; Cabannes, 34.5 percent; and Castillon, 41.4 percent).

⁹ "Observations presented by the mayor of Massat," n.d., ADA, Pe 45. The rising price of wood is noted by Agulhon, *op. cit.*, p. 46; Clarenc, *op. cit.*, p. 299; and Guy Thuillier, *Aspects de l'économie nivernaise au XIXe au XIXe siècle* (Paris: Colin, 1967), p. 106.

¹⁰ M. Baudrillart, *Recueil chronologique des règlements sur les forêts, chasses et pêches, III* (Paris, 1824); M. E. Meaume, *Des droits d'usage dans les forêts de l'administration des bois communaux et de l'affouage,* I (Paris, 1851); Suzanne Coquerelle, "Les droits collectifs et les troubles agraires dans les Pyrénées en 1848," *Actes du 78e Congrès National des Sociétés Savantes,* 1953, pp. 345–363; Agulhon and Clarenc, *op. cit.* By notables, I am referring to important property-holders, both noble and bourgeois.

¹¹ The number of prosecutions increased in the *arrondissement* of St. Girons from 192 in 1825 to 341 in 1828 (830 in 1833), Baby, *op. cit.*, p. 39. ADA, Pe 45, "Tableau par ordre chronologique des divers attentats commis . . . par les malfaiteurs connus sous le nom de Demoiselles," relates the story of the peasants searching for their deeds. "Rapaciousness" of notables indicated by the *sous-intendant militaire* in Foix to MG, AG D³ 127, August 17, 1829.

¹² AG, E⁵ 2, General Laffite to MG, September 16, 1830. The general was given credit for putting down an uprising in the department in 1815, ADA, Pe 45, "Aperçu sur le service forestier de l'arrondissement de St. Girons"; AG, E⁶ 1, Laffite to FG, August 10.

¹³ ADA, Pe 45, PA to Int., February 3, 1829. Early resistance also was noted in the *arrondissement* of St. Gaudens in Haute Garonne, Commissioner of Forests in Toulouse to PA, July 6, 1829.

¹⁴ ADA, Pe 45, PA to Int., May 30, 1829.

¹⁵ ADA, Pe 45, PA to Int., August 6, 1829; Int. to PA, August 31; and PA to Int., September 7. Marrot apparently was able to buy the forest at a very

low price because of the tradition of the rights of the commune of Moulis in the forest.

[16] ADA, Pe 45, Sub-prefect of St. Girons (henceforth, SPSG) to PA, June 30 and July 20, 1829.

[17] ADA, Pe 45, SPSG to PA, June 7, 1830.

[18] AG, D³ 127, Commander of 10th Military Division (Toulouse, hereafter, 10th) to MG, August 20, 1829; ADA, Pe 45, PA to Int., August 20, 1829, and SPSG to PA, August 18, 1829. All of the administrative correspondence relative to the *demoiselles* is gathered in Pe 45, in four dossiers or *liasses*. Hereafter, ADA will refer to Pe 45, unless noted. In addition, the departmental archives include the *procès-verbaux* for ten trials of *demoiselles*, 1829 to 1831, in 2 U 193.

[19] AG, D³ 129 10th to MG, February 14, 1830. Also letters of February 1 and 9.

[20] AG, 10th to MG, February 21, 1830; ADA, SPSG to PA, February 18.

[21] AG, 10th to MG, March 19, 1830, and ADA PA to Int., April 5, 1830.

[22] ADA, Trinqué to PA, July 17, 1829. His first recorded complaint was a letter written to the prefect, June 17, 1829.

[23] ADA, Int. to PA, June 9, 1830.

[24] ADA, Int. to PA, June 9, 1830; PA to Int., May 24, 1830.

[25] ADA, PA to Int., May 30, 1829.

[26] The very first mention seems to be AG, Commander of Gendarmerie to MG, July 16, 1829, D³ 126, which dates their appearance earlier than François Baby indicates. Baby did not consult the useful AG. There is good evidence that the *demoiselles* were active initially in the *arrondissement* of St. Gaudens in Haute Garonne, Commander of Gendarmerie to 10th, July 3, 1829, AG.

[27] ADA, Forest Inspector to Commissioner of Forests, July 6, 1829; ADA, PA to Int., June 12, 1829. One of the most accurate and complete descriptions is from the *arrondissement* of St. Gaudens in Haute Garonne, AG Commander of Gendarmerie of the *arrondissement* to MG, July 16, 1829. This disguise included a hood of cotton cloth.

[28] ADA, Mayor of Saurat to PA, June 5, 1830, and June 8, 1830. Peasants from a nearby commune wore their native straw hoods.

[29] Proclamation in ADA refers to the "criminal association of the *Demoiselles*"; ADA, PA to SPSG, February 23, 1830.

[30] E. J. Hobsbawm and George Rudé, *Captain Swing: A Social History of the Great English Agricultural Uprisings of 1830* (New York: Pantheon Books, 1968), example from p. 206.

[31] ADA, signed "Madamoiselle Lagrande."

[32] The evidence confirms that the *demoiselles* were local peasants; ADA, letter of a justice of the peace to PA, July 16, 1829, and mayor of Saurat to PA, April 30, 1830. Indications of outsiders (Spaniards or deserters from other departments) in or recruitment for the *demoiselles* are slight. The prefect, not normally a perceptive man, agreed that the peasants involved in the July 1829 disturbances were locals (ADA, PA to Int., July 20, 1829, and ADA, PA to Int., May 18, 1830).

[33] Natalie Zemon Davis, "The Reasons of Misrule: Youth Groups and Charivaris in Sixteenth-Century France," *Past and Present,* 50 (February 1971), p. 57.

[34] Professor Davis asserts that "real life was always deeply embedded in these carnivals" and that the "mocking laugh of misrule intended to keep a traditional order" (pages 45 and 65). In her "Women on Top: Sexual Inversion and Disorder in Early Modern Europe," preliminary draft of a paper presented to the American Anthropological Association, 1972, Davis indicates that female attire and titles in collective protest was to be found in Lyon in the 1770s (page 10).

[35] Baby, *op. cit.,* especially pages 126 to 139.

[36] Davis, *op. cit.* It was significant that one important incident of pillage in the forests of the unpopular Astrié de Gudannes came on the day of the local *fête,* ADA, PA to Int., June 12, 1830, which Baby notes (p. 105).

[37] AG, D³ 129, 10th to MG, February 14, 1830; ADA, commander of the first subdivision of the 10th to PA, July 27, 1829. Brawls between the communes and the forest guards were common; e.g., ADA, SPSG to PA, July 16, 1829.

[38] ADA, PA to Int., December 18, 1829; ADA, SPSG to PA, April 23, 1830 (example from royal forest of Bethmale); AG, D³ 128, 10th to MG, November 1, 1829. Other examples of attacks on forest guards and *charbonniers* include, ADA, under-inspector of forests in St. Girons to inspector in Foix, June 28, 1829, PA to Int., June 20, 1829, and July 3, 1829. Weapons usually included scythes, hatchets, sometimes rifles, and even bayonettes (ADA, mayor of Aulus to PA, June 14, 1830). The commander of the 10th complained that it was difficult to find *charbonniers* to go into the forests of the Ariège, AG D³ 126, July 25, 1829.

[39] AG, D³ 126, Int. to MG, July 9, 1829. Secret police were used beginning in June 1829, ADA, PA to SPSG, June 30, 1829.

[40] For example, ADA, lawyer of *propriétaire* to PA, June 14, 1830.

[41] AG, D³ 127, 10th to MG, August 17, 1829, and Int. to MG, August 30. It seems that some members of the National Guard were present among some of the repressive forces in the summer of 1829, but these were certainly the elite in communes which were completely outside of the struggle.

[42] ADA, PA to Int., March 8, 1830; ADA, PA to Bishop of Pamiers, June 30, 1829, and Bishop to PA, September 10, 1829. In addition, the SPSG convoked the mayors from the troubled areas, on orders from the prefect, ADA, PA to SP, September 5, 1829, and the prefect talked to a number of mayors on his tour of the *arrondissement,* ADA, May 18, 1830.

[43] Baby, *op. cit.,* pp. 60–61, indicates that priests sometimes helped the insurgents, and that the communes mentioned, Biert and Soulan, were communes in which the curés were, at least in 1809, members of the "Petite Eglise," which had refused to accept the Concordat and the authority of those priests ordained since 1803.

[44] ADA, PA to Int., September 4, 1829. As the prefect wrote the Minister of Interior, ADA, May 24, 1830, "the commune of Massat wants all rights of pasturing without any exception." In December, the number of incidents sharply

Notes

increased, including those in St. Lary, Augirein, and Villeneuve. This followed a period of relative calm. The Minister of War, whose job was to repress the disturbances, frequently suggested some conciliation, e.g., AG, D³ 129, MG to Minister of Finance, February 7, 1830. Few municipal councils formalized claims in the time following the decree in August, ADA, PA to Commissioner of Forests, November 28, 1829.

⁴⁵ AG, D³ 127, 10th to MG, August 21, 1829; ADA, SPSG to PA, April 12, 1840. Troop movements can be followed in the General Correspondence in the AG, e.g., D³ 125, 10th to MG, May 31, 1829. Baby, *op. cit.*, p. 93, estimates the entire repressive force, including gendarmerie, at more than two thousand or one for every eighty-five people in the department. There were entire companies in communes like Massat, Boussenac, and Rivèrenert.

⁴⁶ This was first suggested by the prefect, who generally preferred the hard line, ADA, PA to Int., September 4, 1829. On complaints, see ADA, Int. to PA, August 31, 1829, and PA to SPSG, September 5, 1829, particularly petition from Castelnau (ADA, SPSG to PA, June 9, 1830), complaining that they were forced to lodge troops in their commune which were used to watch neighboring Esplas.

⁴⁷ ADA, PA to Int., March 8, 1830. Arrests included those in Ustou, where the worksheds of the *charbonniers* were burned (AG, D³ 126, 10th to MG, July 23, 1829); trials involved arrested peasants from St. Lary, Seix, Sentenac-de Sérou, Massat, Esplas, and Buzin, 2 U 19³ ADA, ten *affaires*.

⁴⁸ The most important was the trial and conviction of Bertrand Cointre, *dit* Falot du Company, which was announced and posted throughout the department, ADA, PA to Int., March 8, 1830. For example, one trial of ten *demoiselles* resulted in the conviction and sentencing of three (two got ten years and the other six months); witnesses could not, or would not, establish the identity of the others, ADA, PA to Int., June 7, 1830. On the two major trials, see Baby *op. cit.*, p. 82.

⁴⁹ Proclamation of Prefect, ADA, March 15, 1830; ADA, *Procureur* of St. Girons to PA, April 7, 1830; Int. to PA, June 9, 1830; AG, D³ 130, Int. to MG, April 17, 1830. In the Trinque case, 2500 francs went to the Crown as a fine, and 300 and 75 francs to the two guards. The use of this law, the law of 10 Vendémaire, An 4, was first suggested by the prefect, ADA, PA to Int., September 4, 1829.

⁵⁰ ADA, mayor of Saurat to PA, June 8, 1830. The winter was apparently particularly harsh, including an avalanche in Bethmale, Archives Nationales (hereafter, AN), F⁷ 6767, PA to Int., February 5, 1830. Spring appearances were particularly marked in cantons of Massat, St. Girons, and Oust.

⁵¹ ADA, St. Martin (inspector?) to PA, September 4, 1829, notes the return of four hundred peasants from the Spanish harvests.

⁵² AN, F⁷ 6767, PA to Int., September 10, 1829. Only mention of dissent is the prefect's report that the young of the "*classes aisés* are generally imbued in the principles of independence which the liberal press sanctions and propagates," AN F⁷ 6767, PA to Int., March 11, 1830. Political interest undoubtedly centered in the *arrondissement* of Pamiers, which had 355 electors, as compared with 345 for the *arrondissements* of Foix and St. Girons combined.

[53] ADA, 5 M 44, August 3 proclamation of the prefect; 5 M 62, proclamation of August 5. The wording of this petition may indicate that there was already an outbreak of disturbances in the forests.

[54] ADA, 5 M 62, August 5; AG, D³ 131, Laffite to MG indicates Laffite had arrived in Foix from Rouen.

[55] ADA, 5 M 44, proclamation of provisional committee of administration, August 9, 1830. The departure of Charles X was not known until the eighth, as evidenced by the fact that the committee replaced one subprefect on the seventh because he would not swear loyalty to Charles X. Two more members were added to the provisional committee of administration on the 10th (proclamation, ADA, 5 M 62). Another proclamation on that day asked each commune to report on the local political situation, agricultural resources available to the commune, and whether the tricolor was flying.

[56] Even David Pinkney's excellent political history of the revolution, *The French Revolution of 1830* (Princeton: Princeton University Press, 1972), underplays the impact of the revolution on the common man and largely limits discussion of the events in provincial France to political settling, such as revocations and replacements and the threat of a pro-Bourbon uprising in the West and South. He views the general economic crisis and its popular protest as contributing to the acceptance of the overthrow of the Bourbons (p. 225).

[57] James Rule and Charles Tilly, "Political Process in Revolutionary France," in this volume, pp. 42–85.

[58] ADA, mayor and justice of the peace of commune and canton of Cabannes to *Procureur*, August 11, 1830; petition of communes of Cabannes canton, to departmental commission on the forest question, n.d; AG, E⁵ 1, *Procureur* to MG, August 21, 1830.

[59] AG, E⁵ 1, provisional committee of administration to MG, August 21, 1830; ADA, *procès-verbaux* of events, August 18, 1830. Damages were estimated at 40,000 francs.

[60] ADA, complaint of owners, August 26, 1830. The commune of Fougax, where there was never an appearance of the *demoiselles*, seemed to have provided most of the participants, who were not disguised.

[61] ADA, n.d., mayor of Rabat to the provisional committee.

[62] ADA, mayor of Prayols to PA, September 12, 1830; mayor of Labastide-Sérou to PA, September 23; Marrot to PA, October 9. Other examples, pillage of property to the Mirepoix family, AG, E⁵ 2, 10th to MG, September 23; mayor of Saurat to provisional committee, September 5; and complaint of mayor of Ganac that commune of Brassac was furnishing *demoiselles* who were coming into the forests at night, ADA, to PA, September 22, 1830.

[63] ADA, mayor of Saurat to provisional authority, August 20, cites the threatening letter. Details of forge-burning, ADA, mayor of Luzenac to provisional committee, August 20, and mayor of Ax to PA, August 20; AG, E⁵ 1, 10th to MG, August 22 and August 21; and AG, E⁵ 1, provisional authority to MG, August 21. At the same time, an intriguing incident seems to have occurred in Lavelanet, with Luddite overtones—an anonymous letter to the provisional authority on August 28 mentioned that a machine of some

sort had been destroyed by individuals who claimed that the machine was taking work from them, ADA.

[64] Pamiers incident, ADA, 5 M 44, subprefect of Pamiers to provisional authority, September 1: ADA, mayor of Vicdessos to provisional authority, August 23. The mayor of Vicdessos also claimed, in a letter of August 27, that the *demoiselles* were seen in the town the night before the people came to "do justice" to the tax collectors.

[65] ADA, petition of mayor of Mongailhard to PA, September 2.

[66] ADA, mayor of Mirepoix to provisional authority, and SPSG to PA, September 7, 1830; AG, E[5] 2, de Portes, deputy, to Int. (Guizot, his friend), September 9, 1830.

[67] ADA, mayor of Freychenet to provisional authority, August 28; AG, E[5] 1, Laffite to MG, August 21. News of concessions spread quickly, AG, E[5] 1, 10th to MG, August 26 and ADA, mayor of Cabannes to provisional authority, August 12. Concessions angered the new prefect, who wrote the mayors of two communes that "all acts of usage or of property which are bases on the disposition of this transaction [the concession] will constitute, until authorized by the King, an attack on the property of others and the communes will be held responsible," ADA, September 14, 1830.

[68] ADA, mayor of Ax to provisional authority, August 23; mayor of Prayols to PA, September 12, 1830; AG, E[5] 2, Commander of Gendarmerie of the *arrondissement* of St. Gaudens (Haute Garonne) to MG, September 1.

[69] ADA, mayor of Ax to provisional authority, August 23, 1830.

[70] ADA, mayor of Engomer to SPSG, August 12, 1830.

[71] This attitude seemed to be reflected in Paris in the face of increased militancy of the workers; David H. Pinkney, "*Laissez-faire* or Intervention? Labor Policy in the First Months of the July Monarchy," *French Historical Studies,* 8 (1963), pp. 123–128.

[72] See note 45. There is no evidence that the number of troops and gendarmes in the department changed between April and the months of August and September.

[73] AG, E[5] 2, Laffite to MG, September 16, 1830.

[74] AG, E[5] 1, 10th to MG, August 26, 1830; MG to Int., August 31.

[75] AG, E[5] 2, Minister of Finance to MG, September 23, 1830 and decree of September 27; Laffite to MG, September 26, 1830.

[76] ADA, petitions of Cabannes canton and commune of Montoulieu, n.d.

[77] ADA, petition of commune of Montgailhard, September 2, 1830.

[78] ADA, Inspector of Forests to PA, September 20, 1830, and report of the Commissioner of Forests at Toulouse, November 6, 1830. Amnesty noted by Baby *op. cit.,* pp. 90–91.

[79] ADA, report of the commission, December 18, 1830, in the form of twenty-two *arrêtes,* or decrees. Article 10 provided for a hearing of the mayors and municipal council before the forest administration indicated each year the "defensible" or permitted areas of the forests. The communes were still held responsible for all violations of the forest code as modified. One previously burdensome stipulation was removed—the communes no longer had to attach

a small bell to each animal pasturing (article 19). The tiny commune of Montoulieu finally received some rights in the royal forests (see note 76).

[80] ADA, report of the Commissioner of Forests at Toulouse, November 6, 1830. It also recommended the upgrading of the personnel of the forest guards in response to the public clamor about the guards' behavior.

[81] AG, E⁵ 2, Laffite to MG, September 16, 1830. In one interesting case, again that of Massat, the commune actually purchased the disputed forest from the owners after the revolution (ADA, n.d. "Observations presented by the mayor of Massat"), later losing it back to the former *propriétaires* when the payments could, apparently, no longer be made (Baby, *op. cit.*, p. 89).

[82] ADA, letter of a "captain" of the *demoiselles* to the provisional authority, August 30, 1830.

[83] ADA, PA to mayor of Montgailhard, November 30, 1830; Inspector of Forests to PA, September 26, 1830 (reported that the new forest guard in Ax was being threatened); ADA 5 M 53, Int. to PA, December 14, 1830.

[84] AG, E⁵ 9, 10th to MG, March 22, 1831, particularly in the Massat area. Rumors of their reappearance began in this area as early as August 1830 (ADA, mayor of Massat to SPSG, August 24).

[85] Baby estimates the number of actual appearances, with disguise, of the *demoiselles* at seventeen between 1831 and 1848, most of these in 1831 and 1832 (*op. cit.*, pp. 93, 214–215). The number of forges continued to grow, reaching 57 in 1844 (43 in 1818), Baby, *op. cit.*, p. 35. Armengaud, *op. cit.*, pp. 195–210 describes the depopulation of the Ariège. Between 1841 and 1856 emigration exceeded immigration by 23,362, particularly during the period 1851–1856.

[86] As suggested by Albert Soboul, "La question paysanne en 1848," *La Pensée*, 18 (55–66), 19 (25–37), 20 (48–56), 1948; and more recently in, "The French rural community in the 18th and 19th centuries," *op. cit.* Baby considers the "War of the Demoiselles" to be unique, the "last French revolt to have made folklore its ornament, its motivations and its principal arm" (*op. cit.*, p. 149). He portrays this "war" as "not a revolutionary uprising . . . it is folklore, essentially [p. 147] . . . not a moment of the Revolution of 1830 but a simple *jacquerie* [p. 54]." While the disguise in the Ariège may have been unique, there were similar forest disturbances in many areas of France, recorded most accurately in the General Correspondence in the AG and in the BB¹⁸ series of the AN. Many of these involved the loss of the same rights as in the Ariège (see note 5, Agulhon, for example). The end of this folklore element to protest was itself another indication of the disappearance of the traditional peasant community.

[87] Agulhon, *op. cit.* In the May 1849 elections, the *"démoc-soc"* list won between 40 and 50 percent of the popular vote in the Ariège (Maurice Agulhon, *1848 ou l'apprentissage de la république, 1848–52* [Paris: Seuil, 1973], p. 174).

[88] Charles Tilly, "The Changing Place of Collective Violence" and "How Protest Modernized in France, 1845–55," *op. cit.;* and Tilly, "Collective Violence in the European Perspective," in *Violence in America,* in Hugh Davis Graham and Ted Robert Gurr, eds. (New York: Praeger, 1967).

Robert J. Bezucha

The Revolution of 1830 and the City of Lyon

The new government was faced with a variety of challenges to its authority. In Lyon, France's second largest city and one of the most concentrated industrial centers in the world, this challenge came from a resurgence of a tradition of municipal autonomy and from the thousands of silk workers who rose up in insurrection in November 1831 and April 1834.

In his study of the impact of the Revolution of 1830 on the city of Lyon, Robert Bezucha challenges the view that the revolution was ended by December of that year. Citing the similarities between Lyon and Paris, he supports James Rule and Charles Tilly's contention that the revolution inaugurated a crucial period of political and social struggle. He argues that the revolution in Lyon was finished only in June of 1834, after municipal resistance to central authority in Paris had been deflated, the silk workers had been crushed by the bourgeois National Guard and the army, and a slate of conservative "men of order" had been returned by Lyon's enfranchised political elite in the elections of June 1834.

Robert Bezucha teaches at Syracuse University. He is the editor of Modern European Social History *(Lexington, Mass., 1972) and the author of* The Lyon Uprising of 1834: Social and Political Conflict in the Early July Monarchy *(Cambridge, Mass., 1974). He is currently studying the development of voluntary associations in France in the nineteenth century.*

Whereas historians once considered the Revolution of 1830 to be an open and closed case, they are now debating whether it was an open *or* a closed case. In support of the latter interpretation, David Pinkney sees the publication of the July Ordinances as triggering an explosion of accumulated popular grievances; more by chance than intention, the violence in the streets broke the constitutional deadlock between Charles X and the Chamber of Deputies, forced the Bourbons to flee Paris, and permitted the political opposition to offer the crown to Louis-Philippe. Suggesting that it was basically a transfer of power between two groups of socially similar elected and appointed officials, Pinkney sets December 1830 as "the close of the revolution."[1] James Rule and Charles Tilly contend, however, that *les Trois Glorieuses* marked "the beginning, rather than the climax of a turbulent period. . . ." According to them, it is more accurate to say that the Revolution of 1830 opened a complex competition for political power which took years to be resolved.[2]

Perhaps this scholarly disagreement can be settled by leaving Paris to examine the Revolution of 1830 from the perspective of the provinces. This essay uses evidence from the history of Lyon to test both interpretations and, ultimately, lend support to that of Rule and Tilly. In 1833 an obscure Lyonnais journalist named Joseph Beuf was sent to prison for writing an alleged "Confidential Letter from His Majesty Louis-Philippe the First, King of the French, to His Well-Beloved Cousin Nicholas, Emperor of All the Russias," in which the Citizen King was made to say: "My Royalty having been proclaimed in Paris by 219 persons[*], it only remains to make France accept it."[3]

Lyon, the second city of France and *chef-lieu* of the Rhône department, stands at the confluence of the Saône and Rhône rivers, three hundred miles southeast of Paris. Famous as a manufacturing center (more than a quarter of the population of nearly two hundred thousand was engaged in the production of silk cloth), her political life during the Restoration began with the election of Ultra-Royalists to the *Chambre introuvable* in 1816 and was characterized, thereafter, by the steady growth of

---

* This is a reference to the number of deputies who had registered their opposition to Charles X and Polignac.

opposition to the Bourbons. In 1829, General Lafayette visited the so-called "capital of liberalism" and was feted at a banquet attended by five hundred persons. Introduced by Dr. Prunelle (who would become mayor within a year), the hero of two revolutions heard his praises sung by local deputies. In June 1830 the voters of the Rhône department, like those of the Seine (Paris), sent a solidly liberal delegation to the Chamber of Deputies, which would be dissolved by the July Ordinances. Local candidates who had supported Charles X and Polignac received only 595 of the 1,813 votes cast.[4]

When the news of the July Ordinances reached Lyon by telegraph on the 27th, local liberals reacted without any knowledge of events in the capital. The *Précurseur*, the leading opposition newspaper in the provinces, ignored an order from the prefect and refused to halt publication until its presses were seized by the police. By then it was too late for supporters of the Bourbons, because liberal leaders had not only called for the immediate mobilization of the National Guard but also encouraged the master silk weavers to close their shops and send their journeymen into the streets. On the morning of the 31st, an armed crowd raised barricades in the Place des Terreaux, the site of the Hôtel de Ville, and the mayor and prefect decided to capitulate in order to avoid a pitched battle. The members of the National Guard elected a Provisional Government and the tricolored flag was raised over the Hôtel de Ville.

The July Days in Lyon paralleled those of Paris with the obvious and important exception of the absence of bloodshed. One might say that the Lyonnais liberals achieved what the Parisians had desired: a revolution "lead by members of a . . . prudent middle class—businessmen, lawyers, doctors—who had no intention of disturbing capital or property because they were capitalists and property owners themselves."[5] On 4 August, the local Provisional Government staged a military review for the new garrison commander. As the troops marched by the crowd began to sing. "What is that song?" asked a young officer. "Ah, don't you know it?" replied his superior. "It is the *Marseillaise*."[6]

The Revolution of 1830 swept new men into the Hôtel de Ville in forty-seven of France's fifty largest towns. Pinkney believes, however, that these municipal revolutions were relatively unimportant because mayors had little independent power.[7] They were nominated by prefects and appointed by the king during the Restoration, and the July Monarchy only modified this dependence on the national government: under the Municipal Law of 1831, the king or prefect (in the case of small towns) selected the mayor from the members of the locally elected Municipal Council.[8] Nonetheless, it would have been difficult to convince the first three post-revolutionary occupants of the Prefecture of the Rhône that the new man in the Hôtel de Ville was simply a political creature of Paris. As late as 1834 the Minister of the Interior commented: "It is not easy to be Prefect in Lyon when M. Prunelle is Mayor."[9]

Dr. Gabriel Prunelle held two offices simultaneously. When he sat in the Chamber of Deputies for the neighboring Isère department he was a staunch supporter of Louis-Philippe, or (to steal a phrase from Rule and Tilly) a member of the successful revolutionary coalition which was seeking to reestablish routine government over the French nation. When he presided over the Municipal Council in Lyon, however, he personified the belief that the July Days had reopened the route toward local autonomy.

The first Orléanist Prefect, Paulze d'Ivoy, arrived in Lyon on 6 August 1830 and found Prunelle already in office under the authority of the local Provisional Government (his position was subsequently confirmed in Paris). D'Ivoy was recalled on 11 May 1831, having been told: "The differences raised between you and the municipal authority have convinced the King's government to send a successor."[10] The second prefect, Bouvier-Dumolart, departed in disgrace in early December. He was charged with mishandling a wage dispute between silk merchants and weavers in Prunelle's absence and, thereby, contributing to the famous worker rebellion of November 1831. The third prefect, Gasparin, arrived with what one observer called "the special mission of preventing a [second] insurrection."[11] The stage was set for a power struggle between a strong-willed mayor and a determined prefect, who represented the centralized national bureaucracy.

Because of the overlapping jurisdictions and complex procedures that plagued French law enforcement in this period their conflict frequently focused on the responsibility for maintaining public order in Lyon.[12] Prefect Gasparin correctly concluded that the Commissioner of Police was incompetent. Mayor Prunelle admitted that "he is not a man of great capacity," but steadfastly refused to dismiss him.[13] A stream of suggestions about police reform from the Minister of Justice and the Minister of War were either ignored or else rejected as too expensive. Gasparin was frustrated, but the Minister of the Interior warned him: "The Mayor is jealous of his rights. . . . The Municipal Police belong to him. Seeking to remove a man who has his confidence will launch an open battle which you risk losing."[14]

When he learned to expect little cooperation from the Hôtel de Ville on this matter, the prefect devised a way to go around the mayor. He successfully recommended to Paris that the local National Guard be dissolved for a year on the grounds that only a fraction of the bourgeois units had responded during the November rebellion and those in worker neighborhoods had actually joined the insurgents. The citizen militia was replaced by an increased garrison and regular troops were given certain police powers. In addition, the prefect relied on the departmental *Gendarmerie* over which he had administrative control.

Mayor Prunelle bitterly opposed these tactics because he considered the National Guard to be the symbol of the July Days. As soon as a year had expired he held elections for National Guard officers without waiting for permission from Paris. To his embarrassment the turnout was low and with a concerted effort the local Republicans elected several of their candidates, including a battalion commander. Confronted with these "imperfect results," as Prefect Gasparin ironically described them, the government decided to keep the Lyonnais militia on inactive status indefinitely. Prunelle had no alternative but to agree, his anger now compounded by questions raised in the Republican newspapers: If only monarchists could be officers, why not call it the Royal Guard? Did Louis-Philippe really consider his fellow citizens too dangerous to trust them with weapons?[15]

The issue of public order in Lyon has been used to illustrate the conflict between the municipal and national authorities because it resembles the post-July situation in Paris. Pinkney considers the Revolution of 1830 to be truly "closed" when General Lafayette was forced to resign as commander of the National Guard, thereby removing the potential of armed resistance from the king's leading rival.[16] Another issue, such as disagreement over taxation, might have been used with similar results. At one point, for example, the mayor wrote the prefect: "MM. Thiers and Laffitte [who supported a controversial municipal tax bill in the Chamber of Deputies] will not be able to prevent us . . . from being massacred in a riot."[17] In any case, it is essential to recognize that Prunelle and Gasparin were both members of the Orléanist party. Yet their rivalry went on for years. In January 1834 the mayor neatly captured what separated them: *"M. le Préfet, you are accountable only to the Government for your conduct; I must justify myself to my fellow citizens."*[18]

". . . [A]gainst the capital's attempts at political domination . . . Lyon had no equal among provincial cities in waging a stubborn resistance."[19] This statement refers to the situation in France in 1870, when the collapse of the Second Empire brought about the declaration of communes in several towns. It suggests two important things about the post-1830 period. First, in the most centralized of European nations any temporary weakening of the government in the capital was accompanied by a test of its continued authority in the provinces. Second, Mayor Prunelle's attitude was not the result of a personality quirk but, rather, resulted from the fact that he consciously represented a tradition of "municipal liberty."

The July Days made decentralization a topic of widespread community discussion in Lyon. In 1833, a printer named Léon Boitel published a collection of essays by local authors called *Lyon vu de Fourvières* (the name of a hill overlooking the city) in order "to combat literary and artistic centralization." As one contributor wrote: "There have been a host of attempts in the departments since the Revolution of 1830 to create . . . a local literary instinct. . . . Lyon is certainly the city in France where this spiritual movement has been the most rapid. . . ." In 1835 Boitel founded the *Revue du Lyonnais* to compete with the *Revue des Deux Mondes* of Paris. For the rest of the century the city's learned societies reported their achievements, and amateur poets and writers published their work in its pages. For example: Lyon had revolted against the policies of the Committee of Public Safety in 1793 and during the Restoration the Bourbons had declared the subsequent siege by the revolutionary army to be a part of the city's royalist heritage. Lyonnais historians now told a different story:

> Those who took up arms . . . did not support the cause of Louis XVI so much as the cause of Lyonnais nationality. Struggling against the Convention . . . they were struggling against the invasion of men and things from Paris, against monopoly and centralization; they were fighting for her independence and liberty.[20]

Or, to cite another example, the *Revue du Lyonnais* asked: "Why does the second city of France not have a Sorbonne of its own? If there is a sacrifice to be made, it is one which . . . Lyon should make in the interest of her dignity." In 1838 a *Faculté des Lettres* opened the doors of its temporary quarters across the street from the Hôtel de Ville.[21]

Closely linked to these cultural trends was the conviction that political and administrative decentralization were necessary if they were to become permanent. We have seen how the mayor tried to deliver this message to Paris. Others, who were outside the successful revolutionary coalition and, therefore, Prunelle's political enemies, agreed with him on this matter. The moderate, or Girondist, faction of the local Republican party endorsed a program of "federalism." One of its spokesmen proposed Lyon as the center of an Association of the East. In a notice sent to newspaper editors in the region he argued:

> Our departments, isolated from the influence of Paris, having different resources and interests, need such an association. . . . Moreover, it is time to give the provinces an independent life of their own. The geographical division of our country . . . will eventually force us there later, if our political interests do not direct us there now.[22]

Lyonnais Republicans resented taking orders from the capital for many of the same reasons that the men in power did. One of them responded to a letter from the National Committee of the Society for the Liberty of the Press with an angry statement: "All I ever hear is 'They want this meeting in Paris. The provisional committee will be chosen in Paris. Finally, the money will be spent in Paris. . . .' "[23] At first, the self-appointed national leaders of the Republican party attacked "this mania of decentralization and federalism" and accused the Lyonnais of playing into the hands of the Carlists (those persons still loyal to the deposed Bourbons);[24] later they learned how to defer to their sensibilities:

> What you have said about centralization appears just and well-taken to us. . . . Lyon should be considered as the headquarters of the French proletariat and a school for the application of new theories of social reform. . . . What we mean by Parisian centralization is not the absorption of all ability and intelligence at a single point. . . . We are counting heavily on you.[25]

There is substantial evidence, in other words, that the Revolution of 1830 opened a period of Lyonnais resistance to outside direction over local affairs.

It would be fruitless to debate whether the July Days of Lyon were more the result of accumulated grievances against the Bourbons or the previous success of their local opponents. It is certain, in any case, that political equilibrium was not rapidly established in the city. Once the common foe had been defeated the fragile liberal coalition began to unravel in a manner strikingly similar to the "political process model" proposed by Rule and Tilly.[26]

The story is familiar when projected on the national level. After a period of accommodation with the moderate Left (a broader coalition is needed to seize power than to maintain it), Louis-Philippe chose Casimir Perier to head the Council of State in March 1831. Perier introduced a policy of judicial attack on the King's enemies wherever they stood on the political spectrum. In June 1832, having already faced a challenge from the Right (an attempted pro-Bourbon revolt in the south), the government met one from the radical Left (a Republican-inspired riot in Paris). By then the divergence in long-term objectives was fully apparent and the revolutionary coalition of 1830 had split into what contemporaries called "the Party of Order" (backers of Perier and his successors), "the Party of Movement" (men loyal to Louis-Philippe but critical of his programs), and the Republican party, which desired the fall of the July Monarchy itself.

On the local level the breakup was revealed in the very forms of respectable activity on which liberals previously had built their unity: elections, banquets, and newspapers. An initial schism occurred with the elections of July 1831, in which three of the five men sent to Paris by the voters of the Rhône were formally allied with Casimir Perier; one of them, a new deputy named Fulchiron, quickly acquired a reputation for his speeches baiting the handful of Republicans in the Chamber.[27] Electoral politics, thereafter, became so poisoned that local Republicans described the candidates for the departmental and municipal councils as "traitors, renegades, 'sold' men, and bad patriots."[28]

The same phenomenon can be seen in the changed atmosphere of a series of banquets. All Lyonnais liberals supported the Polish rebellion against Russia in November 1830. A *Bazar polonais,* with a bust of Louis-Philippe in the place of honor, was established with the approval of the municipal government and raised 17,000 francs by the time Warsaw fell in September 1831. As refugees arrived in France, however, the government's failure to intervene became a divisive issue. Noting Mayor Prunelle's absence at a banquet for Polish patriots in February 1832, its sponsors recalled his own attack on his predecessor for failing to attend the banquet in honor of General Lafayette in 1829: "Who has changed in so little time, the people or the orator? Who has betrayed the eternal principles of liberty and humanity . . .?"[29]

Since Prunelle, Fulchiron, and their supporters were now a local "Party of Order," there was private discussion in the fall of 1832 about a banquet to seal an alliance between "the two [no longer three] nuances of Lyonnais liberalism."[30] The guest of honor was to be a local deputy, Couderc, a backbencher of the Party of Movement. When the Republican papers excitedly leaked word of the negotiations, however, Couderc reconsidered the political consequences of the company he would be keeping and withdrew his name, stating: "I share many of their ideas, but experience has robbed me of the illusions which color the happy period of youth."[31]

Among the members of the revolutionary coalition of 1830, only the Republicans continued to use banquets as an opposition forum. In the spring of 1833 the Lyonnais Association for the Liberty of the Press announced a mammoth one for Garnier-Pagès, a Republican deputy who was in the city to defend a radical paper before the Assizes Court. When the Banquet Committee began to distribute free tickets, Prefect Gasparin banned public assemblies until further notice and sent troops to guard the hall.

The *Courrier de Lyon*, a spokesman for the government, applauded his action with the observation that "the July Monarchy is more often compromised by the weakness of its friends than by the . . . real strength of its enemies."[32]

Before the Revolution of 1830, Lyonnais liberals had clustered around the *Précurseur* like moths around a flame. A new editor was hired in the fall of 1831 and, although approved by a committee that included Mayor Prunelle and *Procureur Général* Duplan, some stockholders considered his ideas too advanced;[33] in January 1832 they founded a rival paper, the *Courrier de Lyon*. There is no evidence to sustain or disprove the allegation that the government gave the *Courrier* an initial subvention, but it is certain that it later helped it through a financial crisis: in August 1833, the Minister of the Interior promised Prefect Gasparin secret funds for "a journal which has rendered great services and can render them still."[34]

The *Précurseur* was the local voice of Movement in the winter and spring of 1832: it opposed Casimir Perier but condemned all conspiracies, supported the reformed Charter by hoped for the perfection of political institutions. The suppression of the June riots in Paris, however, caused the paper to break with the Citizen King: "The government of July . . . is now stained by [the] blood . . . of those who founded it. . . . Today there are no more 'divisions' between us: a river of blood separates us from our enemies. . . ."[35]

This declaration led to the final step in the disintegration of the Lyonnais liberal coalition: the majority of the *Précurseur's* stockholders transferred their money and allegiance to the *Courrier de Lyon,* and those who remained became identified as the moderate wing of the Republican party, forced into an uneasy alliance with the city's tiny band of radical Republicans and their newspaper, the *Glaneuse*. As the *Précurseur* became the target of a concerted attack (eight trials before the Assizes Court in the second half of 1832 alone[36]), persons who once had defended it from the Bourbon courts now raised funds to save it from a legal system controlled by their former friends. Pledging he would pay one percent of any newspaper's penalties, a wealthy engineer named Jules Seguin proclaimed: "A fine is a tax on the convictions of partisans of liberty."[37] The July Monarchy had become "the counterrevolution" in the eyes of those who published controversial opinions in Lyon.[38]

The Revolution of 1830 upset the city's political equilibrium not only by inducing the breakup of the anti-Bourbon coalition, a narrow world of respectable men devoted to modern forms of politics, but also by mobilizing a broad community of persons who were not considered respectable and whose means of expression were often traditional (Maurice Agulhon uses the term *folklorique*[39]): in other words, a popular form of politics.

In one café workers sing the glory of Napoleon, in another they grumble about the government's failure to support the Belgian revolution; a tree is decorated with a white handkerchief with a *fleur de lys* pinned to it, another is topped by a Phrygian bonnet; two men are arrested for displaying a medal bearing a portrait of Henry V, another is brought to trial for shouting "I want a Republic, I don't want a King" in the streets; the local deputy Fulchiron is forced to flee a friend's house in disguise when a crowd gives him a *charivari*, a raucous serenade to protest a recent speech: the archives are laced with incidents that illustrate the entry of ordinary Lyonnais onto the political stage.[40] Orléanist officials were dismayed by this harvest they themselves had helped to sow during the July Days because, as they sanctimoniously announced, "much time and care is necessary to inculcate the masses with a feeling for the law and . . . respect for institutions."[41] The *Courrier de Lyon* put it another way: "We do not invite the workers to rally to our flag because we consider them workers and not party men."[42] The government's desire to restore politics to their pre-1830 boundaries can be seen in its changing attitude toward two post-1830 local ceremonies.

In September 1830 a memorial service was held at the grave of General Mouton Duvernet, who, like Marshal Ney, had been executed by the Bourbons in 1815; for the first time in fifteen years the patriotism of this Lyonnais hero was publically praised. Ceremonies were held without official notice in 1831 and 1832 because the local authorities no longer felt comfortable associating themselves with the memory of a man who represented resistance to an established government. And in 1833 the police declared the crowd that gathered in the Loyasse cemetery an unauthorized assembly and arrested three Republicans for making speeches hostile to the regime.[43]

A similar evolution occurred with regard to the commemoration of the July Days. The first anniversary of the Revolution was a festival of harmony featuring a parade by the National Guard, speeches lauding those who had endangered their lives in the Place des Terreaux, and the sale of a special medal with the motto "From the Patriots of Lyon to their Polish Brothers, 27, 28, 29 July 1831."[44] By 1833, however, the official ceremony was more a show of force than the celebration of a patriotic holiday. As the prefect and the commander of the Seventh Military Region reviewed the garrison, local Republicans protested the government's plan to build a ring of forts, their guns trained on the city, around Lyon. That evening the *Procureur Général* reported there were bands of workers "chanting 'Down with the Bastilles,' energetically singing the *Marseillaise*, and looking for trouble. . . ."[45]

The Lyonnais authorities discovered it was not an easy matter to demobilize these new contenders for power and influence. As they continued to test the dimensions of the post-revolutionary polity with threats and violence, the government responded with increasingly open repression: the result was a general politicization of conflict. What Rule and Tilly have postulated in theory was so in reality.[46]

Belgium and Poland were not the only national causes in the effervescent period after the July Days. Because Lyon was near the border and had a large foreign population, there was considerable sentiment for the liberation of Savoy, which France had surrendered to the Kingdom of Piedmont in 1815. An invasion force called the Legion of the Volunteers of the Rhône was recruited with government complicity in worker cafés decorated by interwoven French and Italian tricolors. On 25 February 1831, this motley regiment of perhaps seven hundred men marched out of the city. Louis-Philippe having reconsidered its diplomatic repercussions, however, the regular army was sent to intercept the expedition.[47]

Some legionnaires took the government's advice and enlisted for service in Algeria; the others returned to Lyon and on Sundays the companies of the Ex-Volunteers of the Rhône, as they now called themselves, drilled in the suburbs under the direction of their elected sergeants. Constantly apprehensive over their presence, Prefect Gasparin called them "our *sans culottes*" and explained to Paris that he could neither arrest their leaders, because no local jury would dare convict them, nor disband their units, because of the danger of armed resistance.[48] The police commissioner unintentionally captured something of the politics of the inarticulate when he reported: "Their goal is completely political; they do not want what exists. If they ever were victorious they would be embarrassed to have to say what they actually want."[49]

Lyonnais officials wrestled this Frankenstein monster for at least two years: during the rebellion of November 1831 the leaders of the Ex-Volunteers of the Rhône belonged to the so-called Provisional General Staff, which briefly seized the Hôtel de Ville; in March 1832 Prefect Gasparin believed their companies were going to march on Grenoble in response to news of trouble there between troops and civilians; in May 1832, soon after the local National Guard had been dissolved, he rejected their offer to protect the city in its stead; and in May 1833 he feared that their remnants would take to the streets to protest his cancellation of the banquet for Garnier-Pagès.[50] References to the Ex-Volunteers of the Rhône disappear from the prefect's correspondence during 1833 and, beyond an occasion when the government purchased five hundred guns from them,[51] there is no information how or when this popular army was finally demobilized.

Certainly for Lyon—and in some respects for France as a whole —the most important events in the uneasy years after 1830 were the worker rebellions of November 1831 and April 1834. Although I have shown elsewhere that they are fully understood only within the context of the economic and social structure of the silk industry,[52] here we shall concentrate on how the July Revolution brought about the politicization of an essentially industrial conflict.

The rhetoric as much as the circumstances surrounding the beginning of the reign of the Citizen King raised the expectations of the Lyon silk workers, or *canuts* as they were called. Specifically, they wanted the renewal of a *tarif*, a fixed minimum rate for finished cloth, as had been established under the Empire and which the Bourbons had neglected to enforce. In October 1831 the master weavers convinced Prefect Bouvier-Dumolart to convene negotiations between their representatives and those of the silk merchants, during which he cajoled the latter into signing a wage agreement. Although the prefect told Paris that his intervention had sealed the canuts' loyalty to the new regime, Casimir Perier, who had received an angry petition from the merchants and feared to lose their political support, not only chastised him for meddling in a private dispute but also ordered him to announce that what the weavers thought was a binding tarif should be considered merely "an engagement of honor."

On 21 November a National Guard unit composed of silk merchants and their clerks fired on a crowd of canuts on its way to the prefecture, and the worker neighborhoods exploded. Street fighting raged for two days: the Hôtel de Ville was besieged, the garrison suffered more than three hundred casualties, and, shortly after midnight on the 23rd, the Municipal Council recommended that the army evacuate Lyon. Because their intention was not to overthrow the July Monarchy, the rebels soon surrendered the fruits of their unexpected victory. Rejecting the appeal of those seeking to establish a revolutionary municipal government, most of them rallied to a council of sixteen master weavers, who administered the city in cooperation with the prefect, whom they had captured and released during the uprising. By the time the Minister of War arrived at the head of the returning army the gates of Lyon were open to welcome him.[53]

The men who had come to power in 1830 were alarmed by the canuts and their motto, "Live Working or Die Fighting." The *Journal des Débats* warned: "The barbarians who menace society are neither in the Caucasus nor on the Tartar steppes; they are in the suburbs of our manufacturing cities."[54] François Guizot, whose notion of the *juste-milieu* became a semiofficial philosophy of government, said:

> The July Revolution raised only political questions. . . . Society was by no means menaced. . . . What has happened since? Social questions have been raised. The Lyonnais events have raised them. . . . [T]oday we have the difficulty of constructing a government and defending a society.[55]

The November rebellion, in other words, raised the specter of the Social Question in its starkest terms.

Informed by Casimir Perier that they could "expect no remedies other than patience and resignation,"[56] the Lyonnais workers kept the image of 1830 in their minds as they adopted the tactics of community organization, principally newspapers and semi-secret associations, in order to achieve their economic goals. Attacking Prefect Gasparin for tampering with the composition of the local labor conciliation board, the weavers' journal, the *Écho de la Fabrique*, said it was "for the workers of Lyon what the July Ordinances were for France as a whole, that is to say a veritable coup d'État."[57] The journeymen tailors offered this defense for this new society:

> Nobody can forget the numerous peaceful meetings . . . which took place after the July Revolution. It appeared to the people then . . . that the thoughts of our legislators would turn toward the laboring classes. . . . It is not our fault if we are now forced to associate in order to combat the rapacious spirit which seeks to exploit our misery so long as we continue to remain isolated.[58]

Conversely, because it considered them to be illegitimate contenders, the government harbored the image of 1831 whether the workers acted legally (Prefect Gasparin described the canuts' preparations for elections to the labor conciliation board as "the spirit of November, no more and no less"[59]) or illegally (the Minister of the Interior condemned a small strike as "the spirit of coalition, or rather of revolt"[60]).

The canuts inevitably drew the attention of Lyon's small Republican party, which attempted to convince them that "the worker seated at his loom is the EQUAL of Louis-Philippe on his throne" and that a future Republic would intervene to solve their plight, whereas the July Monarchy had abandoned them to the evils of laissez-faire.[61] It is a moot point how these ideas were received in the workshops and cafés: most historians have assumed (without much evidence beyond government claims) that the workers were easily converted, but I have found them remarkably resistant to radical solutions and intensely pragmatic in their programs.[62] In February 1834, for example, the master weavers' Society of Mutual Duty called a general strike which idled every loom in Lyon in a demand for a tarif; when the association's leaders learned that Republican tracts were being read in some lodges they warned:

> . . . it is the intention of the authorities to make a completely industrial affair degenerate into politics. Reflect wisely, Brothers. We must be prudent . . . Beware of police tricks, of cries you may hear day or night. Do not leave your homes. We must remain calm and silent. . . . We beg this of you in the very name of Mutual Duty.[63]

In any case, the government saw in the general strike an opportunity to demobilize conclusively its enemies by attacking the base of their power: on 25 February it introduced a bill banning all unauthorized associations of any kind. Painting a picture of the canuts "blindly obeying higher orders" from the Republicans, Fulchiron told his fellow deputies, "you cannot leave . . . our manufacturing centers under the dread of the sword of Damocles."[64] Adolphe Thiers, soon to become the Minister of the Interior, also defended the repressive measure: "The day after the July Revolution . . . we saw our duty to moderate it. In effect it was no longer liberty, but order which was in danger."[65]

For Lyonnais workers and Republicans alike the law on associations was final evidence of the betrayal of the heritage of 1830. "What they want," said the *Écho de la Fabrique,* "is to force workers back into the primitive state of isolation where they can be exploited with full security."[66] The *Précurseur* declared: "If France resigns herself to it, if we consent to pass under the yoke of a power which we created with our own hands, . . . then she will have become the most imbecilic nation of Europe."[67] On 9 April, the day before Louis-Philippe signed the bill that the *Courrier de Lyon* had confidently called "the demarcation line between the past and the future,"[68] the second city of France was torn by violence once again. Unlike the November rebellion, however, the authorities were prepared for the trouble they had done so much to induce; the fighting lasted for six days, but the outcome was never in doubt. As an aide to the Minister of War stated with pride: "The garrison of 1834 has revenged the one of 1831."[69]

By examining the *dénouement* of the major themes of this essay we can see how the complex competition for power, which the Revolution of 1830 opened, in Lyon was finally closed after the uprising of April 1834.

Mayor Prunelle was attending the Chamber of Deputies in Paris when the trouble began, and the Minister of the Interior informed him that he need not return to Lyon because Prefect Gasparin was already in command. Prunelle angrily submitted his resignation as mayor and to his chagrin it was accepted. Although he begged for and received his job back, the Prefecture of the Rhône had triumphed over the Hôtel de Ville.[70]

The law on associations proved an effective weapon against the Republican and worker societies: the former were forced to abandon public demonstrations and return to the tactics of the secret societies, which had characterized the radical opposition during the early Restoration; the latter were stripped of all means of effective organization for at least a decade. Politics had truly been restored to their respectable pre-1830 boundaries. "The victory of public order over anarchy in Lyon," announced the *Procureur Général* "has borne happy fruit."[71]

Elections were held in June 1834 to replace the Chamber of Deputies chosen in 1831. The voters of the Rhône responded to what Minister of the Interior Thiers called "the great question of the past four years" by selecting a delegation uniformly pledged to the party of Order, or "the constitutional cause" as it was now described.[72] When the *Précurseur* succumbed to a series of judicial attacks that fall, the symbol of the old liberal coalition itself disappeared. A new political equilibrium had been wrought and the Revolution of 1830 was closed in Lyon.

Notes

[1] David Pinkney, *The French Revolution of 1830* (Princeton: Princeton University Press, 1972).

[2] James Rule and Charles Tilly, "Political Process in Revolutionary France, 1830–32," in this volume, p. 70.

[3] "Lettre confidentielle de S. M. Louis-Philippe Ier, roi des français, à son bien-aimé cousin Nicolas, empereur de toutes les Russes" (n.p.n.d.).

[4] F. Dutacq and A. Latreille, *Histoire de Lyon de 1814 à 1940*. Vol. III of *Histoire de Lyon*, A. Kleinclausz, ed. (Lyon: Librairie Pierre Masson, 1952), pp. 66–78; F. Baud, "Les Caractères généraux du parti libéral à Lyon sous la Restoration," *Revue d'histoire de Lyon*, 12 (1913).

[5] Dutacq and Latreille, *ibid.*, p. 77; Fernand Rude, *Le Mouvement ouvrier à Lyon de 1827 à 1832* (Paris: *Les Éditions Sociales*, 1969; orig. ed. 1944), pp. 173–178; M. Buffenoir, "*Le Précurseur* et la Révolution de Juillet," *Revue d'histoire de Lyon*, 6 (1907), pp. 351–362.

[6] Cited by P. Montagne, "Aspects du comportement de l'armée à Lyon sous la Monarchie de Juillet et la Seconde République," *Actes du 89e congrès des sociétés savantes, Lyon, 1964* (Paris, 1965), p. 405.

[7] Pinkney, *op. cit.*, pp. 286–287.

[8] Félix Ponteil, *Les Institutions de la France de 1814 à 1870* (Paris: Presses Universitaires de France, 1965), pp. 30–36 and 156–164.

[9] F. Dutacq, "L'Extension du cadre administratif et territoriale de la cité lyonnaise" (Lyon, 1922), p. 34.

[10] Rude, *op. cit.*, p. 256.

[11] J. B. Monfalcon, *Histoire des insurrections de Lyon en 1831 et en 1834 d'après des documents authentiques précédée d'un essai sur les ouvriers et sur l'organisation de la fabrique* (Lyon and Paris, 1834), p. 164.

[12] Alan B. Spitzer, "The Bureaucrat as Proconsul: the Restoration Prefect and the *Police Générale*," *Comparative Studies in History and Society*, 7 (1965), p. 372; Howard C. Payne, *The Police State of Louis-Napoleon Bonaparte, 1851–1860* (Seattle: University of Washington Press, 1966), Chapter One.

[13] *Les Archives Municipales de la Ville de Lyon: Les Documents Gasparin* (hereafter AMDG), t. 13; Prunelle to Gasparin, 10 March 1834.

[14] *Ibid.*, Minister of the Interior to Gasparin, 9 May 1832.

[15] *Ibid.*, Prunelle to Gasparin, 25 and 28 May 1832; t. 11: Gasparin to Minister of the Interior, 3 May 1833; *Le Précurseur*, 3–4 April and 20 July

1833; Monfalcon, *op. cit.*, pp. 176–179; Louis Girard, *La Garde Nationale* (Paris: Plon, 1964), p. 225.

[16] Pinkney, *op. cit.*, p. 365.

[17] AMDG, t. 13: Prunelle to Gasparin, 22 December 1831.

[18] *Ibid.*, 20 January 1834.

[19] Louis Greenberg, *Sisters of Liberty: Marseille, Lyon, Paris and the Reaction to a Centralized State, 1868–1871* (Cambridge, Mass.: Harvard University Press, 1971), p. 215.

[20] *Revue du Lyonnais*, 2⁰ série, 1 (1850), p. 95.

[21] M. Roustan and C. Latreille, "Lyon contre Paris après 1830," *Revue d'histoire de Lyon*, 3 (1904), pp. 21–42, 109–126, 306–318, and 384–402.

[22] Anselme Petetin, "Lettre circulaire: Association de l'Est, avril 1833" (Lyon, 1833).

[23] Girod de L'Ain, *Rapport fait à la Cour des Pairs*, 4 vols. (Paris, 1834), 4: annex 55, p. 117.

[24] *Les Archives Nationales de la France* (hereafter AN), CC 612, registre 1: correspondence of the *Association en faveur de la presse patriote*," circular dated 6 October 1832.

[25] *Société des droits de l'homme et du citoyen: Comité de correspondence générale et d'affiliation républicaine: Aux sections lyonnais* (2 March 1834).

[26] Rule and Tilly, *op. cit.*, pp. 42–85.

[27] Dutacq and Latreille, *op. cit.*, p. 83; *Le Courrier de Lyon*, 30 June 1833.

[28] *La Glaneuse*, 1 December 1833.

[29] *La Précurseur*, 17 February 1832; M. Brisac, "Lyon et l'insurrection polonaise de 1830–1831," *Revue d'histoire de Lyon*, 8 (1909), pp. 161–204.

[30] *La Glaneuse*, 30 October 1832.

[31] *La Précurseur*, 1 November 1832.

[32] *Le Courrier de Lyon*, 13 May 1833.

[33] AN, CC 572, dossier Petetin: *Mémoire justificatif*, p. 5.

[34] AMDG, t. 9: Minister of the Interior to Gasparin, 22 August 1833. The allegation was made in the *Précurseur* on 28–29 March 1832.

[35] *Le Précurseur*, 9 June 1832.

[36] AN, BB²⁰ 61: *Comptes rendus d'assises (Rhône)*, 1832.

[37] *La Glaneuse*, 1 October 1833.

[38] *Ibid.*, 14 October 1832.

[39] Maurice Agulhon, *La République au village: les populations du Var de la Révolution à la Seconde République* (Paris: Plon, 1970), p. 266.

[40] AN, BB¹⁸ 1318: *Avocat Général* Lyon to Minister of Justice, 6 November 1830; AMDG, t. 4: Gasparin to Minister of the Interior, 7 October 1832; AN F⁷ 6782: report by Commander of Rhône *Gendarmerie* to Minister of the Interior, 11 March 1831, 1 January 1832, and 29 April 1833; AMDG, t. 2: Minister of the Interior to Gasparin, 6 May 1832; *L'Écho de la Fabrique*, 9 December 1832.

[41] *Le Courrier de Lyon*, 11 June 1833.

[42] *Ibid.*, 13 July 1833.

[43] Rude, *op. cit.*, p. 180; Monfalcon, *op. cit.*, p. 195; AMDG, t. 9: Minister of the Interior to Gasparin, 9 November 1833.

[44] Brisac, "Lyon et l'insurrection polonaise," p. 188; AN, F⁷ 6782: report by Commander of Rhône *Gendarmerie* to Minister of the Interior, 4 August 1831.

[45] AN, BB¹⁸ 1217: *Procureur Général* Lyon to Minister of Justice, 3 August 1833.

[46] Rule and Tilly, *op. cit.*, p. 67.

[47] F. Rude, "La Première Expédition de Savoie," *Revue historique*, 189 (1940), pp. 413–443.

[48] AMDG, t. 4: Gasparin to Minister of the Interior, 30 January, 26 May, and 10 June 1832.

[49] *Ibid.*, t. 10: "Rapport sur les differentes sociétés établies à Lyon" [April 1833].

[50] Rude, *Le Mouvement ouvrier, op. cit.*, pp. 465–470; AMDG, t. 4: Gasparin to Minister of the Interior, 20 March and 26 May 1832; t. 10: Gasparin to Minister of the Interior, 9 May 1833.

[51] Rude, *Le Mouvement ouvrier, op. cit.*, p. 620.

[52] Robert J. Bezucha, *The Lyon Uprising of 1834: Social and Political Conflict in the Early July Monarchy* (Cambridge, Mass.: Harvard University Press, 1974).

[53] Rude, *Le Mouvement ouvrier, op. cit.*, chapters 5–9.

[54] *Le Journal des Débats,* 8 December 1831.

[55] *Le Moniteur Universel,* 22 December 1831.

[56] Rude, *Le Mouvement ouvrier, op. cit.*, p. 695.

[57] *L'Écho de la Fabrique,* 14 July 1833.

[58] *La Glaneuse,* 3 November 1833.

[59] AMDG, t. 4: Gasparin to Minister of the Interior, 16 April 1832.

[60] *Ibid.*, t. 9: Minister of the Interior to Gasparin, 16 July 1833.

[61] *La Glaneuse,* 8 December 1833.

[62] Bezucha, *op. cit.*, chapters 3–4.

[63] AMDG, t. 13: "*Ordre du jour,* 16 Union, AN 6 [16 February 1834]."

[64] E. Laurent and J. Mavidal, eds., *Les Archives parlementaires de 1787 à 1860: receuil complet des débats legislatifs et politiques des chambres françaises. Deuxième série: 1800 à 1860* (Paris, 1862–1913), t. 87, p. 393.

[65] Adolphe Thiers, *Discours parlementaires, 1830–1836,* 3 vols. (Paris, 1879), 2, p. 359.

[66] *L'Écho de la Fabrique,* 9 March 1834.

[67] *Le Précurseur,* 11 March 1834.

[68] *Le Courrier de Lyon,* 29 March 1834.

[69] *Les Archives du Ministère de la Guerre,* E⁵ 51: *Aide de camp du ministre en mission* to Minister of War, 18 April 1834.

[70] AMDG, t. 5: Prunelle to Thiers (copy of personal letter), 15 May 1834.

[71] AN, BB¹⁸ 1354B: *Procureur Général* Lyon to Minister of Justice, 23 May 1834.

[72] AMDG, t. 5: Minister of the Interior to Gasparin, 19 May and 3 July 1834.

Christopher H. Johnson

The Revolution of 1830 in French Economic History

*The opposition to the last Restoration government included a
strong representation of commercial interests. The bourgeoisie is
often identified with the political change in 1830 and with the
July Monarchy. To what extent did the July Monarchy, then,
consciously pursue an economic policy that favored the bourgeoisie? The answer to this question should help clarify the controversial "bourgeois revolution" hypothesis.*

*Christopher H. Johnson's study finds that the July Monarchy
maintained an economic policy that favored capitalist economic
development. This commitment of the regime to "order" and
"résistance" helped create a mood of economic expansion and
achievement. Although most wealth was still in the land and in
aristocratic hands, a "culture" of capitalism was created that may
explain the image of a "bourgeois monarchy" held by contemporaries and many historians.*

*Christopher H. Johnson teaches history at Wayne State Univer-
sity. His publications include "Communism and the Working
Class before Marx: the Icarian Experience"* (American Historical
Review, 73, 3 [1971], pp. 642–689) and Utopian Communism in
France: Cabet and the Icarians, 1839–1848 (Ithaca, N.Y., 1974. He
is currently engaged in research relating to the Enquête sur le
travail agricole et industriel *of 1848 and has begun work on rural-
urban migration in nineteenth-century France.*

Le crédit, c'est la confiance
Emile Pereire, 1833

Since the Villèle ministry, the system of Administration has been hostile to industry: this Administration resolutely proclaims its preference for the interests of the landed proprietors, and while it reduces the land tax by 120 millions, it increases indirect taxes by 200 millions; and this unjust measure was further accompanied by a profound disdain for industry, which encounters among the agents of the Administration nothing but a complete ignorance of and a profound hatred for its interests. Our consuls, chosen in a lamentable way, shackle our exports instead of favoring them. Moreover, in consequence of such a state of things, industrial capital has been little by little swallowed up by the *fisc* and by the grievous fortunes of commerce; and in these times when lack of credit leads toward general liquidation, one finds to his astonishment that industry, in spite of its discoveries and immense works, is poor.

Thus did Charles Lamouroux, a Parisian manufacturer and commission agent residing in a wealthy quarter near the Stock Exchange, excoriate the troubled government of the Restoration in a brochure written shortly before the July Revolution.[1] The discontent evidenced in this bitter statement was widespread on the eve of the revolution[2] and surely figured prominently in the ready acceptance of the *Trois Glorieuses* and the black-coated new king by businessmen throughout France.

To what extent were their expectations justified? To what extent did the regime that issued from the Revolution of 1830 develop policy favorable to capitalist economic growth in France? Two decades ago the answers to such questions might have seemed self-evident. This was, after all, the Bourgeois Monarchy. It ushered in definitively the domination of modern capitalist interests over the destinies of the nation, and if the ruling clique was a bit narrow (limited largely to *grand bourgeois* of finance, commerce, and industry) in pressing their own interests, they simultaneously guided France through the essential first steps of an industrial revolution.[3] Then, after regrouping in 1848–1849, a somewhat reconstituted *grande bourgeoisie*, now led by its most progressive elements, found in Louis-Napoleon Bonaparte and his chief advisers the instruments for thoroughly "recasting society in its own image" and fulfilling the long-awaited promise of the Revolution of 1789. This thesis was refined and altered only in particulars by French social and economic historians during the 1950s, although some, like Guy Palmade, manifested certain doubts about just how economically progressive the July Monarchy had been and preferred to see it as largely preparatory to a vast expansion during the Second Empire. But the "reign of the *grande bourgeoisie*" seemed secure as a characterization of the reign and received a major new formulation in 1960 in a remarkable analysis by Jean Lhomme, a prominent economist-sociologist.[4]

But British and American economic historians had in the meantime been raising hard questions about the performance of the French economy in the nineteenth century. Without seeking to challenge the bourgeois monarchy thesis directly, this research tended to underline the "retardation" of Fernch economic growth when placed in comparison with that of Britain, Germany, and even Belgium. The comparative study of economic growth reached a maniacal level among economic historians in the late 1950s, and one of the central questions seemed to be "what was wrong with France?" Rondo Cameron capped off this discussion with a brilliant article in 1958 in which he stressed France's relative deficiency in the essential resources of nineteenth-century growth, coal and iron, which were furthermore neither easily accessible nor proximate; the low level of aggregate demand resulting from slow population growth and wide income differentials; and, at least by implication, difficulties in channeling capital into productive enterprise as a result of inadequate credit facilities during the first half of the century.[5] One author, however, did introduce a social variable rather early on; David Landes argued that French growth in the nineteenth century was severely handicapped by a failure of entrepreneurial daring among French capitalists, citing in particular the continuation of *Ancien Régime* habits of making safe investments in government bonds and especially land, thence to retire as bourgeois of old—that is to live "nobly" on their incomes rather than plowing their profits back into their businesses.[6] Although no one really thought through all its implications at the time, Landes' thesis brought together the economic and the sociopolitical issues. And

141

the work of all the "retardation" or "slow growth" theorists
posed an essential set of questions. If French growth was not
impressive in the first half of the century, the July Monarchy
included, what should one make of the bourgeois (that is pro-
capitalist) monarchy of post-1830? Was the regime really that
supportive of capitalist interests? Alternatively, even assuming
that the wealthy grande bourgeoisie ran the country, did their
policies really promote national economic growth? Or finally:
maybe state policy and who directed it had little to do with the
problem of growth at all.

The last dozen years or so have yielded an impressive harvest of
works in French social and economic history relevant to the problem this essay seeks to illuminate. Above all, they have witnessed
the coming of age of economic history in France itself,[7] and the
meticulous and imaginative work of individuals like Claude
Fohlen, Bertrand Gille, François Crouzet, Pierre Léon, Maurice
Lévy-Leboyer, and the inheritors of François Perroux at the Insti-
tut de Science Économique Appliquée, Jean Marczewski, Tiho-
már Markovitch, and J. C. Toutain, have taken the subject of
French economic growth to a new level of analysis. The most
important consequence of their work has been a more solid
understanding of the pattern, rates, and nature of this growth.
Although full agreement is naturally wanting, their research
points to the following conclusion: the July Monarchy, especially
after 1840, *was* a period of significant economic development—
not only for industry but for agriculture as well. Fohlen is less
certain, giving much greater emphasis to the Second Empire. Perhaps the most persuasive view is that there was a major spurt in
growth from around 1840 to 1857, with a deep trough caused by
the economic and political crises of 1847–1850. Nevertheless it
would be unwise to speak of a "take-off" in French nineteenth-
century experience. It was a question instead of slow, steady
growth marked by certain periods of speed-up and lag. (All seem
to agree that the first thirty years of the Third Republic were
unimpressive.) Unquestionably the French economy was "revolu-
tionized" from the eighteenth century to World War I; but
an industrial revolution, in the sense of a fairly short period of
massive conversion to mechanical processes, high rates of growth

in overall production, and a sustained high level of net capital investment, is very hard to find.[8]

The "retardation" question has been put in a new light as well. Crouzet stresses that per capita growth rates, given France's slow population growth, compare favorably with that of the rest of Europe for much of the nineteenth century.[9] But perhaps the central fact is that the nature of French economic growth in the nineteenth century must be set against two primordial factors: the negative influence of the French Revolution on the economy and English competition. Lévy-Leboyer has underlined both, concluding that French growth does not appear nearly so weak if it is understood that France lost nearly a generation of potential growth because of the revolutionary upheaval, while England simultaneously surged forward, in part benefiting from the flight of capital during the revolution and the capture of formerly French-dominated foreign markets.[10] It seems probable that the Empire saw a decade (1800–1810) of revival, and, therefore, Lévy-Leboyer's "massive deceleration" thesis for the whole Revolutionary-Napoleonic era needs some modification.[11] Still, in 1815 as in 1830, French industry was at a severe competitive disadvantage vis-à-vis the giant across the Channel.

France adapted to this situation in the first place by restrictive tariff policy, which prohibited the entrance of many English industrial products. This was the principal contribution of the Restoration as landowners and industrialists alike rallied to protectionism.[12] Less appreciated until recently are the other adaptive strategies to which French businessmen resorted. The stock-in-trade of British industrial production were common, mass consumption goods, especially in textiles. Capital-intensive production was the mainspring of success in this realm. But in higher quality items, *articles de goût*, France had a historic reputation and, more importantly, a competitive chance. Basic economic analysis demonstrates that quality, at least in that day and age, related directly to the proportion of labor in the final cost price; moreover, later stages of production took progressively greater amounts of labor input. But on a general level French industrial wages were approximately two-thirds of those paid in England.[13] This meant that the higher the quality of goods produced, the greater the labor input and therefore the stronger the relative position of French industry. France quite logically took its stand on this level. Thus *indiennages* and cotton prints, *nouveautés* in woolens, and silk textiles had the greatest possibilities of success. Alsace enjoyed the best position in this regard, benefiting from wages lower than much of the rest of the country and focusing very early on quality cottons.[14] All this meant that handwork, particularly in weaving, maintained its significance much longer in France than it did in England. Moreover, the better part of the first half of the nineteenth century witnessed a phenomenon that, at first glance, seems strange indeed for a country undergoing industrialization—the massive development of rural outworking in the textile industry. The reason, of course, was not hard to find. Rural labor was cheaper.[15]

In a way, however, this focus on quality and the efficient exploitation of hand labor should be seen more as a survival technique than as the motor of industrialization. Perhaps the most important fact in the economic history of the July Monarchy was the reversal of this trend around 1840. Alsace led the way. The number of handlooms operating in the Haut-Rhin, after increasing from 1,903 in 1812 to 31,000 in 1834, dropped to 17,000 in 1844. Simultaneously, capital-intensive production increased rapidly during the July Monarchy.[16] Markovitch's estimates of total industrial production indicate the same process at work. (And in line with our earlier comments, it is the period bridging the July Monarchy and the Second Empire that is important.) While the share of capital-intensive, "pure" industry remained less than half the total value of industrial production, its share nevertheless advanced from an average of 25.2 percent to 37.2 percent of the total during the twenty years from 1835–1844 to 1855–1864. Moreover, in *industrie pure,* the share of wages in total revenue reduced from 44 percent to 36.6 percent. Conversely, while artisan production continued to increase during this period, its share in the total industrial revenue reduced. Finally, Markovitch estimated that auto-consumption of (largely peasant) industry declined absolutely, a good indication that this was also an important era of change in the peasants' market orientation as consumers. As he sums it up:

The growth of total industrial production between the two

periods was about 50%. Consequently, the "pure" industry sector grew at a rhythm two times as rapidly as the total mass of industrial production, and more than five times more rapidly than artisan and family production. We therefore have a very clear indication of the acceleration of the process of industrialization in the course of that crucial period in French history which links the July Monarchy and the Second Empire.[17]

Crouzet goes beyond the decennial averages of Markovitch and helps us develop a more precise picture in his annual index of industrial production. While less optimistic about the overall growth rate in nineteenth-century France than Markovitch or Lévy-Leboyer (his index fixes the average at about 1.6 percent per annum, though he thinks 1.8 percent is closer to the reality), he demonstrates that "French industry experienced its most rapid growth phase during the middle of the nineteenth century. That phase is centered on the period of the *Empire authoritaire,* but it had begun during the July Monarchy."[18] This estimate is based on two indices and their deviations from the secular trend of the whole period 1815–1914. The deviation for his index 8b, which removes heavily weighted and retrogressive linen and hemp textiles as well as woolens and jute, moves from a —10 to a +10 from 1831 to 1838 and then, after a dip for the depressed year of 1839, rises to a +22 in 1843 and +30 in 1846. After the predictable decline—but only to normal (zero deviation)—by 1848, the deviation reaches +37 in 1853 and then hovers between 10 and 20 from 1857 to 1869. Index 8a, closer to the global reality of French growth and including the more backward textile industries, showed positive deviations during the early years of the Restoration, fell below normal between 1825 and 1839 (generally between —5 and —10) and then experienced the same rapid rise after 1839 as index 8b. It was clear that "modern" industries (mining, metals, chemicals, and at least cotton among the textiles) were pulling more than their weight, but even so, deviations here reached a peak of only +5 in 1846. The '50s were the longest period of positive deviation from the norm (though never more than +11) during the nineteenth century.[19]

From almost every point of view, therefore, 1840 seems to have been a major turning point for French industry, and whatever "revolution" it may have experienced was nurtured in the later years of the July Monarchy and came to full bloom in the '50s.[20] Furthermore, these statistical evaluations correlate well with a variety of other, softer evidence contributing to an appreciation of economic development during the July Monarchy, including concentration and integration of industrial structures, the rise of ready-made products, and the increasing division of labor in formerly purely artisan industries such as clothing, the greater ease of company formation and mobilization of capital despite the reigning conservatism of the Bank of France, and, of course, the increasing application of mechanical power to the problems of production. Finally, it is fairly certain that agriculture experienced real progress as well. Of all this more will be said later, but again, the 1840s seem to have been the era of rapid evolution.

In general, then, there is a certain optimism about the performance of the French economy in the first half of the nineteenth century and an appreciation of the realism of French capitalists in making the best of a general situation of competitive disadvantage. The July Monarchy tends to reemerge as a crucial turning point in the process of overall development, if not the wellspring of an economic miracle. It would appear that earlier hypotheses about the "bourgeois monarchy" are not so much in contradiction with the economic realities of the era as one might have thought, given the retardation themes of the 1950s.

But, ironically, the thrust in French social history has been to modify the *"grande bourgeoisie au pouvoir"* thesis. Without a doubt, the crucial works here have been A. J. Tudesq's monumental *thèse de doctorat, Les grands notables en France (1840–1849)* (1964) and Adeline Daumard's *La bourgeoisie parisienne de 1815 à 1848* (1963). Read with an eye bent on destroying the older dogma about what happened after 1830, these works can serve the purpose well. Alfred Cobban, for instance, found in them enough material to extend his onslaught against the Lefebvre school on the nature of the Great Revolution well into the nineteenth century—claiming that Lhomme's thesis is a myth.[21] Not only was the French Revolution not a bourgeois (capitalist) revolution, but neither was the Revolution of 1830. Instead "the bourgeoisie" of Paris became *more* conservative with their investments (this he draws from Daumard) and in general it was the *notables,* a group whose wealth essentially was derived from land and whose social preeminence rested on this, their family name, and their local networks of influence, who dominated France politically during the July Monarchy (Tudesq). Cobban found support in the studies of David Pinkney and P. B. Higonnet, who argued that the social background of both administrators and national elected officials did not change appreciably after the Revolution of 1830, thus throwing further doubt on the alleged transfer of power that accompanied it. Pinkney sees a revolution to be sure, but an ideological one: "Indeed, the Revolution of 1830 may have come close to being a Bonapartist revolution."[22] Overall, the goal of the revisionists—but not really of either Tudesq or Daumard—is to dispense with Lhomme altogether. What the Cobban school is striving for, of course, is to undermine the socioeconomic interpretation of French political evolution from the late eighteenth century at least to 1848, to remove "Marxist" conceptions of class struggle from the debate, and to reassert liberal historical relativism.

Aspects of this historiographical conflict are broached in this collection, and it is beyond my purview to enter into it directly. What I wish to examine, however, is how businessmen seemed to view the Revolution of 1830, especially in terms of its impact on their immediate interests, what they sought from the new regime, how the regime responded (and what elements in it seemed most willing to respond), and the extent to which this response proved efficacious for economic development. The state's role in the economic development evident after 1830 is the central issue at hand. The question of who came to power in 1830 will not be answered in this analysis; but perhaps the question of what those who did come to power (whomever they might have been) did to stimulate capitalist economic growth during the July Monarchy through executive policy and legislation—or lack of it in certain areas—can be clarified.

The reaction of French businessmen to the Revolution of 1830, their concerns about the economic conditions that followed it, and their desires in the realm of future public policy have never been adequately analyzed. Obviously such information would be of great value not only in understanding the nature of the revolutionary developments subsequent to the July Days, but above all in assessing the extent to which the government of the July Monarchy responded to the business interest in the longer run. Fortunately, an extremely important set of documents that assists in probing these issues is available. On February 19, 1831, the Minister of Commerce, the Comte d'Argout, initiated an "inquiry on the state of commerce and industry" in which he asked the following questions: (1) What was the situation in manufacturing and commerce early in 1830? (2) What are the changes since the revolution of July? (3) What permanent causes of economic distress can be identified? (4) What "accidental" causes? (5) What means can the government employ to improve conditions (*atténuer les causes*)? The circular was sent to Chambers of Commerce and Chambres Consultatifs des Arts et Manufactures in selected French cities as well as prefects in certain departments. In all, we have responses from thirty-five of the former, seven prefects, and one mayor (Bolbec). Finally, there is a special, and quite detailed, report from the Chamber of Commerce of Paris. The list is not exhaustive, to be sure, but the range of cities and regions included makes this an excellent sample.[23] While the chambers were sometimes closely connected to the official bureaucracy, there is little reason to believe that they did not come close to representing the opinions of the more prominent members of the local business community. These reports, therefore, can serve as a kind of rudimentary set of businessmen's *cahiers* concerning the most crucial months of the revolutionary era. Nearly all of them were produced in March or April 1831 and make retrospective analyses stretching back over about one year.

Notwithstanding the complaints of a Lamouroux, the most striking preliminary point to be made concerning this survey is that the picture painted of the pre-revolutionary situation in industry was by no means universally bad. France was certainly not enjoying the prosperity she had in 1825 and many respondents spoke of flagging fortunes thereafter. But several noted that 1830 witnessed a new upswing. Of the thirty-eight respondents indicating a position, thirteen described their situation as good (Troyes and Avignon were "flourishing") and six more used terminology ("satisfying enough," "industry maintaining itself advantageously enough," "business was picking up") indicating that their towns were not badly off. Two others, the textile cities of Tarare and Bolbec, spoke of difficulties, although employment remained steady and sales continued. In Paris none of the industries surveyed could call the first half of 1830 a great period (though the important woolens branch of *nouveautés* was beginning to boom again in 1830, and woolens in general followed the trend), but none save irons and chemicals complained bitterly about the situation. Nine provincial respondents estimated that times were bleak, and eight others could express little enthusiasm about their mediocre output. Thus, overall, this cross section of French economic life split about evenly between positive and negative assessments of their economic situation in the last months of Charles X's reign.

But this is not the essential fact. Many of those on the negative side had witnessed difficulties all through the Restoration. Givet (Ardennes) had never recovered from the loss of Napoleonic territories across the "Belgian" border. The Niort (Deux-Sèvres) *chamois* industry and related skin manufactures suffered grievously from the elimination of army contracts in 1815.[24] Mende (Lozère) and Loudéac (Côtes du Nord), heavy woolens and linen *toile* producers respectively, were facing irreparable decline in face of cotton and modernized woolens production. Nantes and Bayonne had been languishing for many years.[25] Indeed, among the seventeen cities or departments presenting negative positions, only Montpellier (speaking for the department of Hérault), Sedan, Angers, and Ste.-Marie-aux-Mines could warrant the term "progressive" in normal times. But all the major industrial cities in France—with the possible exception of Paris, and she was "industrial" only in a peculiar sense—viewed their situation before the revolution as at least decent. The Lyon Chamber of Commerce, happy about the recovery of silk exports, thought their city to be experiencing "progressive prosperity." Things in Rouen were untroubled since conditions of international peace reigned; they groused a bit about the Restoration's apparent disinterest in helping to procure new markets. Troyes had full employment and "consequently" happy woolens workers. Lille and Mulhouse both saw early 1830 as an important upward turning point in the demand for their cotton goods. Mulhousiens were especially enthused about new Mexican export prospects.

Avignon, the major outlet for dye products (alizari and madder root) in the south, waxed ecstatic about their success, and silk commerce was responding well to the new Lyon demand. Nîmes, the second silk city of France after Lyon, had nothing to complain about. Even Carcassonne, already facing serious competition from better and more cheaply produced northern woolens, could remark: "The manufacturing establishments were, in 1830, in a state of remarkable development" because of the low price of raw materials, itself a result of the prodigious crop of wool induced by the unseasonably cool winter of 1829–1830.

This is not to say that there was no industrial crisis in France in 1830. But from these remarks and other evidence[26] it is clear that the spring of 1830 saw somewhat of an upswing after difficult times in many semi-modernized industries. The woolens industry seemed to be generally well off, in part because of a big internal demand stimulated by two cold winters in a row. Even Sedan, not at all happy with its situation early in the year, was looking forward to important autumn sales. The remarks from Limoges restore a sense of proportion, however. The prosperity of the porcelain industry in the 1820s had induced many manufacturers to overextend themselves, incurring massive debts for investment in plant. They were on the brink of trouble at the moment of the revolution, thus facing conditions that had beset other cities and other industries two or three years earlier. Nor can it be denied that Restoration policy in the years of crisis (and longer) was resented by many respondents. Comments in this vein are all the more significant in these documents because the inquiry actually focused on the post-July period and did not specifically request opinions on the question. Nevertheless, out of seventeen responses discussing "permanent causes" of economic distress as of 1831, ten alluded to unrectified Restoration policies. Nantes violently attacked the colonial system, which undermined general foreign commerce. Boulogne and Châlons-sur-Marne were distressed by smuggling, and several others felt that tariff policies were either too restrictive or ill-conceived. Ste.-Marie-aux-Mines, for instance, was galled by the heavy duties on machines and machine parts, especially since no compensation was then allowed by the system when they went on to sell their products at artificially inflated prices. St.-Maixent was quite blunt: "In 1830 and before, the orientation of the government set itself against the prosperity of commerce."

If a spread in opinion concerning the pre-July economic scene existed, the business community of France was almost unanimous on the impact of the revolution and its troubled aftermath. Thirty-five provincial respondents answered the question and thirty-two indicated that economic conditions worsened in the months that followed the revolution. The three others—prefects of the rural departments of Landes, Cantal, and Finistère—saw little change. In Paris opinion was also unanimously negative. But, in many cases, there was an interesting chronology to the collapse. It is clear that the time of the inquiry was the lowest point yet reached, but July-August was not necessarily the turning point. Instead, the autumn of 1830 seemed to be the era of disaster. Let us examine this in more detail because it tells us a great deal about the overall revolutionary process and its fruit in terms of July Monarchy policy orientations.

Argout penciled in red the following assessment from Lyon: "The events of July, in shaking credit, have impaired the transactions market since; numerous bankruptcies have aggravated our position by the mistrust that they have inspired. Commercial transactions have been arrested and all branches of industry have felt the effects of this state of things."[27] Nancy went from bad to worse: "Early in 1830, the conduct of the government inspired anxiety and commerce suffered greatly. Since the July revolution, business activities have been even more retrograde than before. . ." In Sedan, recovery was on the horizon in the woolens trade, "but the events of July destroyed this hope. Orders stopped entirely, production was curtailed and is now threatened with total cessation due to the difficulties in collecting debts." St. Quentin and its region had 100,000 textile workers at their looms and in the shops early in 1830. Sales collapsed after July, and March of 1831 saw "nine-tenths" of this largely rural proletariat without work. The Chamber "feared the consequences" of their distress.[28] Aubusson followed a similar pattern of boom and bust. Her rug industry was apparently little affected by the crisis of 1827–1829. But the revolution stopped everything: warehouses were full and without hope of sales. Today the situation of entrepreneurs and workers alike "could not be worse." On and on go the tales of woe: no credit, no sales, or sale at low prices (Languedoc wines had dropped 15 to 20 percent), unemployment, bankruptcies galore.

A closer analysis, however, takes the onus off July itself. Lyon's situation was indicative: the decline was gradual, aggravated by mounting problems. The Avignon and Nogent reports remarked that business picked up briefly after July only to collapse in September and October. Several Paris industries saw hope in July, but it was dashed in the fall. In fact, wherever a more detailed discussion of the recent months of economic crisis was made, it was clear that a developing process was at work, one which made the era of the "fatal Ordinances" and the days of Parisian revolution pale into insignificance.

It is at this point that we must look at the causes of this distress, at least as perceived by the French business community. The reporter for the cloth printing industry (*toiles peintes*) of Paris, M. Baumgarten, presented an analysis acceptable to large numbers of his fellow manufacturers. The revolution itself, he said, did not really hurt his industry. Instead it was

> the movements that have occurred since. [The revolution's] principle was great and noble; its watchword: Liberty, Public Order, had reassured all. Already, resulting from a tranquility of some time, business seemed to be tending to pick up once more, and then came the days of October and of December, and later those of February 14 and 15, which destroyed all hopes for the spring, not only because of the evil they did to Paris itself, but still more because of the exaggerated reports that the newspapers made of them in the provinces, which in turn stopped merchants from making purchases. . . . [Business will revive] only when such evils reach their end, when the government senses the entire evil, and when they are prevented with greater energy.
>
> Industry is the friend of order and tranquility; it can prosper only under their shadow, and no interest desires their maintenance more because none has more to lose since a greater part of its capital is invested in machines, which lose their value at the moment when they can no longer be employed.[29]

Baumgarten was, of course, referring to the popular "days," uprisings that punctuated the months after the revolution; the last saw the sacking of the venerable old Parisian church St.-Germain-l'Auxerrois.

So the secret was out: business failed in the post-July era (after a month or so of optimism) because of popular upheaval. It is not really my purpose to debate the extent to which this was really true. Elsewhere in this volume, however, the reader will find extensive evidence of the high level of collective violence, of full-scale insurrection, of broad left- and right-wing political agitation, of labor organization, strikes, and Luddism—in short, of an era of upheaval that extended well beyond the date at which our Chambers of Commerce were preparing their reports. The Revolution of 1830 was at least the Revolution of 1830–1832, and James Rule and Charles Tilly's analysis of its essential pattern of development is most persuasive (see pages 42–85). Paul Gonnet doubts the significance of the revolution itself and is leery of the ongoing popular agitation thesis as well when writing about the industrial crisis. His central theme, certainly warranted as *one* explanation, is that the high price of essential foodstuffs reoriented demand and industrial sales suffered, especially in the longer run.[30] Moreover, deeper structural factors (overproduction, overextension of credit) and the international financial crisis precipitated by the British depression that began in 1825 no doubt played a continuing role.[31] But the overwhelming concern about internal disorder and the resultant *faute de confiance* among businessmen (who after all were doing the business) evidenced in these reports forces us to argue at least that this problem gave substantial reinforcement to the other, perhaps deeper, forces behind the depression.[32]

There was also another element, again pressed by our businessmen, that is often lost in the analysis of the economic crisis of 1830–1832: the international political situation. The multiple revolutions which followed that in France (Belgium, Poland, Italy, etc.) not only destroyed markets but, especially during the winter of 1830–1831, seemed to be putting France on the verge of war with the defenders of the Vienna settlement. Republicans chided Louis-Philippe for his failure to support the Belgian revolutionaries with greater verve, and several foresaw, with some glee, a new, massive war of national defense. Visions of Valmy, Jemappes, the *levée en masse* abounded.[33] At the very least, perhaps one could arrange a tariff union with liberated Belgium. All of this euphoria was received in horror by businessmen. "Com-

merce lives only by confidence and peace," said the Chamber of
Nantes. (The Belgian tariff union idea provoked another inquiry
by the government and, receiving an overwhelming "non" from
the Chambers throughout France in 1831, the idea was uncere-
moniously dropped.)[34]

Disorder at home, the threat of war abroad, these were the fundamental concerns of French business in 1831. Although the historian can hardly doubt their real significance in aggravating the
economic crisis, what is important for now is the significance that
businessmen *attached* to them. The evidence is overwhelming.
The following enumeration of the responses mentioning these
and other "accidental causes" of economic distress tell the story.

Number of responses: 33   *Total number of statements*:   62
1. Internal unrest—31
   a. "Popular"—28
   b. Legitimist agitation—3
2. International political situation—24
   a. Threat of war—20
   b. Revolution elsewhere—2
   c. Belgian union discussions—2
3. Government instability—7

Thus more than 90 percent of those organs responding to the
question listed internal unrest as a cause of the current withdrawal of capital and uncertain future of French business. These
men certainly *thought* they were still in the midst of a revolution
in the spring of 1831. It is worth noting that the Chamber of
Deputies had already voted 30 million francs in credits (October
17, 1830) to distressed areas of industry and commerce, with 2
million reserved especially for immediate distribution to newly
created *comptoirs d'escomptes* for the purpose of discounting
bills as rapidly as possible. Four million more were allocated to
the Paris *comptoir* in December. There was some debate over the
effectiveness of such measures,[35] but in the judgment of Maurice
Lévy-Leboyer, they did some good in restoring credit, at least
temporarily.[36] But obviously such pump-priming was not the
real solution in most of their minds. As the Chamber of Commerce of Carcassonne remarked, "we think, with all *bons esprits*,
that the intervention of the Government into the details of com-

merce is neither useful nor desirable. Commerce asks of it only (tariff) protection, freedom, and external markets. Thus, in this time of crisis, when all commercial transactions are paralyzed, the government can remedy it by making all the sacrifices compatible with national honor for the sake of peace and by repressing internal disturbances."[37]

And so the answers rolled in: Le Havre—"without [public] order neither credit nor commerce can exist"; Lyon—"Let the government, by its firmness, render new troubles impossible, make our foreign relations certain, and commerce and industry will resume a new phase of growth"; Troyes—"repress the audacious behavior of the parties of popular disorder," shackle the press, maintain peace, and confidence and credit, the "sources of public prosperity," will return. Lille, Rouen, Avignon, Châlons-sur-Marne, St. Quentin, Angers, Limoges, Nantes, Amiens, even the Basses-Alpes, everywhere the answer was the same. Finally, all but one of the seventeen responding Parisian industries took a similar stand. Although none of the respondents actually ranked causes and remedies, those invoking a single cause invariably stressed repression of popular disturbances. Only Niort specifically gave more emphasis to the peace issue than to the other. It was also made clear that the danger was on the Left. Only Angers, apprehensive of "civil war fomented by the clergy and the nobility," and Niort, on the southern border of the western stronghold of legitimism, looked to the Right.[38]

Seven respondents remarked about the disorder or lack of direction within the government itself as a factor shaking business confidence, although many more scolded the new regime for not maintaining law and order effectively. But none of the seven failed to include the internal disorder theme. Vienne was typical (and Argout red-penciled it): "Among the permanent [sic] causes, the chamber calls attention to the uncertain orientation of the Ministry and the lack of unity it seems to exhibit. It announces its confidence in the civic dedication (*civisme*) of those ministers who are most disposed to recognize the source of the evil and to remedy it." One should not infer from this that there was a vague preference for the fallen regime. Besides the ten respondents that blamed the Restoration for their economic problems, several others made specific reference to the promise of the new government for the economic future of France. The Chamber of Commerce of Bayonne perhaps summed up the general feeling in its brief remarks:

> The July Revolution found the commerce of Bayonne and its environs in a state of decadence which had anterior causes, but which could only get worse with the uncertainty, inseparable from the unexpected changes, and with the unfortunate complications which have led to the forced adjournment of most of the immense advantages that will sooner or later, but unfailingly, result from this revolution.[39]

These voices of French business had delivered a message to the new regime at a crucial juncture of its existence. Some of the reports were already in and others were still in the making when the "unstable" ministry of the banker Jacques Laffitte (himself nearly destroyed by the post-revolutionary financial crisis) was replaced by that of the banker Casimir Perier (March 12–13). On the 18th, Perier delivered the essentials of his policy in a speech before the Chamber of Deputies: "Order internally, without the sacrifice of liberty; peace externally, without cost to honor."[40] This was to be the "government of resistance," whose energy in repressing popular outbursts, republican political organization, the radical press, and labor organization and strike activity during the following year has become part of the folklore of French history. We shall return to this and the subsequent history of law and order during the July Monarchy. For now, it should simply be noted that whatever one may say about the influence of the business community on July Monarchy policy, the "reign of the bourgeoisie," and all the rest, in the spring of 1831 business got what it wanted most of all: a government that would keep the poor, the working people, and their defenders in line. And Argout, who was retained in the new ministry, in responding to the mayor of Bolbec's request for extra public assistance funds in June, exhibited a serene air of certainty that confidence would soon return, employment would revive, and aid for the "indigent class" would not have to be renewed.[41]

The inquiry of February 19 concluded with recommendations to the government on how to remedy the economic crisis. The significance of repression, peace, and ministerial stability as businessmen's preoccupations is made all the more clear by the Chambers' hesitancy to introduce other concerns. Only tariff reform rivaled them, with thirteen responses mentioning it. It is interesting that no one called for higher tariff protection and only one, St. Dié (Vosges), a none-too-prosperous cotton, iron, and paper manufacturing city, stressed the need to maintain the highly restrictive system of the Restoration. While there is no doubt that all respondents would have opposed unfettered free trade, eight sought selective decreases either to cheapen raw materials or to ease retaliatory tariffs in other nations. Predictably, the three respondents from Haut-Rhin (Mulhouse, Colmar, and Ste.-Marie) were all favorable to such action, thus announcing to the July Monarchy an ongoing Alsatian demand. Other concerns included revision of the harsh bankruptcy law (three), the regulation of peddling (three western towns concerned about its effect on local industry), the reduction or elimination of excise taxes (three), and Carcassonne urged the government "to make good use of Algeria, which has cost us so dearly." Surprisingly, demands for improved communications were found only in the recommendations of the prefect of the Meurthe (canal to the Rhine) and the Chamber of St. Dié, which wanted a rail connection. Finally, only Ste.-Marie mentioned the need for provincial banks.

Considerable space has been given to the *Enquête* of 1831. More than an introduction to the problem of this essay, it shows the overriding concerns of businessmen as they entered the era of the July Monarchy. This regime was doubtless an improvement on the one that had just collapsed. But the continuance of popular revolution, unleashed by the July Days, had to cease. Credit, the mainspring of business enterprise, could not exist without confidence in the future, and the latter rested on social stability. For the business community, this meant an orderly, disciplined, and powerless work force. Why was this so overwhelmingly important? Because at that moment for France, whose industrial resources were expensive, whose credit facilities were mediocre, whose company law hindered large-scale capital formation, whose communications system left much to be desired, and whose position in foreign trade was vastly inferior to her great rival across the Channel, the efficient exploitation of labor resources—relatively expensive anyway because of only moderate population growth and aggravated by the nasty proclivity of French peasants to remain so—was a matter of economic life and death.

Thus the desire for repressive social policy among French businessmen was more than an accident of troubled times. It represented a deeper need lodged in economic reality. In 1831 low-paid labor was the key to profits, and it was the business of government to assist in maintaining business prosperity. But without question this government could do more. Indeed, one of the principal grievances against the Restoration had been its generally tight-fisted fiscal policy—public works had languished dismally despite wide-ranging canal and road proposals, government contracts had been curtailed, export subsidies were lacking in many industries injured by high duties on needed raw materials, the administration of commerce and agriculture (then a branch of the Ministry of the Interior) lay virtually dormant for lack of funds. Henri Sée pointed out the excellent fiscal management of the Restoration—it operated normally with an excedent and maintained a nearly constant budget of between 900 million and 1 billion francs per year. "It avoided expenses, but lived *une vie assez étriquée*." Strictly speaking, laissez-faire, if interpreted as nonsupport for economic interests, reigned during the Restoration as never before or since.[42] But as Rostow and many others have stressed, "a very high proportion of total capital investment in the preconditions and take-off period must go into social overhead capital; and this fact lays a heavy burden on the role of the state in the early states of industrialization."[43] This means, at the very least, input into education, including the collection and provision of economic information, and public works, especially transport facilities. It will become clear that the government of the July Monarchy largely understood its task in this regard. Moreover, while the volume of specific economic legislation was not large during the life of the regime, most of that which was passed must be classified as progressive, even in the realm of tariff policy. Finally, in many respects the administration winked at much past legislation (particularly regulatory law developed during the Napoleonic era) that fettered capitalist freedom and, conversely, interpreted narrowly and acted harshly upon law relating to labor.

There seems to have been a fairly clear chronology to all this. In the early years of the regime, government policy focused principally on labor repression. Beginning in 1833–1834, however, its determination to deal positively with investment in social overhead capital became evident as the Guizot primary education law and the law on expropriations were passed and as the Administration des Ponts et Chaussées undertook to formulate an overall program for vast improvements in communications. Then from about 1836 to 1840—although further detailed research would be necessary to clarify the process—the administration guided, cajoled, and sometimes bullied the Chambers through a stormy period during which both localist-traditionalist and excessive laissez-faire opinions were often undermined, and rational railroad policy, business law, and agricultural improvement orientations were forged. Banking and credit policy was liberalized, although the Bank of France itself remained a formidable obstacle. Labor policy was still as tight as ever but receded into the background as these more positive moves were made. In a way, this period can be viewed as one during which state policy created crucial legal and social preconditions for the economic boom of the 1840s.

During these years both "liberal" and "étatist" orientations can be distinguished. But there was really no contradiction between the two. In the first place, it has been a long time since economic historians have claimed that the definition of what is "capitalist" rests exclusively on laissez-faire. Indeed, the economic theory of early capitalist industrialization virtually dictates that state investment in social overhead capital must be made. Secondly, as Claude Fohlen has so perfectly phrased it, the French "bourgeoisie makes use of [the notion of economic] freedom when it profits from it, and thus makes a weapon of it against its adversaries —the unorganized and thus inoffensive masses; this same bourgeoisie makes a clean sweep of this same freedom when its interests are threatened and when non-intervention of the state puts profits in peril. This completely subjective conception of economic freedom will be imposed progressively all through the nineteenth century."[44] There is, therefore, nothing "anti-capitalist" about state intervention, especially in France. This holds, incidentally, even for intervention in support of the unemployed in times of severe crisis, for the alternative might well be bloody upheaval.

Thus the short-lived *ateliers de charité* of 1830–1831 in Paris and many other parts of France, other public works projects for indigents during the July Monarchy, and the whole structure of public assistance in France were perfectly reasonable in light of the higher costs and threat to profits that public disorder might bring.[45]

This trend toward rational, growth-oriented policy can be roughly indexed by the changing attitudes of the Pereire brothers, those arch-promoters of economic progress, to July Monarchy policy. Their criticism of it moderated perceptibly during the '30s. As Saint-Simonians they did not worry about state intervention. Only let it be competent. But alas, as of early 1832, the highest level of economic policy formation was far from that: "After the July Revolution, a ministry of commerce and public works was created, and the direction of it was confided to M. d'Argout: this was to destroy the effect of a good measure with a bad." Argout seemed to know nothing of the realities of economic life and less about technics. If "the administration of Becquey [the key figure in Restoration economic policy] was somnolent, never has it seen such incompetence."[46] Argout was in fact a kind of high-class political hack, a wealthy conservative *doctrinaire* who owed his title to the Empire; in short, the complete notable. The same year, however, four Saint-Simonian friends of the Perieres published an important book on public works and showed that the ministry already included a man whose competence they could only admire, B.-A.-V. Legrand, recently elevated to the position of director-general of the Conseil des Ponts et Chaussées. Legrand, *polytechnicien* and engineer, like so many of the Saint-Simonians, became their hope for the economic future of France.[47] As we shall see, it was a hope well founded. This division of sympathy underlines a central issue of this essay: there seems to have been, throughout the 1830s, a marked difference of orientation on economic questions between the politicians, either in the Chamber of Deputies or, as ministers, reliant upon it, and the career bureaucrats. The latter, as the regime consolidated itself, generally stood at the forefront of pro-capitalist policy, while the politicians often dragged their heels, especially in defense of local interests. Bureaucrats like Legrand spoke for the "national interest," which in their minds meant the creation of prosperity through carefully conceived and developed state policy. By and large, this approach coincided with the desires of large-scale capitalism, or at least of the industrial and commercial grande bourgeoisie (if not always *la haute banque*), and of Paris and other large cities as opposed to the rest of the country. The politicians on the other hand naturally tended to represent their constitutents, which meant greater attention to local interests and to landed proprietorship—in short, to the much more varied and amorphous interests of the notables who comprised the electorate. The fascination of the problem lies in the extent to which the former increased its power at the expense of the latter as time went by. In any case, it is clear that the Pereires, beginning with their guardedly favorable reaction to the expropriation law of 1833, found more and more good things to say about policy orientations of the administration and of the legislation it managed to get passed.[48]

Let us now examine some of the specifics of July Monarchy policy, beginning with labor. Perier's government of resistance and its continuators did their work. Popular outbursts were dealt with by a policy of overkill. The Lyon insurrection of November 1831, the troubles in Grenoble in March 1832, and the reprisals taken in the June 5–6 rebellion in Paris are exemplary.[49] Concerted policy to destroy all popular republican associations courting workers was generally successful as the Société des Amis du Peuple was hounded out of existence in 1832 and the Association Libre pour l'Education du Peuple in December of 1833. Finally, the great Société des Droits de l'Homme was crushed by law, then by military force in 1834.[50] Simultaneously, the government imposed the letter of the law on strikes and trade unions (both were illegal by virtue of revolutionary and Napoleonic legislation) and, more importantly, moved against legal mutual aid societies that it suspected of using their organizations for future strike activities. The summary dissolution of the Société Philanthropique des Ouvriers Tailleurs in 1835 was typical.[51] The Law on Associations of April 1834 served to destroy both popular political and worker defense organizations. It may be true that government officials mediated certain labor disputes in 1830–1831,[52] but as time passed, article 1781 of the Code, which specified that the word of a master would be taken over that of his worker, was applied with rigor. By 1840 government policy had taken its full development. Not only was the great strike wave in Paris snuffed out by force of arms, but master coalition (among the tailors for instance) was accepted even though it clearly violated the law.[53]

Perhaps more important were the multiple abuses that workers suffered at the hands of their employers (and the system in general) that went unrectified in the course of the July Monarchy despite continuous outcry against them.[54] A few examples will have to suffice. *Marchandage*, subcontracting of work to intermediaries for a lump sum, had tremendously negative effects on wages in a variety of industries, particularly construction and rural outworking in textiles, and spread like wildfire in the 1840s. It is no accident that its elimination was the first major act relating to work by the provisional government in 1848. A central issue in all outworking trades was the exclusive right claimed by entrepreneurs to weigh and judge the quality of finished goods returned to them and then make deductions for underweight and flawed materials.[55] One of the most startling, and little appreciated, abuses of the day was wage advances made to workers when they took employment from which a virtual system of peonage could develop. Only in 1850 would this problem be addressed by the government.[56] Even though the guild system was officially dead, the ancient practice of restricting ascension to master status was universal and became especially vicious in declining craft industries.

Masters and workers alike suffered from trends toward "big business" practices in formerly purely artisan industries. The July Monarchy held pride of place in French history in the rise of ready-made clothing (*confection*). Under this system, hoards of low-paid seamsters (often foreigners and women) worked for large-scale entrepreneurs who had the cutting done in their own shops. The latter then sold their products at prices much below those of the bespoke tailors, either in their own "department stores" or through a sophisticated organization of traveling salesmen.[57] In general, *colportage* (peddling) went unregulated —save for newspapers!—during the July Monarchy, much to the dismay of local artisans throughout France. Merchandising was experiencing a real revolution, one whose dimensions unfortunately have not yet been adequately researched.

Finally, phenomena of integration and concentration were manifest all through the July Monarchy but especially after 1840.[58] Small business and artisan industry naturally suffered the most from it, but larger outfits collapsed before its onslaught as well. Collusion—expressly forbidden by law—went on unimpaired. The most famous example was that between the two giants of highway passenger and light freight service, the Messageries Royales and Laffitte and Caillard's Messageries Générales, who together destroyed all competition. For example, in 1837 one Pénicaud, an employee of both lines overseeing their joint route from Angoulême to Bordeaux, had the audacity to set up on his own. Because of his close local contacts, especially with the *maîtres des postes* who rented teams to the highway companies, he rapidly took over much of the traffic, so the big companies simply responded with a rate war. They took major losses (made up for by their profits elsewhere) and killed off the upstart by the end of 1838. Then came the interesting part. He sued his great adversaries on the legitimate grounds of collusion. The case went from court to court. He won before the Tribunal d'Instance de Police Correctionelle de la Seine, but the decision was reversed by the Cour Royale de Paris. Poor Pénicaud appealed to the Cour de Cassation, which referred it to the Cour de Lyon. The latter, in the midst of some very strange proceedings, finally rejected his suit and charged him with all the court expenses. This became somewhat of a *cause célèbre* and Baron Dupin, arch-notable, could not be constrained from condemning such injustice before the Chamber of Peers. We will probably never know what actually went on behind the scenes in this scandalous affair, but it is clear that the court system succumbed to the power of big business.[59]

Concentrations and mergers were especially significant in the coal mining industry, which was responding to a massive increase in demand as metallurgy developed in the course of the July Monarchy. The government actually seems to have encouraged the reduction of competition, especially through an act in 1838 forcing several companies of Rive-de-Gier to cooperate in flood prevention while simultaneously easing the process by which small concessions could be absorbed by major companies like Anzin. The great Compagnie des Mines de la Loire, a monopoly in Rive-de-Gier, was formed in 1845: although provoking strikes and bloody protest from the miners and widespread public outcry, its existence was not troubled by the regime.[60]

The clear impression is that with abuses in both industrial relations and business collusion, the government opted for a hands-off (if not really a laissez-faire) policy and rarely heeded the complaints of injured parties. Without question big business benefited and so, it would appear, did the general growth process.

The July regime combined action with inaction in dealing with banking and credit facilities and business law. Considerable research has been devoted to banking and the problems of capital investment in France during the July Monarchy. Rondo Cameron and Bertrand Gille, the leading authorities on the question, feel that inadequate credit facilities were an important drag on French growth down to 1848. Cameron has rightly laid the principal blame on the Banque de France, which possessed exclusive rights to issue notes valid throughout the country and followed extremely conservative reserve practices. Moreover, it discounted bills payable only in Paris and required elaborate guarantees. The Bank of France, its structure and high personnel, was one of the few institutions to undergo no change at all after 1830. In 1840, when so much else seemed to be changing, its charter was renewed almost without revision. The small number of departmental banks then in existence had petitioned the Chamber of Deputies "for permission to discount bills drawn on any city in which an authorized bank existed, to accept one anothers' notes and to form a nation-wide note exchange, to substitute deposits of their own shares for the third signature on bills of exchange, to pay interest on deposits, to liberalize the use of current accounts, and to issue notes for as little as 100 francs." (The bank allowed minimum notes of 1000 francs.)[61] The Chamber paid no heed to these progressive proposals. It should nevertheless be appreciated that between 1835 and 1838 six new departmental banks *were* chartered. These and three others authorized early in the Restoration seem to have played a fundamental role in developing local and regional commerce, especially through their discounting services. As Gille writes, for instance, "the Bank of Marseilles [authorized by Royal Ordinance, Sept. 29, 1835] appears to have enjoyed an excellent reputation in Marseilles commerce, whose transactions it notably facilitated."[62] Such success frightened the Bank of France, however, and it waged quiet war against these upstarts. But even the bank made a fundamental contribution, one which anyone who recalled the 1790s had to appreciate: French currency remained stable; indeed the solidity of the franc made it nearly as sought after in international exchange as the pound sterling.

By and large, however, real investment banking was virtually nonexistent during the July Monarchy. Only Laffitte's Caisse Générale du Commerce et de l'Industrie, founded in 1837, played any kind of an important role in this regard, investing in French plaster and haulage businesses as well as railroads. Moreover, his competition appears to have "forced amelioration in the market for short-term commercial credit," including the discount operations of the Bank of France itself.[63] Mobilization of capital therefore came largely through direct individual investment in firms, although private banking houses like the Rothschilds and Foulds or groups of financiers played an increasingly important role in industrial capitalization after 1840.[64]

Their investment was heavily oriented toward safer *sociétés anonymes* (limited liability companies) and it is one of the honored verities of French economic history that the governments (specifically the Conseil d'état) of the whole period from 1815 to 1848 were reluctant to authorize such companies.[65] Laffitte had applied and been denied in 1837. Still, there was a palpable increase in the number and the amount of capitalization of sociétés anonymes during the July Monarchy, especially after 1837. A peak of twenty-eight firms and a capitalization of 569,-108,000 francs for twenty where the figures are known was reached in 1845.[66] The great bulk of société anonyme capital, however, went into rail companies, where the interest was generally guaranteed by the state and the impeccable credentials of the original investors was all but assured by the adjudication for the concession in the first place.

Much more important, and less appreciated, was the vast extension and legal liberalization of the other principal joint-stock form of business organization, the Société en Commandite par Actions, during the July Monarchy. It did not require government authorization, but simply registration with the local Tribunal de Commerce. This type of company was organized under one or more managers (*gérants*) whose liability was unlimited. Capital, however, largely came from shareholders, whose liability was limited to the amount of their investment. Their penalty was that they could not legally share in the direction of the enterprise, which was left solely in the hands of the active partners. Such companies were relatively rare under the Restoration, however, because of a fundamental legal disability: the trading of shares on the market was hamstrung by the fact that Restoration jurisprudence condemned *bons au porteurs* (bearer shares), thus vastly complicating transfer. Charles Lamouroux had complained loudly about this in 1830. But in a landmark decision in 1832, the Cour Royale de Paris confirmed a decision of the Paris Tribunal de Commerce allowing the issuance of such shares. This naturally posed the danger of excessive speculation, but a true market in negotiable shares on business enterprise was created. Abuses were rampant, however, and the Chamber of Deputies even considered the abolition of *commandites* altogether during the speculative year of 1838. While total figures on commandite formation are lacking, it is clear that this form of enterprise lubricated industrial investment significantly during its heyday under the July Monarchy. Finally, it naturally follows that the number of transactions on the Paris Stock Exchange multiplied many times over during the July Monarchy: in many respects France entered the modern age of stock exchange during this era.[67]

One of the key demands of Charles Lamouroux and many other businessmen in 1830 was the reform of the articles of the Code de Commerce relating to bankruptcy (*faillites*). Typically eighteenth century, the Code "treat[ed] the *failli* as a criminal" and totally destroyed him; moreover, the liquidation process was very costly to the creditors because of government fees.[68] Stringent bankruptcy law was a fundamental obstacle to the willingness to take risks and hence an important impediment to capitalist development. The July Monarchy acted to modify it as the

Ministry of Commerce proposed a new law in 1835 that was finally promulgated after much debate on May 28, 1838. Its principal virtue was the expeditious handling of each case. Costs were therefore kept to a minimum. One judge from the Tribunal of Commerce (instead of the whole court) oversaw each case and the investigation was carried out by selected *syndics* within the confines of a specific timetable. While the *failli* was in principle stripped of all his goods, he was allowed a subsistence income from his liquid assets during the course of the proceedings, and was not likely to spend any time in prison, and if the bankruptcy involved no fraud, could immediately apply for "rehabilitation" papers from the public prosecutor (*procureur du roi*). If successful, he could then "present himself *à la Bourse*." The moral opprobrium of bankruptcy remained, but with good faith and some luck a clever entrepreneur could now recover from Balzac's "ultimate disaster."[69] Less fundamental for the future of French capitalism but an important encouragement to innovation was the patent law of 1844. Its significance for property law was underlined by Georges Ripert: "in giving the author of a discovery the exclusive right to exploit it to his profit, the legislator created a new form of property, which has taken the name of *industrial property*."[70]

Many historians have criticized both the Restoration and the July Monarchy for the maintenance of blanket tariff protection for French industry; moreover, all through the July Monarchy certain industries such as silk, wine, and Alsatian cotton prints, whose competitive position in the world market was strong, cried out for freer trade.[71] But "free trade" as a general panacea has always been the ideology of those dealing from a position of strength. Naturally English industry as a whole should promote it. It is clear that most French industry would have been crushed by English competition had not the Restoration government rendered it protection. The July Monarchy followed the same principle, but with greater intelligence. In a major inquiry in 1834, the Ministry of Commerce (then under the more competent Duchâtel) sought the opinions of French business on tariff reform and found nearly universal opposition to major steps toward free trade. But specific reductions on primary materials, machines and machine parts, and certain grades of thread whose production costs were expensive in comparison to England were sought by interested parties. Selective reduction did indeed follow—though significantly by virtue of royal ordinance rather than statute. Thus were fine-gauge cotton thread duties diminished in August 1834, coal in January 1836, and certain needed grades of wool yarn in July 1837. Lévy-Leboyer points out that the yarn reductions benefited weaving immensely without hurting spinning. French spinning simply focused more on lower thread numbers, which it could produce more effectively.[72] The lifting of excessive coal restrictions was a boon and was largely responsible for the major shift from charcoal to coke in iron smelting so evident in the 1840s. Simultaneously, the foreign competition forced the French coal industry toward greater efficiency in terms of techniques (improved pumping systems above all), concentration of ownership, and, unfortunately, the ever greater exploitation of one of the most oppressed work forces in the nation. In the '40s, machinery and machine part duties were reduced as well. Thus the July Monarchy maintained a high tariff framework, but selectively reduced duties on certain products crucial to French industrial growth. It is evident also that the administration was at the forefront of this endeavor, the Chamber of Deputies maintaining a kind of knee-jerk conservatism on the entire subject.

The balance sheet regarding state action short of direct investment in the economy thus appears to find a surplus in the assets column. To be sure, much more could have been done to improve banking facilities, to ease the financing of business, and to rationalize the tariff system, although the situation was not as bad as is often claimed. The law nevertheless largely favored business and left it free to exploit its labor resources virtually at will. Only three measures remotely in the interest of the working classes were passed during the entire reign. But the law authorizing the creation of savings banks (1835), motivated out of the reigning self-help philosophy, could hardly hurt business, nor could that law reducing the number of artisans having to pay the *patente,* a tax on operating business enterprises (1844). In any case the former benefited only that minority of working people who *could* save anything and was designed to reduce the need for potentially dangerous mutual aid societies, while the latter had its major effect among rural handloom weavers, whose days were, by then, numbered anyway. This leaves the law of March 22, 1841, regulating child labor and stipulating previous and/or simultaneous primary education for the working child, which was passed by the Chambers over the strong opposition of many manufacturers.[73] But it is well-known that the application of this law was, at best, confused and, at worst, simply inoperative because of a woefully inadequate inspection system which was not rectified until 1874.

Let us move finally to the question of state provision of social overhead capital and its direct role in stimulating economic growth. The budgets of the July Monarchy were, on the annual average, 42 million francs higher than those of the Restoration. More importantly, the total budget expanded by nearly 50 percent during the reign, running at a deficit throughout the '40s, and the share of the Ministry of Commerce and Public Works increased dramatically, as did that of Public Instruction.[74] In particular, the volume of business handled by the Conseil Général des Ponts et Chaussées multiplied rapidly. This can be gauged by the number of dispatches from the various departments under its administration that it registered from 1833 to 1841.[75] The total number of dispatches increased from 32,295 to 57,425 (the figure had been 27,078 for 1830), or 78 percent. The personnel and accounts offices' dispatches predictably increased at about the same rate. Business relating to roads and bridges expanded by nearly 50 percent with a marked favoritism shown to roadwork in the northern half of France.[76] Internal Navigation went from 4,660 to 7,591, or 59 percent, and mostly concerned works in progress. The somewhat smaller number of dispatches relating to factories and mines as they affected the public interest rose the least, just under 20 percent. The major increases came from Ports and Maritime Works (from 1,898 to 3,048 or 61 percent) and above all from railroads and *police de roulage* (a tiny proportion of the total), which expanded from virtually nothing—the first figure given is 243 in 1835—to 6,932 in 1841. The overall pattern of development shows the years 1837 to 1840 to be the period of the most rapid expansion, with railroad business leading the way. As of 1841 each of the major capital-absorbing branches of the Administration registered the following proportions of dispatches.

Routes et Ponts	14,059	*dépêches*	44%
Chemin de fer et Police de roulage	6,932		22
Ports et Travaux maritime	3,048		10
International Navigation	7,591		24
	31,630		100

There is little question, then, that the positive role of the state in economic development increased, especially during the later 1830s. Moreover, the structure of the administrations relating to economic affairs was progressively rationalized. As already noted, a separate Ministry of Commerce and Public Works was one of the fruits of the July Revolution. Simultaneously high advisory councils of agriculture and manufactures and the Conseil Supérieur de Commerce were organized anew, and election procedures to the Chambres de Commerce and Chambres Consultatifs throughout France were altered to give them greater independence from government influence. Ideally, the opinions of the local chambers would flow directly into the various *conseils* and thence to the ministry. The ministry was encumbered at first by the responsibility of administering hospitals, prisons, and the regulation of begging, but these were removed from its competence by ordinances of 1834 and 1836. In 1840, Public Works was separated and awarded ministerial status—a further indication of its growing significance in French life.[77] In 1834 the Chamber of Deputies authorized a fund for the creation of a special bureau of statistics within the Ministry of the Interior. On this basis the first efforts in the development of modern national statistics—which produced the published volumes of the *Statistique générale de la France* in subsequent years—were generated.[78] The Commerce ministry also provided independent informational services concerning new foreign products and techniques in industry and agriculture, new market opportunities, the transfer of useful information from one part of France to another, etc. It underwrote the publication of the *Annales des Mines,* the *Annales des Ponts et Chaussées,* and other technical journals and sponsored numerous specific research projects. The many

Enquêtes on economic questions that dot the July Monarchy were largely promulgated by the same ministry. Finally, local Chambers of Commerce, often at the urging of the central administration, undertook inquiries of their own.[79] As social overhead capital, such work can hardly be overestimated, especially in view of the long-range return on such a modest investment.

The direct educational services that evolved under the July Monarchy are dominated, of course, by the *loi Guizot,* the primary education act of 1833. Basic literacy is unquestionably one of the essential prerequisites of economic modernization and this was not the least of the motivations behind the act. The law has been justly criticized because it made education neither free nor compulsory, because of the laughably low salaries provided for teachers, and because it transferred so much of the financial and administrative responsibility to the communes. But, while a full study of literacy in France during the July Monarchy remains to be written, local research, the analysis of the growing number of army recruits knowing how to read and write, and the subjective estimates made by the local committees who conducted the *Enquête* of 1848 all attest to the growing percentage of literate French men and women during the July Monarchy.[80] High quality technical education at the university level was a long-standing French tradition and was given a massive boost by revolutionary and Napoleonic legislation.[81] Intermediate technical instruction was lacking, however, and apparently received only desultory support from the July regime. Much research is needed in this area but if the responses to the *Enquête* of 1848 are any indication, *ferme-écoles,* model farms, secondary vocational and technical schools, and the like *had* been developed, but their numbers were small. Perhaps one can hypothesize that the thrust of educational policy under the July Monarchy was to produce fine crops of engineers and other professional technicians on one hand and to give workers only the bare educational essentials for getting on in the industrial world on the other, leaving out the intermediate stage of developing real expertise in the practical arts among the masses at large. If so, while consistent with social policy already examined, this must certainly be condemned from the point of view of global economic growth.[82]

The central consideration in assessing the positive role of the state in stimulating economic growth is the progress of public works, above all in transport. Here the work of the Conseil Général des Ponts et Chaussées was crucial.[83] No one doubts that the orientation of this body changed rapidly after the Revolution of 1830, although some historians maintain that it was too submerged in technical details to appreciate the larger economic needs of the country.[84] I hope to show that this simply was not so. Indeed, if the future of public works policy had been left to the Chamber of Deputies or even the Ministry of Commerce operating without the Conseil's advice, progress might have foundered altogether. In reading the deliberations of the Conseil during the 1830s,[85] it became increasingly clear to me that these men possessed not only remarkable technical capacities, but a profound sense of the national economic interest. Often for this reason they found themselves in conflict with the Chamber of Deputies, local chambers of commerce, municipal and departmental councils, and with many individual businessmen and landowners, in short, with the particularist concerns of a majority of the notables of the era. But most interestingly their focus seemed to coincide more often than not with the great capitalists of France who sought, as they did, policy promoting the national interest, at least in the sense of developing a nationwide market for the goods and services large-scale capitalism alone could provide. The evolution of railroad policy brought out these differences most clearly.

The composition of the Conseil Général des Ponts et Chaussées saw a massive turnover from 1830 to 1831. Two out of seven inspectors-general, the highest ranks beneath the director, were replaced and a third had been dropped by 1832. Two of the three replacements, however, were former divisional inspectors, who oversaw operations of the public works districts in France and certain special problem areas. The very top positions, while changing somewhat, thus kept important functionaries from the Restoration. But at the divisional inspector level, replacements were rampant. Of the fifteen in office in 1829–1830 only two remained in 1832, though Dutens and Cavenne had been promoted to inspector-general. Eleven men seem to have left the administration altogether. Moreover, of the twelve new faces that appear in the ranks of the divisional inspectors by 1832, only five held high positions in the administration beneath the Conseil level (all were departmental engineers-in-chief).[86] Finally, Becquey—who had doubled as head of Ponts et Chaussées and as kind of *de facto* minister for economic affairs—was replaced by Simon Bérard, a liberal industrialist, former Napoleonic official, and ally of Jacques Laffitte. Whether he or Guizot was responsible for the purge is difficult to say.[87]

But one man stayed right where he had been: secretary of the Conseil was Baptiste-Alexis-Victor Legrand. Bérard's star faded in 1832 as his critical attitude toward the government of resistance hardened, and on June 8 (was Bérard implicated in the rising of June 5–6?) Legrand became provisional director-general. He was already renowned for his bearing, modesty, intellectual powers, and super-efficiency. For the next ten years he would be the soul of public works development and is rightly regarded as the architect of the French railroad system.[88]

Although it is impossible to recount the details, it is evident from an examination of the weekly proceedings of the Conseil Général[89] during the early years of the July Monarchy that Legrand's rise to power changed the atmosphere considerably. Even with the influx of new men, the excessive caution as regards technical details seemed to override considerations of rapid economic progress. Moreover, there is little indication that a majority had been won to the concept of the railroad. The harassment of the great pioneers of early French rail development, the Séguin brothers, proves both points.[90] But even in 1831 Legrand, supported by the recently promoted Dutens and Cavanne, demonstrated an acute appreciation of businessmen's motivations and the need to promote the railroad. In the session of August 9, 1831, a stormy argument developed in which some members, led by Tarbé, a Restoration inspector-general, thought that temporary and renewable rail concessions were "safer for the state and the public interest," while Legrand and his allies felt that "speculative investment in railroads is not yet sufficiently accepted in France for the government not to look for all the means at its disposal to support and to promote it: one of these means is the perpetual concession," which, by giving the capitalist a sense of security, has "a moral advantage that will make the purchase of shares easier and thus favor the success of the operation."[91] His position lost to the more cautious majority.

Legrand's permanent appointment was confirmed during the summer of 1832 and previous difficulties relating to rail concessions began to fade, although badly prepared *cahiers des charges* (technical provisions with cost estimates) were summarily dismissed. Thus the Talabot proposal for a line from the mines of Alais to the Rhône port of Beaucaire sailed through without a hitch on July 24, 1832, while a sloppy cahier presented by an unknown for a concession from Bordeaux to Laubusse was quickly rejected; the Conseil nevertheless recommended that a proposal for Bordeaux-Bayonne be prepared. More to the point, on December 18, 1832, a majority of the Conseil supported Legrand in the name of practicality against the legal scruples of several older members in authorizing that a link between the St. Etienne-Andrézieux and the Lyon-St. Etienne lines, both now controlled by Mallet et Henry, be constructed by that company without competitive adjudication.[92] And so it began. Whether Emile Pereire influenced Legrand or the latter arrived at his position independently, it was rare thereafter for the director-general to take a position that did not find at least partial favor with perhaps the most farsighted capitalist of the era. By 1836 they were fast friends.[93]

But the problem was not at Ponts et Chaussées. At every turn, attempts to develop rational public works policy ran into opposition from local interests. The latter were most powerfully represented in the Chamber of Deputies. There they were often joined by individuals perhaps of broader vision, but who feared the power of the central administration and the great interests it seemed to represent: we might call them the moralists of left and right—men like Garnier-Pagès and Arago or Berryer, the great voice of legitimism. The battle was first joined in 1833 over an administration project to streamline the Napoleonic law on expropriation for public necessity, which left responsibility to the judiciary and hence led to interminable court battles. The goal was to eliminate this and to substitute special departmental juries, chosen from among electors by the prefect. Almost immediately it was amended to create juries in each *arrondissement*, thus assuring greater influence from local proprietors. Then came a parade of legists, condemning the proposal as a destruction of the individual right to suit in court in defense of property. But the most fascinating episode (indeed, one that may be a minor turning point in French history) concerned a well-supported amendment defended by the conservative Parent. The ministerial project took the position that compensation to dispossessed landowners should be determined by a bargaining process in which the state and the proprietor register their respective claims and the jury then decides on an amount, also taking into account the commodity value of the land. The amendment sought to abandon the obligation of the proprietor to lodge his claim on the grounds that he often would not really be able to establish a value on the "succession of his fathers"; it had a *valeur d'affection* which could not be easily expressed in money. One might make fun of such a position, but it is interesting that the two main proponents of the government bill, Bernard (de Rennes) and Teste, felt obliged to argue long and hard against it. At issue was a conception of *moral* economics regarding land values as opposed to the idea of land as simple, disposable property.[94] The Chamber opted for the government in this case, but the substantial backing received by the amendment was a significant indication of the struggle in defense of capitalist values that the administration would have to continue to wage. The government finally got its law, but it was so watered down that a new law expediting expropriation procedures had to be rammed through eight years later.[95]

The unfolding of French rail policy and the incessant battles fought for general principles and for the concessions themselves by the Conseil Général des Ponts et Chaussées in the Chamber of Deputies during the later '30s are well enough known only to require brief comment.[96] The idiocy of granting two lines to Versailles, one from the right bank and one from the left (the latter pushed by the Chamber ostensibly out of "fairness" to the merchants on the left) evoked the rage of the Pereire-Rothschild consortium that was assured the right bank line and evoked the famous discourse of Legrand in which he remarked to the legislators: "I do not know what the principles of my predecessors were; for my part, I declare that the direction of a road, canal, or railroad is an economic question before it is a technical question; that under my leadership, the technical side will be subordinated to the economic."[97] Almost out of frustration, Legrand proposed in 1838 a master plan for French rail development beginning with four great lines radiating from Paris and financed by the state. This project was soundly defeated, but as much out of acrimony for the Molé ministry and concern that this or that electoral district might be left out as for the idea of state ownership.[98] The crisis of 1838–1839 hit several of the young railroad companies hard (especially the Paris-Versailles left bank), and the government was obliged to make low interest loans to bail them out. Simultaneously Legrand sought to restimulate rail investment by another tactic, the guaranteeing of interest on capital sunk in railroad companies. This developed as established practice and naturally had a positive effect. The principle was continued even when the great law of 1842 finally created the essentials of the French national system. Under this law it was further stipulated (a kind of perfect marriage between the technocratic Legrand and the great capitalists) that the state would purchase the right of way and construct the roadbeds and buildings; it would then lease the actual operation of the lines to private companies that would provide the rolling stock. The state maintained broad regulatory powers over rates.[99]

What is most striking about this story is the generally close coordination of goals between state functionaries, most of them coming to power after the Revolution of 1830, and national capitalist interests. It would be unsophisticated to say that Legrand was "controlled" by these interests; he was in fact a technocrat, and his willingness to call for full state ownership—which even won him charges of being a "communist"—indicates that the rail system, with all its long-range benefits for France, was even more important than assuring healthy profits for rail investors. Still, he came around to the concept of interest guarantees and a mixed system of rail exploitation. More importantly, his whole emphasis on rationality and efficiency is bureaucratic to be sure, but it is also the root mentality of capitalist economic development. Perhaps the personnel that flowed into the vast administration of France after 1830 had been trained largely in the Napoleonic era.[100] But they possessed two other qualities as well: they were overwhelmingly from old regime *roturier* backgrounds and they were (usually) competent. They could run a state in an orderly fashion, they could do it efficiently, and they had enough vision to recognize that at this juncture in French economic history the state needed to play a stimulative role. As for their relationship with the representative bodies of France, it is of great interest that the number of functionaries who also held legislative office (either in the national Chamber or the departmental *conseils généraux*) increased dramatically in the later '30s and early '40s. Perhaps it was through them that the grande bourgeoisie gravitated toward power—or, at least, that their interests began to be satisfied.

There is no reason to doubt Tudesq's analysis of the continuing strength of the notable and his particularist interests during the July Monarchy. We have seen their conservatism on the railroad question as we saw another kind in the defense of the position of the Bank of France. But in areas where the notable and great capitalist found their interests to coincide, there we find also the greatest thrust for economic development. Labor policy, so crucial for growth in this phase of French economic history, is the clearest example. And with regard to highway extension and improvement, in the history of which "the July Monarchy holds a privileged place,"[101] to the massive work of completing the canal system initiated by the Restoration, to most of the economic legislation that has been discussed, the notable was often enthusiastically supportive, but at the very least, indifferent. The most obvious sector of the economy where capitalism and the more amorphous economic doctrines of the notable would coalesce was on agricultural improvement. We have indications that the period from 1835 to 1845 may have seen the most rapid development of agricultural production in nineteenth-century French history.[102] Yet its causes remain obscure. No doubt the "return to the land" of great landowning legitimists after 1830 had something to do with it. But clearly the informational services of the department of agriculture (especially the campaign to eliminate fallow), the government push for the leasing of communal lands after 1836, the definitive abolition of *droits de parcours* and pressure against vain pasture, and the vast improvement in the quality of horses through government sponsored stud service played a role. The record of public works in agriculture was also impressive. Irrigation, either directly financed by the state or through encouragement of associations of proprietors; the drainage of swamps and lowlands; the planting of pines for wood and resin on the dunes of the Atlantic; general expansion of forest conservation (despite popular opposition); and the encouragement, rendering of technical assistance, and sponsorship of land clearance throughout France provide a partial list of accomplishments.[103] Such activity no doubt reflects the continuing power of the landed interest. But if Lévy-Leboyer is correct in a recent hypothesis, then not only did large numbers of French peasants benefit but so did industry, possibly in a respect as important as all the other elements that have been discussed combined. From a global point of view, the terms of exchange between agriculture and industry, especially in the period 1835–1845, increased rural buying power markedly, thereby provoking "a more vigorous development of the economy."[104]

This essay has emphasized the successes of state economic policy during the July Monarchy, although there has been no attempt to gloss over its shortcomings. It is probable that much more detailed research, particularly on the actual mechanisms by which businessmen influenced government policy within both the administrative-judicial and legislative branches, will have to be done before definitive answers about the impact of the Revolution of 1830 on French economic development can be given. But there is little question now that the July Monarchy was an era of economic progress and that state policy represented an advance over that of the Restoration. It certainly helped to stimulate that progress more than it hindered. There seems to have been a chronological relationship between policy and progress. The negative policy of repression restabilized the economy early in the regime and helped to kindle the industrial revival of the middle '30s. This was thoroughly in line with the quality production and labor-intensive orientation of industry inherited from earlier years. Then, starting in some respects in 1833–1834, building after 1836, and doubtlessly spurred on by the economically troubled years of 1838 and 1839, the state's role became more positive as enabling legislation, judicial support, and social overhead capital provision created an improved framework for capitalist enterprise. The economy appeared to respond to this stimulus in the 1840s, an era of major growth and perhaps the fundamental turning point in the process of French economic modernization, although it would be senseless to deny that factors unrelated to state policy played just as important a role.

The very nature of economic policy also helps us to appreciate the variegated nature of the power structure in France during these years, and thus what had happened in 1830. Despite clear signs of agricultural advance, a complacent gentry who mainly sought stable income and social prestige from their landed holdings dominated one pillar; protectionist, subsidy-seeking but often brilliantly imaginative manufacturers another; and *la haute banque* of Paris, torn between defense of vested interests (above all the rights of the Bank of France) and the profits to be reaped in transport and industrial investment, controlled a third. But another, and possibly more important, kind of split can be found in the edifice of power, one that goes a long way in explaining the shortcomings of July Monarchy economic policy: between Paris and the country. In social terms this division amounted to a confrontation between grand bourgeois, and local notable, and in political terms one between Administration (including much of the regional and local appointive apparatus) and legislative organs, from the Chamber to the various elected conseils. Local and particular interests versus the grander designs of the great capitalists and the "technocrats"; legislative defeat or obfuscation of successive reform or organizing measures sponsored by the center of power: such also was the fruit of another kind of polarization at the top of this transitional society.

But despite such fissures, the July Monarchy, as a regime, presented something perhaps more important than all the policy-making and legislation in the world, the *image* of a bourgeois monarchy. Few contemporaries doubted that the name was appropriate or that *le poire-roi* himself was the perfect bourgeois king, least of all the businessmen whose efforts initiated the rapid growth of the '40s. Moreover, a glance at the responses to the *Enquête sur le travail agricole et industriel de 1848* shows that in canton after canton throughout France hoards of employers as well as employees, rural as well as urban, had been won to the idea of economic progress. A kind of mania for improvement seemed to have captured the nation. And perhaps, after all, as Schumpeter, Gerschenkron, and indeed Marx himself would argue, it is this atmosphere of confidence, the *culture* of capitalism, that makes for its triumph.

Notes

[1] Charles Lamouroux, *De quelques griefs de l'industrie* (Paris: Chez Delangle, Libraire, Place de la Bourse, 1830), p. 7. Archives Nationales (hereafter AN), F^{12} 2401.

[2] David Pinkney, *The French Revolution of 1830* (Princeton, 1972), pp. 61–63; Louis Girard, *Etude comparée des mouvements révolutionnaires en France en 1830, 1848 et 1870–71* ("Les cours de Sorbonne"), (Paris, 1960), pp. 92–101.

[3] See especially Henri Sée, *Histoire économique de la France, les temps modernes (1789–1914)*, 2nd ed. (Paris, 1951), pp. 107–231; Eugène Fournière, "Le règne de Louis-Philippe," in J. Jaurès, ed., *Histoire socialiste* (Paris, 1906); C. E. Labrousse, *Le mouvement ouvrier et les théories sociales en France de 1815 à 1848* ("Les cours de Sorbonne") (Paris, 1948); and a longer-range view of bourgeois supremacy, E. Beau de Loménie, *Les Résponsabilités des dynasties bourgeoises*, vol. I, *De Bonaparte à MacMahon* (Paris, 1943).

[4] *La grande bourgeoisie au pouvoir (1830–1880)* (Paris, 1960).

[5] He gave greater stress to the latter in subsequent publications—to which we shall return. Cameron, "Economic Growth and Stagnation in France, 1815–1914," *Journal of Modern History*, 30 (1958), pp. 1–13.

[6] Landes, "French Entrepreneurship and Industrial Growth in the Nineteenth Century," *Journal of Economic History*, 9 (1949), pp. 45–61.

[7] Rondo Cameron, "Introduction," *Essays in French Economic History*, R. Cameron, ed. (Homewood, 1970), pp. 1–8.

[8] I will return to some of the aspects of these men's work. For now, the reader is referred to P. Léon, "L'industrialisation en France en tant que facteur de croissance économique, du début du XVIIIe siècle à nos jours," in *First International Conference of Economic History (Stockholm), Contributions, Communications* (Paris and The Hague, 1960), pp. 163–204; J. Marczewski. "The Take-Off Hypothesis and French Experience," in W. W. Rostow, ed., *The Economics of Take-Off into Sustained Growth* (New York, 1963). pp. 119–138; and above all T. Markovitch, *L'industrie française de 1789 à 1964, Conclusions générales* (Paris, 1966), vol. 7 of *Histoire quantitative de l'économie française, Cahiers de l'I.S.E.A.*, especially pp. 213–215, 310–323.

[9] F. Crouzet, "French Economic Growth in the Nineteenth Century (1815–1914): Data and Interpretations," paper delivered before the *Society for French Historical Studies*, Ottawa meeting, April 1972.

[10] M. Lévy-Leboyer, *Les banques européennes et l'industrialisation internationale dans la première moitié du XIXe siècle* (Paris, 1964), pp. 23–115.

[11] Louis Bergeron, "Problèmes économiques de la France napoléonienne," *Revue d'histoire moderne et contemporaine*, special issue on La France à l'époque napoléonienne," 17 (1970), pp. 467–505, particularly p. 504.

[12] See especially Shepard Clough, *France: a History of National Economics, 1789–1939* (New York, reprinted 1964 [1939]), pp. 91–122.

[13] It is very difficult to establish international wage differentials with any accuracy. Lévy-Leboyer dealt with the question in some detail and this figure seems reasonable in light of his research; for cotton spinning workers (common grades) the difference for a 69-hour week was larger: 37 francs in Great Britain and 19 francs in France; *op. cit.*, p. 65.

[14] *Ibid.*, p. 74ff.

[15] *Ibid.*, pp. 83, 142. Among the many works addressing this problem, see especially A. Démangeon, *La plaine picarde* (Paris, 1905), p. 265ff; J. Sion, *Les Paysans de la Normandie orientale* (Paris, 1909), pp. 301–317; and Mme Kahan-Rabecq, *La classe ouvrière en Alsace pendant la Monarchie de Juillet* (Paris, 1939), chapter III. One of the best sources for gauging the significance of rural outworking even in 1848 (although it was then beginning to decline in many places) is in the *Enquête sur le travail agricole et industriel* ordained by the National Assembly in May 1848. AN, C 943–69.

[16] See table in Lévy-Leboyer, *op. cit.*, p. 87.

[17] Markovitch, *op. cit.*, pp. 78–79. There has been some criticism of the Marczewski school for their considerable use of extrapolations and interpellations to fill out their indices. Thus despite the apparent hardness of their figures, they themselves admit (indeed underline) that they are only approximations.

[18] F. Crouzet, "An Annual Index of French Industrial Production in the Nineteenth Century," in Cameron, *op. cit.*, pp. 245–278.

[19] *Ibid.*, Chart 11, p. 274.

[20] See also Claude Fohlen, "The Industrial Revolution in France," in Cameron, *op. cit.*, pp. 201–225.

[21] Cobban, "The 'Middle Class' in France, 1815–1848," *French Historical Studies*, 5 (1967), pp. 41–56.

[22] Pinkney, *op. cit.*, p. 293. Higonnet, "La composition de la Chambre des Députés de 1827 à 1831," *Revue historique*, 239 (1968), pp. 351–378, especially p. 363.

[23] Réponses à l'Enquête du Ministre du Commerce sur l'état d'industrie et de commerce," AN, F^12 2713 and two misplaced responses in F^12 2401. Responses from *Chambres*: St. Lô (Manche), Bolbec (Seine-Inf.), Le Havre (Seine-Inf.), Lyon (Rhône), Vienne (Isère), Troyes (Aube), Nogent-le-Rotrou (Eure-et-Loir), Rouen (Seine-Inf.), Lille (Nord), Givet (Ardennes), St. Maixent (Deux-Sèvres), Boulogne (Pas-le-Calais). Avignon (Vaucluse). Nîmes (Gard), Carcassonne (Aude), Châlons (Marne), St. Quentin (Aisne), Mende (Lozère), Montpellier (Hérault), Bayonne (B.-Pyrénées), Nancy (Meurthe), St. Dié (Vosges), Nantes (Loire-Inf.), Sedan (Ardennes), Lou-

déac (Côtes-du-Nord), Amiens (Somme), Tarare (Rhône), Bar-le-Duc (Meuse), Angers (Marne-et-Loire), Aubusson (Creuse), Limoux (Aude), Niort (Deux-Sèvres), Mulhouse (Haut-Rhin), and Tours (Indre-et-Loire). Prefect's reports concerning the entire department came from Landes, Cantal, Basses-Alpes, Meurthe, and Finistère, while three others related to the capital city: Puy-de-Dôme (Hte.-Loire), Limoges (Hte.-Vienne), and Colmar (Ht.-Rhin). Finally the report from the Chambre de Commerce de Paris included seventeen major industries.

[24] This is made clear by the "Rapport de M. Petit-Crétal sur la chamoiserie de Niort," (1852), AN, F^{12} 2266.

[25] See Ange Guépin, *Nantes au XIXe siècle* (Nantes, 1835), *passim*.

[26] A careful reading of Paul Gonnet, "Esquisse de la crise économique en France de 1827 à 1832," *Revue d'histoire économique et sociale*, 33 (1955), pp. 249–291 and Jean Bruhat, *Histoire du mouvement ouvrier français*, vol. I (Paris, 1952), yields this impression even though neither author seems willing to admit the point. It is especially clear that early 1830 saw a drop in the number of violent outbursts and this correlated closely with the easing of the food crisis. See note 32.

[27] Chambre de Commerce de Lyon, 17 March 1831, AN, F^{12} 2713 dos Réponses. They went on to note that the English and American market had helped make things bearable for the silk industry and that hats and *passementerie* (lace and braids) survived only because of the demand from the National Guard.

[28] *Ibid.* Response of the *Chambre consultatif* of St. Quentin. Large numbers of rural and urban handloom weavers in this area worked for the cotton spinning entrepreneurs of Rouen and its smaller industrial neighbors (Bolbec, Yvetot, etc.). Their situation was much more precarious than that of weavers in the Rouen area itself. This is made clear by the fact that Rouen tended to ride out the crisis with greater ease.

[29] *Ibid.* Response of *toiles peintes* (summary), Chambre de Commerce de Paris, 16 March 1831.

[30] Gonnet, especially pp. 290–291.

[31] See Bruhat, pp. 212–215. He virtually ignores the *crise de subsistances*, however.

[32] The collapse of the economy in later 1830 and early 1831, whatever its causes, is abundantly documented. See Lévy-Leboyer, *op. cit.*, pp. 479–487, especially the chart showing the deluge of bankruptcies during the period on p. 482.

[33] These sentiments were summarized by Etienne Cabet (then still a moderate republican) in his *Révolution de 1830* (Paris, 1832).

[34] AN. F^{12} 2401.

[35] See the negative remarks of Emile Pereire in *le National*, January 11, 1833, reprinted in *Oeuvres de Emile et Isaac Pereire*, P. C. Laurent de Villedeuil, ed., Series D, *Le crédit public moderne et la politique française*, tome 2e (Paris, 1913), pp. 605–606.

[36] Lévy-Leboyer, *op. cit.*, p. 489.

[37] AN, F¹² 2713 dos Réponses, Carcassonne, 13 April 1831.

[38] Nogent-le-Rotrou (Eure-et-Loir) and St. Maixent (Deux Sèvres), also in the legitimist "belt" of the country, looked at the situation somewhat differently. In the former, the *Chambre consultatif* claimed that rich nobles had stopped purchasing and withdrawn their capital from enterprise, while the problem in the latter was the failure to remove Restoration officials. Finally, while focusing on the left, Vienne also mentioned legitimist sedition.

[39] AN, F¹² 2713, Bayonne, 6 April 1831.

[40] A. Jardin and A. J. Tudesq, *La France des Notables, 1815–1848*, vol. I, *L'evolution générale* (Paris, 1973), p. 132.

[41] Argout to J. Pouchet, mayor of Bolbec, 5 June 1831, AN, F¹² 2401.

[42] See, *op. cit.*, pp. 111–114.

[43] W. W. Rostow, "Leading Sectors and the Take-Off," in Rostow, *op. cit.*, pp. 15–16.

[44] Fohlen, "Bourgeoisie française, liberté économique et intervention de l'état," *Revue économique* (1956), p. 415.

[45] This was often very carefully calculated. The mayor of Bolbec wondered whether 10,000 francs for public assistance would be enough to keep the poor from rioting in May 1831. Argout figured it would. See above, footnote 41. Even where more humanitarian considerations were brought to bear, it was the public order question that remained primary. For instance, Odilon Barrot, then Prefect of the Seine, pled with the Municipal Council of Paris for matching funds in order to continue "charity workshops" in 1830 as follows: "if the existence of these *ateliers* is an evil (*plaie*) that could get worse, if the basis of their necessity is calamity, their brusque and stormy suppression would pose dangers that might trouble public tranquility. It would be, besides, an act of inhumanity against the suffering and unfortunate class of our population." From his *Mémoire* on the subject, reprinted in Georges Bourgin, "La crise ouvrière à Paris dans la second moitié de 1830," *Revue historique*, 198 (1947), p. 211. See also David Pinkney, "Les ateliers de secours à Paris (1830–31): précurseurs des ateliers nationaux de 1848," *Revue d'histoire moderne et contemporaine*, 12 (1965), pp. 65–70. The primacy of the law and order rationale—though moderated by the Christian humanitarianism of Villeneuve-Bargement and others—was also evident in Lille when such works were created. See René Van Berkel, "Les ateliers de charité dans le département du Nord (première moitié du XIXᵉ siècle)," *Revue d'histoire économique et sociale*, 47 (1969), pp. 77–91.

[46] Isaac Pereire, "Sur l'état des travaux publics," *Le Globe*, February 21, 1832, in *Oeuvres*, Series G, *Documents sur l'origine et le développement des chemins de fer (1832–1870)*, tome 1ᵉʳ (Paris, 1920), p. 4.

[47] Lamé, Clapeyron et Stéphane et Eugène Flachat, *Vues politiques et pratiques sur les travaux publics en France* (Paris, 1832), pp. 13–16.

[48] See below, note 95, and Pereire, *op. cit.*, pp. 91–92, 168, 172, 350–371.

[49] Fernand Rude, *Le mouvement ouvrier à Lyon de 1827 à 1832* (Paris, 1944); Charles Breunig, "Casimir Périer and the 'Troubles of Grenoble,' March 11–13, 1832," *French Historical Studies*, 2 (1961–62), pp. 469–489;

Georges Weill, *Histoire du parti républicain de 1815 à 1870* (Paris, 1928), p. 72ff.

[50] Edouard Dolléans, *Histoire du mouvement ouvrier (1830–1871)* (Paris, 1957), pp. 78–107 summarizes the process.

[51] See above all the works of Octave Festy, *Le mouvement ouvrier au début de la Monarchie de juillet* (Lyon, 1908) and "Dix années de l'histoire corporative des ouvriers tailleurs d'habits (1830–1840)," *Revue d'histoire des doctrines économiques et sociales*, 5 (1912), pp. 166–199.

[52] David Pinkney, "Laissez-faire or Intervention? Labor Policy in the First Months of the July Monarchy," *French Historical Studies*, 3 (1963–64), pp. 123–128.

[53] See Festy, "Le mouvement ouvrier à Paris en 1840," *Revue de l'école libre des sciences politiques*, 6 (1913), pp. 216–247 and on the general problem, Henri Hauser, "Les coalitions ouvrières et patronales de 1830 à 1848," *Revue socialiste*, 33 (1901), pp. 539–548.

[54] The best overviews of questions relating to conditions of work in this era will be found in Georges Duveau, *La Vie ouvrière en France pendant le Second Empire* (Paris, 1946), p. 233ff. and Rémi Gossez, *Les ouvriers de Paris*, livre 1er, *L'organisation, 1848–1851* (Paris, 1967), pp. 48–110.

[55] See, for example, R. J. Bezucha, "The 'Pre-industrial' Worker Movement: the *Canuts* of Lyon," in Bezucha, ed., *Modern European Social History* (Lexington, Mass., 1972), p. 102 and *Enquête* of 1848, Tourcoing (Nord), Archives départementales du Nord, M 547/1.

[56] "Enquête sur les avances aux ouvriers" (1850), AN, F^{12} 2354.

[57] The best analysis of *confection* in its early years is Lémann (*négociant confectionneur*), *De l'industrie de vêtements confectionnés en France* (Paris, 1857). See also Christopher H. Johnson, *Utopian Communism in France: Cabet and the Icarians* (Ithaca, 1974), Chapter IV.

[58] Bertrand Gille, *Recherches sur la formation de la grande entreprise capitaliste (1815–1848)* (Paris, 1959), pp. 47–94.

[59] Henri Cavaillès, *La route française: son histoire, sa fonction* (Paris, 1946), pp. 235–237.

[60] See Arthur Dunham, *The Industrial Revolution in France, 1815–1848* (New York, 1955), pp. 103-109 and Gille, *Recherches*, pp. 56–65.

[61] Cameron, "France 1800-1870," in Cameron, *et al.*, *Banking in the Early Stages of Industrialization* (New York, 1967), pp. 125-126. The law of June 10, 1847, had finally reduced this minimum to 200 francs.

[62] Gille, *La Banque en France au XIXᵉ siècle* (Paris, 1970), p. 73.

[63] Cameron, *France and the Economic Development of Europe* (Princeton, 1961), pp. 118–119 and Gille, *ibid.*, pp. 119–120.

[64] Lévy-Leboyer, *op. cit.*, pp. 704–705.

[65] Each limited liability company had to apply for specific authorization until the relevant articles of the Napoleonic *Code de Commerce* were repealed in 1867.

[66] Charles Freedman, "Joint Stock Business Organization in France, 1807–1867," *Business History Review* (1965), Table, p. 200.

[67] *Ibid.*, 193–195, 202–204, and C. Lescoeur, *Essai historique et critique sur la législation des sociétés commerciales en France et à l'étranger* (Paris, 1877), pp. 41–50, 60. The fascinating story of the *commandite* needs much further research. On the *Bourse*, see Charles Freedman, "The Growth of the French Securities Market, 1815–1870," in C. K. Warner, ed., *Essays in the History of Modern France in Honor of Shepard B. Clough* (New York, 1969).

[68] Lamouroux, *De quelque griefs*, 8; "Enquête de 1831," Paris, Limoges, St. Dié, St. Lô.

[69] "Loi sur les faillites" in J. B. Duvergier, ed., *Collection complète des lois, décrets, ordinnances, règlements et avis du conseil d'état, année 1838* (Paris, 1839), p. 363ff.

[70] Ripert, *Aspects juridiques du capitalisme moderne* (Paris, 1951), p. 27. Other legislation designed to improve the economy included the law of July 4, 1837, reconfirming metric standards in weights and measures (this was important for consumers as well), the reorganization of Tribunals of Commerce, increasing their efficiency, in 1840, and a series of laws encouraging French merchant shipping (1833, 1835, 1841). See Duvergier, *Collection*, in relevant years.

[71] Dunham, *op. cit.*, 388–389, summarized the principal objections. On the latter, excellent evidence may be found in official inquiries, especially the *Enquête relative à divers prohibitions établies à l'entrée des produits étrangers*, 3 vols. (Paris, 1835) and the *Enquête* of 1848, AN, C 943–69.

[72] Lévy-Leboyer, *op. cit.*, pp. 158–159. An important table (note 74, p. 159) shows a major jump in British thread imports after 1834 and 1837 respectively, but they leveled off in the early 1840s as a new equilibrium was reached.

[73] This does not gainsay the fact that action on this legislation was originally stimulated by a petition from the *Société industrielle de Mulhouse*, a cotton city noted for its paternalism—and its prosperity. See above all, A. J. Tudesq's outstanding analysis of the stance taken by various elements of the notability on this law. *Les grands notables*, vol. II, pp. 581–598.

[74] Sée, *op. cit.*, II, pp. 114–116. For some specifics, see Michel Chevalier, "Statistique des travaux publics sous le Monarchie de 1830," *Journal des économistes* (October 1848) and Dumon, "Equilibre des budgets sous la monarchie de 1830," *Revue de deux mondes* (September 1849).

[75] "Tableau comparatif de l'enregistrement des divers bureaux pour les neuf derniers années: nombre des dépêches enregistrés," AN, F¹⁴ 11053 dos Archives. It also included figures for 1830–32, but the departments were reorganized in 1833, so constant comparative analysis from 1830 is not possible.

[76] This is quite significant. The *Enquête sur le travail agricole et industriel* of 1848 will see many more complaints about the state of roads from the Midi than from the north.

[77] See especially C. A. Costaz, *Histoire de l'administration en France de l'Agriculture, des arts utiles, du commerce, des manufactures, des substances, des mines et usines*, 3rd ed. (Paris, 1843), I, pp. 230–234 and AN, F¹² 4551

dos 1159, "Etat des attributions et du personnel de l'administration centrale du Ministère de Commerce et des Travaux publics, 1er septembre 1831."

[78] See the comments of Markovitch, *op. cit.*, p. 11.

[79] The great *Statistique de l'industrie de Paris* begun by Paris Chamber in 1846 is the finest example. It was finally published in 1851.

[80] In all but the most backward and inaccessible parts of the country, the cantonal committees noted (in responses to question 20) that the youth was more literate than their parents and often cited the Guizot Law. AN, C943–69.

[81] Cameron, *France*, pp. 45–63.

[82] The Saint-Simonians recognized and condemned this double standard and its harmful influence on growth potential.

[83] Unfortunately, no detailed modern study of public works, like that of Louis Girard on the Second Empire, exists for the July Monarchy. It remains a fruitful area of research. Girard, *La politique des travaux publics du Second Empire* (Paris, 1951).

[84] Arthur Dunham attacked this myth twenty years ago but it reappears with some regularity: the most important recent example is Tudesq, vol. II, pp. 634–635. See Dunham, *op. cit.*, pp. 400–404, 426–427.

[85] F^{14}* 10912[86–95].

[86] All this information is drawn from the *Almanachs officiels de la France*, 1829–33. Further research would obviously be necessary to develop in-depth profiles of these men. Such wholesale shake-ups were universal in the administration throughout France. See note 87.

[87] Bérard no doubt approved of the revamping given his background, but Guizot appears to have masterminded much of the general purge. See Ch. Pouthas, "La réorganisation du ministère de l'intérieur . . . en 1830," *Revue d'histoire moderne et contemporaine*, 9 (1962), pp. 243–258 and Guizot's general report on changes as of early 1831, AN, C 745 dos 9.

[88] Little has been written on Legrand (1791–1841). Parisian born, he was a scholarship student at the Lycée Impérial and perhaps came from a less-than-wealthy family. After the Ecole Polytechnique, he went on to the Ecole des Ponts et Chaussées in 1811 and thence into the corps. He was associated with the bureaux in Paris almost exclusively from 1815 on and was well-regarded by Becquey. It appears that very early on he showed a strong concern for the economic significance of public works—specifically regarding the canal system. *Dictionnaire de biographie français*. In 1832 he was also appointed to the *conseil supérieur de commerce*, thus giving *Ponts et Chaussées* a direct entrée into the highest economic policy-making unit in the government. AN, F^{12} 2493A.

[89] The *procès verbaux* of the *Conseil* are well kept and provide much valuable information on the general development of policy; they are not merely collections of technical data—as is the case with the *Annuaire*.

[90] AN, F^{14}* 10912[85] (several sessions in late 1830).

[91] AN, F^{14}* 10912[86].

[92] AN, F^{14}* 10912[87].

[93] A. Audiganne, *Les chemins de fer aujourd'hui et dans cents ans* (Paris, 1858), vol. I, p. 376.

[94] One is reminded of Karl Polanyi's central criterion for gauging the triumph of capitalism: the commoditization of land, labor, and capital and the end of moral attributes attached to them. *The Great Transformation* (Boston, 1957). See also E. P. Thompson, "The Moral Economy of the English Crowd in the Eighteenth Century," *Past and Present* (February 1971), pp. 76–136.

[95] See above all the magnificent articles on this in *Le National* (February–May, 1833) by Emile Pereire in *Oeuvres*, Series D, pp. 663–886 (intermittent).

[96] See especially Georges Lefranc, "The French Railroads, 1823–1842," *Journal of Economic and Business History*, 2 (1931), pp. 299–331; Audiganne, *Les chemins de fer*; A. Picard, *Les chemins de fer français*, 6 vols. (Paris, 1884) (annotated primary documents); Dunham, *op. cit.*, 49–84; and Richard de Kaufmann, *La politique française en matière de chemins de fer* (Paris, 1900).

[97] *Le Moniteur*, June 14, 1836, p. 1424.

[98] Tudesq, II. p. 636.

[99] The law is conveniently reprinted in J. M. Jeanneney and M. Perrot, eds., *Textes de droit économique et social français, 1789–1957* (Paris, 1957), pp. 164–165. See also Dunham's unenthusiastic comments, *op. cit.*, pp. 73–75.

[100] This is Pinkney's thesis, *op. cit.*, pp. 274–295.

[101] Cavaillès, *op. cit.*, p. 201. The major conquest came in the area of making existing roads usable more than in the extension of mileage (pp. 206–207). Departmental roads were a special target, although success was not always forthcoming. See the grim description of the departmental road through Mazières-en-Gâtine at this time by Roger Thibault, *Education and Change in a Village Community*, trans. by P. Tregear (New York, 1971), pp. 42–44. Rural roads (*chemins vicinaux*) were also given attention in a major way for the first time in 1836. Progress tended to be most rapid in areas where farming was itself progressive and vice-versa (pp. 210–211). Howls of outrage over local roads were still common in 1848. *Enquête* of 1848, AN, C 943–69.

[102] This is not to say that an "agricultural revolution" really occurred. But, according to Toutain, 1835–1844 saw the highest annual rates of growth in the final agricultural product of any decade in the nineteenth century (1.47) and was even higher if related to population growth. Productivity seemed to be significant as well. *Le produit de l'agriculture française de 1700 à 1958*, II, *La croissance* (Paris, 1961) in *Histoire quantitative de l'économic française*, vol. 2, *Cahiers de l'I.S.E.A.*, pp. 204–208. See also M. Morineau, ('Y'a-t-il eu une révolution agricole en France au XVIIIe siècle?" *Revue historique*, 486 (1968), pp. 299–336; and Paul Hohenberg, "Change in Rural France in the Period of Industrialization," *Journal of Economic History*, 32 (1972), pp. 219–240. Finally, Henri Sée, who without the benefit of global statistics, argued persuasively that 1840 marked a fundamental turning point in agricultural production, *op. cit.*, II, p. 137.

[103] Sée, *op. cit.*, pp. 137–150 and above all "Extrait d'un rapport adressé à M. le Ministre des travaux publics sur les travaux d'irrigation, de desséchement, de réglementation d'usines et de plantation de dunes, exécutés du 1er janvier 1831 au 31 décembre 1846," AN, F^{14} 11053.

[104] Lévy-Leboyer, "La croissance économique en France au XIXe siècle. Résultats préliminaires," *Annales, ESC* 23 (1968), pp. 778–807, especially p. 794.

David H. Pinkney

Pacification of Paris: The Military Lessons of 1830

As George Rudé suggested in his influential The Crowd in History; 1730–1848, *the success or failure of the rebellious or revolutionary crowd was often determined by the degree of efficiency and commitment of the repressive forces. In July 1830 an ill-prepared army was defeated by the revolutionary crowd. After the revolution, there was an increase in agitation among the common people of Paris. The government's plans for social control, based upon the army with the elite National Guard backing it up, were tested several times during the early years of the July Monarchy. While the government was successful in dealing with limited insurrections, David Pinkney's study of the plans for social control demonstrates that the lessons of 1830 were not learned by a government which, ironically, was more than ever committed to a policy of resistance against the protest of the laboring poor.*

Much of what historians of modern France know about the Revolution of 1830 has been learned from Professor David Pinkney. His recent The French Revolution of 1830 *(Princeton, 1972) incorporates years of thoughtful research on the revolution. Professor Pinkney, who teaches at the University of Washington and has been editor of* French Historical Studies, *is the author of numerous articles on modern French history and of* Napoleon III and the Rebuilding of Paris *(Princeton, 1958). He currently is turning his attention to the July Monarchy.*

In 1830 the Bourbon regime in France was overthrown in the streets of Paris, the first time in more than a generation that popular violence had forced a change in government. The experience was frightening, especially to a ruling elite that looked upon the lower levels of urban society as savages. It reacted at first with extravagant praise of "the good workingman" and nurtured the myth that he had fought to defend the Charter of 1814, trying to conjure away the threat posed by the populace to any order. Oddly, the government did not apparently think of intensified repression.

Throughout the '20s the army had maintained a sizeable garrison in Paris—in 1830 elements of four regiments of the Line, eleven regiments of the Royal Guard in the city or nearby, and the Royal Gendarmerie of Paris. At the time of the revolution these units included about eleven thousand men.[1] After the revolution the Line was strengthened, a number of cavalry units were assigned to the city, presumably to compensate for the withdrawal of the Royal Guard, which was dissolved, and the new Municipal Guard replaced the Gendarmerie of Paris, but the overall strength was not significantly changed.[2] The principal innovation was the revival of the National Guard, which, beginning at the end of July 1830, assumed many peace-keeping duties. It was regarded by the Orleanists as the great bulwark of the regime, but in the first months after July it was reluctant to act against street disturbances; moreover, it lacked the training and discipline of a professional force, and its ability to contain a rising like the July Days was doubtful. The main burden rested on the army.[3]

The army, despite its heavy responsibility and its conspicuous failure in July, prepared no plan to deal with massive disorders in Paris. Since 1816 it had had a plan for the use of the Royal Guard in case of an "alert" in the capital, and the plan was revised several times in the 1820s. The revision of July 1830 called for the concentration of units of the Guard on the Champs Elysées, the Place Louis XVI, the Place Carrousel, the courtyard of the Louvre, the Place Vendôme, and the Place de la Bastille. If the King were at Saint-Cloud, additional troops were to be shifted to the Champs Elysées, suggesting that the safety of the King, not the pacification of Paris, was the principal concern. No provision was made for use of troops of the Line.[4] The plan proved to be of little practical value in the situation in which Marshal Marmont, the commander of troops in Paris during the July Days, found himself on July 28, 1830. Declaring that he was confronted that morning not with a riot but with a revolution, he appealed to the King for instructions, and when none was forthcoming, he improvised a plan to pacify the city by sending three heavily armed columns of Guard and Line across the city to disperse crowds, dismantle barricades, and occupy key points, a plan inadequate in the desperate circumstances of that day.[5] This disastrous failure and the popular ferment in Paris in the weeks after the revolution, including a serious threat of renewed insurrection in December, would seem to call for fresh thinking and planning to protect the new regime, but nothing was done for two years.

Then, in 1832 the insurrection of June 5–6, in which 70 soldiers were killed and more than 290 wounded,[6] shocked the army into serious planning for such emergencies. A few days after the event a general of engineers, Baron de Valazé, submitted to the Minister of War a memorandum in which he held that the garrison of Paris could suppress such outbreaks with fewer losses if they would, following the tactics of the rebels, fight only from cover. At the first sign of trouble the command should position troops in buildings along the boulevards from the Place de la Bastille to the Place de la Concorde and on key streets between the Palais Royal on the west and the Rue du Temple and the Place de l'Hôtel de Ville on the east. From those buildings they could by musket fire from windows, break up crowds, and prevent the building of barricades. If barricades were erected, they should be attacked only under covering fire from adjacent buildings. The Minister of War sent the memorandum to General Pajol, Commander of the First Military District (which included Paris), and to General Lobau, commander of the National Guard of Paris, with his recommendation that the proposals be given serious consideration.[7]

In the next month, July 1832, the army issued a detailed plan of measures to be taken "in case of a new movement in Paris." The plan was vague on the exact timing of the actions prescribed, but apparently the initial step, at the first threat to the peace, was the confinement of troops of the garrison to their barracks, where they would prepare to march to assigned posts. The National Guard should at the same time don uniforms and make ready to march to prescribed assembly points. Isolated guard posts about the city, the kind that had been overrun and disarmed in 1830, were to be evacuated and guards concentrated on other more defensible posts. The number of firemen on duty was to be doubled, and their posts protected by regular troops if necessary. This reflected the fear, stated in the plan itself, that insurgents might set many fires in the city to distract attention from their revolutionary activities.[8]

Troops in the environs were to be alerted for possible duty in Paris. Regiments at Versailles, Saint-Germain, Saint-Denis, Vincennes, Courbevoie, and Reuil would be made ready to march. More distant regiments in Rambouillet and Beauvais would proceed to within three leagues of the capital and on orders, or at the first sound of gunfire, continue into the capital. The National Guard of the suburbs would throw a net around Paris to intercept rebels fleeing the city or provincials coming to join the insurgents.[9]

Citizens were to be warned that on hearing the general alarm for the call-up of the National Guard they should close their shops and doors to prevent pillage and fire and to forestall rebels' establishing themselves in houses as they had done in 1830 and in 1832.[10]

As soon as menacing crowds were reported anywhere in the city, imposing forces were to be moved against them. The dispersal of unarmed crowds was the responsibility of the National Guard, but regular troops would be used against armed crowds. Attacks on barricades, which should be ordered as soon as they were discovered, should be supported by musket fire from overlooking houses as Valazé had recommended. Artillery would be used only as a last resort and then only after precautions had been taken to prevent injury to peaceful citizens and to troops.[11]

In case of "serious riot," which was not further defined, troops were to occupy nineteen key points in the city. One battalion of the Line and one battalion of the National Guard would take positions at the Place de la Bastille, the Place de l'Hôtel de Ville, the Place du Châtelet, the Place des Victoires, the Place de la

Madeleine, the Boulevard Saint-Martin, and the Boulevard Saint-Denis. The troops on the Place de la Bastille were supported by cavalry and two batteries of artillery. A reserve composed of infantry of the Line, National Guard, cavalry, artillery, and engineers equipped with tools for dismantling barricades was to be assembled on the Place de la Carrousel, near the general headquarters in the Tuileries Palace, and on the Champs Elysées. The National Guard of the suburbs would provide one battalion for each of four city gates—Saint-Denis, Etoile, Trone, and Enfer. On the Left Bank a battalion of the Line and a battalion of the National Guard were assigned to the Luxembourg Garden (supported there by a squadron of cavalry), the Place du Panthéon, the Place Maubert, and the Babylon Barracks. One battalion of the Line was to take position on the Rue Saint-Dominique, and two held the Ecole Militaire.[12]

Drawing on the experience of 1830 the authors of the plan prescribed that troops should occupy houses controlling approaches to the *places* that were potential centers of resistance—the Bastille, the Hôtel de Ville, and the Châtelet. Following the recommendation of Valazé, troops were also to take up positions in buildings at a dozen points along the *grands boulevards*.[13]

In the weeks after the issuance of this plan it was implemented by orders from Lobau, and from General d'Arriule, Commander of the Place de Paris, and Arriule added a few instructions. Troops were to be stationed to guard bridges across the Seine. Units in position for the "serious riot" alert would send out patrols in their areas and maintain communications with troops in adjoining areas. Forty to fifty men were to be left in each barracks to prevent arms stored there from falling into the hands of insurgents. Apparently recalling that the supply of food to engaged units in July 1830 had completely broken down, Arriule ordered that each battalion assure its own supply from the military bakehouse.[14]

The Prefect of Police, after consultation with the military commanders, prepared an order to his forty-eight commissioners to proceed on the first warning of disorder to specified positions. Here they would advise officers on where troops should be sent and then accompany troops to give the required legal warnings to hostile crowds.[15]

On March 21, 1834, Arriule, perhaps moved by disorders on the Right Bank a month earlier in protest against the law restricting public criers and by reports from the police that the Société des Droits de l'Homme was preparing an insurrection, reissued the plan of 1832 under the title "General Disposition for Defense in Case of Serious Troubles" with slight modifications. The instructions were to be put into effect only on specific orders from the Commander of the Place de Paris, but letters to commanders of all concerned units ordering them to occupy the prescribed positions were prepared and kept ready at Arriule's headquarters for immediate dispatch.[16]

In late February and in March and April 1834, in expectation of trouble, police made precautionary arrests and seized arms and shot in apartments of members of the Société des Droits de l'Homme.[17] On April 10 the commander of the Place de Paris, warned by civil authorities of possible imminent disorders, alerted troops in Paris and the suburbs and that night and the succeeding two nights put extra patrols on the streets throughout the city. On April 13 insurrectionaries began to build barricades. The Municipal Guard was unable to stop them, and Arriule ordered the application of his "General Disposition for Defense in Case of Serious Troubles." Troops supported by the National Guard and the Municipal Guard attacked the barricades, which were confined to a few streets in the central Right Bank, and restricted the active insurrection to that area. By seven o'clock the next morning the barricades were taken, the insurgents arrested or dispersed, and the insurrection over. The government's forces had ended the outbreak quickly and with a loss of only eleven killed and thirty-five wounded.[18]

Arriule's plan, proven in battle, remained basically unchanged until 1839. It was reissued with minor alterations in November 1837 and again in August 1838, and the number of foot soldiers permanently garrisoned in the capital or nearby was increased.[19]

The plan had a second trial when the Society of Seasons revolt erupted in the city in the afternoon of May 12, 1839. Again troops and National Guard occupied prescribed positions, dispersed crowds, reduced barricades, and by eleven that evening had apparently ended the revolt. As a precaution, half the troops remained in position throughout the night. Threatening crowds reappeared on the Rue Saint-Honoré and the Rue Saint-Denis early the next afternoon, and additional troops were called out, but there was no resumption of fighting. At 11 P.M. all forces save four companies on the Place de l'Hôtel de Ville were withdrawn. The army and guard had confined the revolt to a few streets in the center of Paris and had lost only eighteen men killed and sixty-two wounded. The modest casualties in both 1834 and 1839 contrasted with the heavy losses in 1830 and 1832, when the government's forces had acted without any comprehensive plan.[20]

A few days after the Society of Seasons revolt, General Pajol made three recommendations to the Minister of War. The experience of May 12 and 13 had indicated, he declared, that a supply of tools for demolishing barricades should be established at the Ecole militaire to avoid repetition of delays in bringing them from Vincennes, where they were at present stored. He also urged that one or two companies of sappers be permanently stationed at Vincennes ready for use in Paris to demolish barricades. He suggested finally that the Grenier de l'Abondance on the Boulevard Bourdon, opposite the Canal Saint-Martin, be converted into a military strong point like the Ecole militaire with infantry, cavalry, and artillery permanently stationed there. This would, he optimistically predicted, make revolt in Paris impossible.[21]

Marshal Gérard, the Minister of War, had taken personal command of the operations on May 12 and 13. He was apparently convinced that such an outbreak could be more quickly suppressed or even prevented, and he charged two officers, one from the army General Staff and one from the National Guard, to draw up a plan for covering Paris with patrols supported by reserves concentrated at a number of strategic points. The two officers delivered their plan to Gérard early in June. It was similar to Arriule's plan, but, following Gérard's charge, it placed more emphasis on the use of patrols, each with an intelligence and an operational role. In an alert, troops of the Line were to occupy seven strategic points on the Right Bank—five fewer than in Arriule's plan—the Place du Carrousel, the Place des Victoires, the Pointe Sainte-Eustache, the Place de l'Hôtel de Ville, the Boulevard Saint-Denis, the Place de la Bastille, and Place de la Concorde. The troops at each point were to mount patrols in the surrounding area, and the plan prescribed the exact itinerary for each patrol. Each was charged with collecting information on developments in its zone and with preventing the formation of crowds and the erection of barricades. In case of trouble each could call on troops at its base strategic point and on the National Guard, which was assigned to support troops at each point. The mounting of patrols and the occupation of key points in the central quarters of the Right Bank were intended to deprive riot and insurrection of its most favorable terrain and to force it into more open quarters, where it could be more readily broken up. On the Left Bank the authors expected no trouble except possibly in support of disturbances under way across the river, and they called for the occupation of only two strategic points there. These troops were charged with exercising surveillance over the Left Bank and with preventing demonstrators from crossing to the opposite side of the river. The entire plan called for the use of about seventy three hundred men, approximately one-half the Paris garrison, supported by at least an equal number of National Guards.[22]

The development of these plans for the use of the army to maintain order in Paris and protect the regime was a manifestation of a changing attitude toward the army on the part of conservatives. Since 1793 they had regarded the army as a revolutionary force, but in the 1830s, confronted with the need to cope with immediate revolutionary violence in the streets and lacking an elite force like the Royal Guard to turn to, they were coming to regard the regular army as the principal defender of the established order, and they gave it a key place in their defense plans, a place it had not occupied earlier.[23]

In February 1848 the government ordered the application of the Gérard Plan, but it failed to stop the popular rising and save the regime. Its failure was owing to the defection of the National Guard, irresolute leadership at the top of the military command, and the hostility of the population of Paris to the existing government. On February 22 and again on the 23rd troops of the Line took up positions prescribed by the plan. Only a fraction of the National Guard responded to the first call; more turned out on the second day, but most were in sympathy with the opposition. The troops, unsupported by the Guard, were unable to disperse crowds or prevent the building of barricades. They found themselves divided and isolated, cut off from help, orders, and supplies, surrounded by a populace hostile to the government and eager to induce the Line to defect. In the absence of resolute direction from the high command they were uncertain on what to do in a situation for which they were not prepared. In the early hours of February 24 a hastily installed new commander of all forces in the capital, General Bugeaud, abandoned the Gérard Plan and ordered four columns across the city, reminiscent of Marmont's improvisation of July 28, 1830,[24] and no more effective.

The Gérard Plan and the similar plans that had preceded it in the 1830s had been adequate for the control of the disturbances of 1834 and 1839, when the populace did not rally to the insurgents and the National Guard fulfilled its assigned role, but it did not suffice to quell a revolution supported by the National Guard and the people of Paris. From the experiences of 1830, 1832, 1834, and 1839 the military had failed to learn how to suppress a real revolution in Paris. Given a hostile populace and less than dependable troops, the charge was probably impossible.

Notes

[1] Archives historiques du Ministère de la Guerre (hereafter cited as AHMG), D³ 131, 1e Div. milit. Etat-major général, "Rapport journalier . . . du 27 Juillet 1830"; Archives du Département de la Seine et de la Ville de Paris (hereafter cited as AS), D 4AZ 1181, "Précis des événemens aux quels a pris part le troisième régiment d'infanterie de la garde royale depuis le vingt-six juillet jusqu'au jour de son licenciement par un officier," p. 2; Archives nationales (hereafter cited as AN), CC 549, Place de Paris, Etat-major, "Casernement des differens Corps Stationnés dans la Capital à l'époque du 21 Juillet 1830"; Auguste de Marmont, *Mémoires du maréchal Marmont, duc de Raguse, de 1792 à 1841*, 3d ed. (Paris, 1857), VIII, pp. 268–269, 431; *Almanach royal pour l'an MDCCCXXX* (Paris, 1830), pp. 601, 647–658, 787; *La Garde Royale pendant les événemens du 26 juillet au 5 août 1830; par un officier employé à l'état-major* (Paris, 1830), p. 5.

[2] AHMG, E⁵ 2, Correspondance générale, September 1830, 1er Division militaire, Rapport journalier à Son Excellence le Ministre Secrétaire d'Etat de la Guerre du 22 Septembre 1830; *Almanach royal et national pour l'an MDCCCXXXI* (Paris, 1831), pp. 622–634, 642, 760–761; Jean Tulard, *La Préfecture de Police sous la Monarchie de Juillet* (Paris, 1964), p. 65.

[3] Louis Girard, *La Garde nationale, 1814–1871* (Paris, c. 1964), pp. 163–164, 167–169; Tulard, *Préfecture de Police*, p. 80.

[4] AN, CC 551, Chambre et Cour de Pairs, Affaire du 25 Juillet 1830, Doc. No. 1029, Note concerning the Duc de Raguse [autumn 1830], Doc. No. 1027, "Note sur l'ordre confidentiel pour le cas d'alerte"; AHMG, D³ 131, Ordre du Major général du Service, Mal. Duc de Raguse, July 20, 1830.

[5] AN, CC 549, Chambre et Cour des Pairs, Affaire du 25 Juillet 1830, Raguse to Roi, July 28, 1830; Marmont, *Mémoires*, VIII, pp. 242–243, 432–433.

[6] AHMG, E⁵ 26, Correspondance gén, du 16 au 30 Juin 1832, Etats des officiers, sous-officiers et soldats blessés et morts dans le journées des 5 et 6 juin 1832.

[7] AHMG, E⁵ 26, Lt.-Gén. du Génie Valazé. Note sur les mesures qu'il conviendrait de prendre s'il arrivait quelque chose d'analogue aux événemens du 5 et 6 juin; Soult to Lobau, June 28, 1832; Soult to Pajol, June 28, 1832.

[8] AHMG, E⁵ 27, Correspondance gén., Juillet-Septembre 1832, Dispositions à prendre dans le cas d'un nouveau Mouvement dans Paris [July 1832].

[9] *Ibid.*

[10] *Ibid.*

[11] *Ibid.*

[12] AHMG, E⁵ 27, Disposition à prendre et emplacement des troupes en cas d'Emeute Sérieuse [July 1832].

[13] *Ibid.*

[14] AN, 221 AP4, Papiers du Général Jean-Luc d'Arriule, Emplacement des troupes de la Garnison de Paris en cas d'émeute, November 16, 1832 [signed by Comte de Lobau]; Arriule to Col., 35ᵉ Rgt. de Ligne, July 11, 1832; Disposition des Troupes en cas d'émeute, November 21, 1832.

[15] AN, F¹ᵃ* 2120, Ministre de l'Intérieur, Circulaires émanées du Cabinet du Préfet de Police (1830–1848), Préfet de Police to Commissaires de police, October 1, 1832.

[16] AN, CC 585, Details exacts des circonstances qui ont amené les événemens de Lyon et de Paris en février et en avril 1834; Henri Gisquet, *Mémoires de M. Gisquet, ancien préfet de police* (Paris, 1840), III, pp. 240–241, 249–256; AN, 221 AP4, Dispositions générales de défense en cas de troubles sérieux, March 21, 1834.

[17] Cour des Pairs, *Affaire du mois d'avril 1834* (Paris, 1834–36), II, pp. 355, 392; III, pp. 342–348, 509, 511; AN, F⁷ 3887, Ministre de l'Intérieur, Police générale, "Bulletin de Paris," March 16, 17, 18, 25, April 12, 1834; Archives de la Préfecture de Police de Paris, A $\frac{A}{422}$ Evénements divers, 1834, "Dossiers collectifs."

[18] AHMG, E⁵ 52, D'Arriule to Ministre de la Guerre, April 18, 1834, Etat des officiers, s.-officiers et soldats des troupes de la Garnison tués et blessés les 13 et 14 Avril 1834; Cour des Pairs, *Affaire du mois d'avril 1834*, I, pp. 364–366; Gisquet, *Mémoires*, III, pp. 385-386; AN, CC 586, Rapport des commissaires de police des quartiers Sainte-Avoie, Lombards, Saint-Martin-des-Champs, etc., n.d.

[19] AN, 221 AP 4, Dispositions générales de défense en cas d'émeute, November 6, 1837, August 13, 1838; *Almanach royal et national pour l'an MDCCCXXXIV* (Paris, 1834), pp. 623, 636–648; *Almanach royal et national . . . MDCCCXXXV* (Paris, 1835), pp. 626, 645–657, 663, 808; *Almanach royal et national . . . MDCCCXXXVI* (Paris, 1836), pp. 630, 652–663, 669–670; *Almanach royal et national . . . MDCCCVII* (Paris, 1837), pp. 639, 663–674, 680–681, 832; *Almanach royal et national . . . MDCCCVIII* (Paris, 1838), pp. 642, 666–677, 683–684, 839; *Almanach royal et national . . . MDCCCIX* (Paris, 1839), pp. 648, 672–683, 689–690, 846.

[20] AHMG, E⁵ 84, Correspondance générale, mai-juin 1839, Lt.-Gén. Pajol, Rapport général sur les événemens survenus les 12 et 13 mai 1839 et la Repression de la Sédition; Etat nominatif des militaires tués les 12 et 13 mai 1839, ou morts de leurs blessures, May 26, 1839.

[21] AHMG, E⁵ 84, Pajol to Ministre de la Guerre, May 1839.

[22] AHMG, E⁵ 84, Rapport sur la reconnaissance militaire de la ville de Paris executée après les ordres de Monsieur le Maréchal Comte Gérard, June 10, 1839.

[23] On the changing attitude toward the army, see Raoul Girardet, *La Société militaire dans la France contemporaine, 1815–1939* (Paris, c. 1953), p. 27.

[24] Girard, *Garde nationale*, pp. 284–286; Paul Thureau-Dangin, *Histoire de la Monarchie de Juillet* (Paris, 1888–1900), VII, pp. 430–435, 451, 459–461; Louis Antoine Garnier-Pagès, *Histoire de la Révolution de 1848* (Paris, n.d.), I, pp. 111–112, 114, 117, 134–135.

Bernard H. Moss

**Parisian Workers and the Origins
of Republican Socialism, 1830–1833**

*During the years immediately following the July Revolution of
1830, French workers emerged as an important social force and
manifested the first real signs of collective consciousness. The
Paris workers, many of whom fought in the streets during the
"Three Glorious Days" for what began, after all, as a political
crisis, became less sure that the glib bourgeois spokesmen of the
liberal cause were speaking for them. They became more militant,
influenced not only by the somber economic depression but also
by the revival of egalitarian Republican ideals, which accompanied the revolution.*

*In this essay, Bernard Moss describes the evolution of Republi-
can socialism among Parisian workers in the years 1830–1833. He
sees the foundation of the Society of the Rights of Man in 1832
and the first attempts to found trade cooperative associations as
important early signs of the evolution of modern working-class
ideology and organization. The author, who teaches at the University of Southern California, is particularly interested in the origins of the French labor movement. He is presently working on a
book,* Origins of the French Labor Movement: The Socialism of
Skilled Workers, *and studying early producers' associations.*

In a controversial book written during the cold war J. L. Talmon sought to uncover the origins of modern "totalitarianism" or socialism in the philosophical postulates of Rousseau and political principles of Robespierre, suggesting further concrete investigations into the democratic, egalitarian origins of nineteenth-century socialism.[1] Though highly metaphysical in his approach to ideological origins, Talman was willing to grant that a political leader like Robespierre might be led by the force of historical circumstances to advocate practical policies that were never intended in his original political philosophy. Thus, during the Civil War and Terror, the struggle against aristocracy had led him to a confrontation with the bourgeoisie and the protection of private property to threats against its vast fortunes.

For the most part Republican and socialist historians have been reluctant to stress the continuities between their rival ideologies, often leaving it to their more conservative censors .to expose the "red menace" lurking in democratic thought.[2] Treating Republicanism as a predominantly middle-class movement with a mild reformist program serving to protect small property, historians have never really emphasized the development of a working-class socialist Republicanism following the Revolution of 1830.[3] For just as the *sans culottes* had forced Robespierre to go beyond the sanctity of private property, so the emergence of the working class in 1830 led the new Jacobins beyond their middle-class democratic framework to a program and organization that could only be described as a working-class Republican socialism.

The *Trois Glorieuses* inspired both a revival of the egalitarian ideals of the First Republic and an unprecedented wave of working-class protest. Responding to this mass movement, the Republican youth of the Friends of the People began to shift the focus of their attacks from the bourgeois "oligarchy" in power to the specific plight of the wage earner within the industrial system, aided in their reflections by Saint Simonian concepts of exploitation that gave economic precision to a class analysis derived from the French Revolution. Eventually dispersed by police, these youths found a more receptive and dedicated following among Parisian workers, who crowded into the revolutionary sections of the Society of the Rights of Man and of the Citizen. Within these sections workers were educated in Robespierre's Declaration of Rights, which subordinated private property rights to the social requirements of security and equality. To trades which had formed their own cooperative workshops during the strikes of 1833, these youths promised a republic that would establish cooperative workshops for all trades, freeing workers from capitalists and the wage system. Thus, the junction of democratic youth with a suffering working class yielded the first socialist program for workers' ownership of capital, which would guide Republican workers for most of the century.

Arising in the midst of a prolonged industrial depression, the July Revolution aroused economic expectations that set off a round of trade assemblies, demonstrations, petitions and strikes lasting from mid-August to November. During the depression elite Parisian trades were suddenly confronted with massive unemployment and depressed wages caused by widespread bankruptcies, technical innovations in the work process—the use of mechanical presses, saws, cutters, sewing machines, etc.—and the substitution of cheaper ready-made goods for finer custom-made suits, shoes, hats, and the like.[4] Especially hard hit after July were the luxury trades—jewelers, *articles de Paris*, saddlers, custom tailors, and bronze workers—who suffered the loss of forty thousand jobs because of the exile of the aristocratic court and the decline of tourist trade. As the supposed victors of July, Parisian workers assembled by trade to formulate demands for higher wages, shorter hours, public works, and restrictions on machines. Expecting their new government to provide the leverage they lacked in a depressed market, they were told public intervention was contrary to the "liberty of industry," and instead of receiving assistance, they were dispersed by police and troops and their leaders arrested.[5]

Toward the end of September appeared a workers' newspaper, which went beyond the trade unionist demands voiced by the assembled trades. For the printers who published *L'Artisan, journal de la classe ouvrière,* these demands actually expressed a deeper protest against the very nature of the working-class condition:

> The condition of the worker . . . is to be exploited by a master
> The trade that belongs to him becomes in the hands of the master

land that he cultivates, a machine that he exploits, and compelled to earn a minimal sum each day, the worker doubles and triples the fortune of his employer. When the profits to be made on one man-machine are too small, large workshops are formed, and the small profits that are obtained from each man become a handsome fortune in the hands of one individual.[6]

By throwing workers into the political spotlight the Trois Glorieuses had revealed them to be the "principal part of society," the creators of wealth, who gave value to capital by exploiting it, and upon whom all other classes, including the "aristocratic petty bourgeoisie," depended. Likewise, the recent introduction of machinery with its potential for relieving men from the necessity of painful physical toil pointed to a new role in society for the worker:

> Until now society only asked what he could contribute as a machine, as a worker, but now that machines do better than he, it reclaims him as a man, as a citizen. Thus we said to the worker: "Since you are ousted from your shops by machines, cease being workers and become masters instead."[7]

Workers would only reap the benefits of machinery when an alternative to capitalist exploitation—analyzed in terms of labor value—had been found. The individual worker could not purchase machinery, but a hundred workers contributing two francs weekly could own and operate a modern shop as a workers' association.

With this rudimentary analysis of exploitation and association program, the *Artisan* laid the ground work for Republican socialism. Surprisingly, the immediate sources and impact of the *Artisan* remain obscure. Certainly, disciples of Owen, Fourier, and Saint Simon, notably, Buchez, had circulated notions of economic association, but none of their theories quite corresponds with this practical suggestion for a workers' association. Though these workers were doubtless aware of Republican and Saint Simonian literature, there is nothing in their simple language, awkward expressions, or professed antagonism to middle-class journalists that would suggest any such outside collaboration. Thus, in the absence of other evidence, one must accept their word that their new consciousness was primarily a result of their own learning experience since July.

To the young Republicans who had fought with the workers on the barricades and formed the Friends of the People, the industrial strife confirmed the need to "obtain truly popular institutions, to improve the physical and moral condition of the people," understood as "all men who work," and achieve an "equitable distribution of goods and enjoyments."[8] Later they denounced the "frightening disparity that exists between work and wages,"[9] which seemed to have gotten worse with the progress of industry. Yet, rather than defend the workers against the masters, they appealed to both sides to unite against the "bourgeois aristocracy, which alone possesses social power," and whose monopoly of financial credit was the cause of industrial ruin and conflict, and promised new institutions that would promote industry and exchange by opening the purse strings of public and commercial credit.

The founders of the Friends of the People, Philippe Buchez, Ulysse Trélat, Charles Teste, Jean-Louis Hubert, the same firebrands who had earlier formed the legions of the French Carbonari,[10] wanted a republic that would serve the material needs and aspirations of the broad masses. To their Jacobin political principles, the Saint Simonians had contributed a language of social reform and an economic analysis of the class conflicts they themselves had observed in French history.[11] As twenty-two-year-old historian Albert Laponneraye explained in a public course to Parisian workers, French history since 1789 had reflected a series of class struggles between a privileged elite, the aristocracy and financial bourgeoisie, and the egalitarian people, including not only peasants and artisans, but also small capitalists and businessmen who "share the work and misery of the people."[12] Having used the people in 1789 and 1830 to overthrow the aristocracy, this bourgeoisie had erected a constitutional system that, with the aid of tariff and fiscal and commercial laws, protected and augmented its fortunes.[13]

The key to its privilege, furnished by the Saint Simonians, was its legal ownership of land, machines, and instruments of labor. By lending these means of production to the small peasants, capitalists, and artisans who put them to work, proprietors were able to extract the wealth they produced in the form of interest and rent. Thus, an idle proprietary class of aristocrats and wealthy bourgeois was able to live upon the revenues generated by all the productive classes—peasants, workers, and capitalists. Hence, the way to end exploitation and industrial disorder was to expand credit and thus gradually transfer means of production from the hands of the idle proprietors into those of the active producers, primarily the capitalist masters responsible for the management of industry.

Theoretically, neither Saint Simonians nor Republicans understood the role of industrial capitalists as an emerging privileged class, as independent exploiters of labor, generators of profit, and possessors of capital. Yet, while continuing to view the old proprietary class as the main source of exploitation, they began to suspect that some capitalist masters were sharing in the benefits of exploitation beyond the useful services they may have performed as managers and, perhaps, even that their substantial revenues might derive not from their useful work but from their possession of capital just like the proprietary class.[14] Since 1830 they had observed these capitalists identifying with the proprietary masters of the new regime; it was not owners but workers who were protesting industrial conditions and demanding greater equality. Thus, without abandoning their traditional proprietary analysis, Republicans, eager to appeal to these workers, began to shift the focus of their program from the "people" to the workers and from proprietary to capitalist exploitation.

This shift was reflected in the weekly broadsheet distributed by the Friends of the People in 1831 to educate people in the causes of their distress. Addressing itself to "laboring men of all professions . . . artisans and peasants of callous hands, who form eleven-twelfths of the population . . . you who work, produce and suffer for the small number who do nothing, consume and enjoy,"[15] the society defined the privileged enemy as the "possessor of land, motor, or the instrument of labor, . . .[who] collects the largest part of the earnings of any enterprise."[16] Responding to major incidents of workers' protest, it applied this general analysis to their specific situation. Commenting on five days of rioting over the introduction of mechanical shawl cutters in Montmartre, Napoléon Lebon, a young medical student, wrote:

> Improvements only profit a small number of persons who hold in their hands the means of industry—capital, land, machines; others

only share in the spoils at the pleasure and dependence of these men. There is a struggle of interests going on in society. It is not a new technique of industry or commerce that will end it but a new principle of organization that must be put forward."[17]

Two months later, after the silk workers had seized control of Lyons, he declared: "The profit of labor must return to the worker. No more will some men serve as the instruments of another man. The laws of society must see to it."[18]

The first practical consequences of this shift had already been drawn by Buchez. Like all Saint Simonians before 1830, he had believed in the useful function of the capitalist master. Since July, however, the emergence of the working class as an independent force—and perhaps contact with the printers of *L'Artisan*—had convinced him that some workers were fully capable of owning and directing their own workshop without the intervention of a capitalist intermediary. In those semi-artisanal industries where skilled labor constituted the major capital and workers themselves directed the process of production, the capitalist who provided the capital—credit, shop, tools, and raw materials—was merely a parasite and exploiter, who extracted part of the value produced by each worker in the form of profit. Leaving the Friends of the People in January 1831, Buchez announced public courses for workers that would change the "regime of labor," "teaching wage earners the method of freeing themselves through association."[19] During discussions with workers, statutes were drafted for associations to free entire Parisian trades from the wage system. To give those associations a more solid economic basis, Buchez suggested the establishment of public credit banks to finance them and the formation of an "inalienable capital" from reinvested earnings to allow for the continual admission of new members without capital.[20]

By the end of 1832 the general idea of association as a remedy for workers' exploitation appeared among the leaders of the Friends of the People. At the trial of the society for illegal association that resulted in its dissolution, Godefroy Cavaignac, citing Rousseau, Saint Simon, Fourier, and Buchez, proclaimed association as the only way to resolve social conflicts:

As for labor, we ask that it no longer be subordinated to the interest of the avaricious and idle. We ask that the worker no

> longer be exploited by capital; that wages no longer be his only
> revenue; that he find in the establishment of public banks . . .
> [and] in the force of association the method to facilitate his task,
> free his activity and compensate his industry and courage.[21]

Announcing the Republican principles of the *Tribune*, the only
Parisian daily close to the society, the new editor, Armand Mar-
rast, denounced the subordination of labor to capital and likewise demanded the expansion of credit institutions and associations that would "gradually transfer the instruments of labor into
the hands of those who work."[22]

This primary concern with workers' exploitation reflected a
decisive shift in the composition and nature of the Republican
movement that had occurred in 1832. Despite ingenious efforts to
reach the Parisian populace through public courses, legal and
medical help, charity relief, and the publication of a weekly journal, the Friends of the People had remained a private debating
society of young students, intellectuals, and professionals. Determined to prevent the society from igniting the fuel of mass discontent, the police had banned its public meetings, harassed its
criers, infiltrated its ranks, and arrested its editorial board. As the
result of this harassment and internal purges, it had dwindled
from four hundred to one hundred members at the end of 1831.
As more moderate professional men departed, it was left in the
hands of students and intellectuals who shared a common faith in
the democratic principles of Rousseau and Robespierre.[23]

One of these Jacobins, Auguste Caunes, who had published a
Moniteur des faubourgs in 1830, decided in November 1831 to
seek out a larger organizational base of support among Parisian
workers, who had continued their violent protests throughout
1831. Convoking workers he had known in 1830, he initiated the
formation of local working-class sections, which adopted Robespierre's Declaration of Rights as their credo. When the parent
society refused to endorse a credo that had proved too radical for
even the Convention of 1793, these local sections became the basis
for an entirely new society, the Rights of Man.[24]

Meanwhile, the insurrection that broke out on June 5, 1832,
following the funeral of the popular Napoleonic General Lamarque, confirmed the worst fears of the police. A small band of
agitators from secret societies had provoked an insurrection that

occupied half of Paris and nearly toppled the Orleanist regime.[25] The crisis nevertheless revealed the failure of Republicans to provide leadership and channel the mass discontent through an organization and program that workers could trust. During the ensuing months of repression, while the Friends of the People remained closed, hundreds of workers began to join the new local sections of the Rights of Man, which remained relatively impervious to police disruption.[26]

The new society was organized on the basis of a local neighborhood section, composed of under twenty men in order to circumvent the law on associations, which elected its own chief and three quinturions to maintain constant liaison with members. Weekly meetings were devoted to the reception of new candidates —investigated on their morality and source of livelihood—voluntary collections for propaganda, and, most importantly, political education, the oral reading, commentary, and discussion of Robespierre's Declaration and other democratic writings circulated by the society. Recruiting in local wineshops and workplaces, the sections often brought together workers of the same trade— tailors, shoemakers, carriage makers, etc. Late in 1833 a deliberate effort was made to create stronger fraternal ties among members by organizing sections along such trade lines. By 1834 the society had perhaps 3,000 members organized into 162 local sections concentrated in working-class quarters bearing such Jacobin names as Robespierre, Saint Just, *Montagne,* and *Chute des Girondins.* A politically conscious army of "devoted," "zealous," and "brave" workers, determined to lead the next insurrection to victory, was in the making.[27]

Following the elimination of more moderate leaders like Raspail, the section chiefs in September elected a central committee of eleven men drawn mostly from the radical rump of the Friends of the People, including the dynamic spokesman Godefroy Cavaignac, the socialist aristocrat and deputy Voyer d'Argenson, three student radicals, Lebon, Camille Berrier-Fontaine, and Jean-Jacques Vignerte, and a mysterious ex-cavalry officer, Guillard de Kersausie, who formed within the society a secret action committee capable of spearheading an insurrection. The new constitutional structure combined a centralized administrative network with the principle of power exercised "from below."

Elected periodically by all the sections and subject to recall, the central committee appointed commissioners for each *arrondissement* and quarter, who transmitted orders, circulated literature, and conducted weekly meetings with local chiefs. Despite the consecrated doctrine of "power from below," however, political decisions were apparently made without consultation by the committee, which after November began to issue weekly political instructions in preparation for revolutionary action.[28]

The significance of Robespierre's Declaration, chosen as the official credo, was that unlike the actual Declaration of 1793 it contained a Rousseauist definition of property as the product of social convention, "that portion of goods guaranteed by laws."[29] By means of inheritance or progressive income taxes, the general will could modify property rights in order to obtain greater equality of wealth and position. Defining equality as "the equal distribution of the advantages and burdens of society among its members,"[30] one commentary claimed that by the nature of political association the state was the master of all wealth and property owners only the depositories of that portion confided to their administration—clearly a theoretical invitation to communism.

As the touchstone of working-class Republicanism, Robespierre's Declaration created alarm in middle-class circles of the party. When Cavaignac requested its approval by the Association for a Free Press, a society of lawyers, doctors, and businessmen, who paid the fines of the Republican press, it rejected the motion. In a tactful report justifying the rejection, Armand Carrel admitted that the Declaration was "the natural product of this Parisian democracy that does not enjoy political representation and lives from its daily work."[31] But while he might concede the need to create more property owners through the extension of credit, he could not accept a redistribution policy that in a property-owning country like France would necessitate a revolutionary dictatorship.

Within the sections there was pronounced hostility to the middle-class professionals who controlled the Republican press. An early brochure warned members against hypocritical Girondist lawyers and professionals who used the gestures and rhetoric of democracy to further their own personal careers.[32] The radical leaders of the society frankly preferred the natural qualities of the workers, who were "simple, upright, sensible . . . and friends of equality":

> Remaining pure in the midst of the general corruption their hearts are exalted and fill with the sublimest sentiments. Every day we have more reason to believe that it is in this fine class of proletarians that reside the hopes of the country and the future of humanity.[33]

Sponsoring the first worker on the central committee, the section of Saint Just declared: "We don't want any of that aristocracy of the society that has infiltrated into the central committee; we want a man of the people."[34] Sending brochures to Epinal, the society advised its provincial affiliate to concentrate "principally on the working class, which, purer and more devoted than any other class, has the greatest need of education."[35]

Distrusting expressions of individualism, the society wanted to create a collective social consciousness. Republican education was supposed to give a "social form" to the mind, teaching children "never to consider themselves except in relation to the body of citizens in the state."[36] Individual differences of opinion springing from middle-class sophistry were not to be tolerated: "An honest man should have only one; that which tends towards the good."[37] A directive barring factions declared, "Any individual acting outside of the circle traced by the will of all is anarchist and destructive of any social existence."[38] Only the working class seemed receptive to this effort to create a uniform collective ideology.

Analysis of membership lists uncovered at St. Pelagie prison allows us to detail the working-class composition of the Rights of Man.[39] Besides the overwhelming predominance of industrial wage-earners, over four-fifths,[40] one is struck by the almost complete absence of middle-class elements—those lawyers, doctors, businessmen, and teachers who filled the ranks of moderate Republicanism. Small also was the number of students and intellectuals—4 percent[41]—nearly all of whom were leaders in the organization. Though the central committee and administrative structure was middle class in origin, a majority of section chiefs were workers—shoemakers, joiners, painters, and saddlemakers in that order. Trades with the largest representation in the society were tailors 7 percent, jewelers 6 percent, painters 5.5 percent, articles of Paris 4.5 percent, shoemakers 4 percent, and joiners 4 percent, of whom jewelers, articles of Paris, and painters stood out in relation to their normal distribution in the population.

The workers with the greatest proportional representation were from those traditional luxury trades, with high rates of literacy and permanent residences, which had suffered extreme deprivation during the depression.[42] Absent were those unskilled and migratory workers who had played roles in the insurrections of 1830 and 1832.[43] While membership reflected normal distribution as to place of birth, the accent on youth was even more pronounced than during those insurrections, with most members between eighteen and twenty-four years of age and nearly three quarters under thirty. These were the young, unattached workers from elite trades who had faced unemployment and subsistence wages upon completion of a long apprenticeship. The Rights of Man then was an organization of workers in their early twenties, led by students and intellectuals in their twenties—a working-class army commanded by young middle-class or *déclassé* generals.

As the labor movement revived in 1833, the Rights of Man drew closer to it as an agency for workers' emancipation. From the end of 1832 the Parisian economy, notably the luxury trades, experienced a sharp recovery that prompted the formation of trade societies and strikes seeking to compensate for losses during the depression. Workers' protest and Republican propaganda had given workers a new sense of dignity. "Made great and powerful by the knowledge they have acquired of the dignity of the man who works to live and to keep alive those who do not work . . . and in the full awareness that the industrial proletarian is the most useful citizen," the Parisian gilders "placed him on the highest rung in the social scale,"[44] imposing a boycott on all shops paying less than five francs daily or allowing painters to do gilders' work. Formed in 1831 to prevent a wage cut, the Société Philanthropique des Tailleurs, or tailors' society, reorganized itself in 1832 into local sections along the lines of the Rights of Man, where its members played leading roles.

As prices rose in the fall of 1833, a new round of strikes began, involving forty thousand Parisian workers, that produced the first attempts to found trade cooperative associations and a national trade federation. In response to a lockout ordered by the largest tailoring shops, the tailors' society opened its own "national workshop" where it employed strikers and sold winter wardrobes at cost. Applying similar pressure on their employers, the box-makers, last-makers, chair-makers, and glove-makers also opened trade workshops after employers refused wage demands. When the shoemakers went out, they planned a vast workshop that would employ all forty-five thousand Parisian shoemakers and initiated the formation of a national federation of workers to provide mutual strike assistance and mutual credit for trade workshops.[45]

Finally, when the printers struck, they approved an association project introduced by Jules Leroux, brother of the Saint Simonian Pierre Leroux, for "an association to make the workers owners of their own instruments of labor." Like the *Artisan*,[46] he argued that illegal strikes and trade unionist restrictions would never improve the basic condition of the working class, suffering from an excess of competition and the institution of private ownership:

> Machines, mattes, stereotype plates, the formation of apprentices are only harmful to us because they are all the property of the masters, because they stand between them and us. Our industry does not belong to us; we have no right to its products; they replace us with inert machines or take advantage of our numbers. . . . Let us act then so that our industry belongs to us. . . . We must form an association that unites the 4,000 or 5,000 typographers of Paris. Money can be collected quickly if we ask one franc per week and the printers can then have their own enterprise.[47]

Arising spontaneously as a strike tactic, a method of employing striking workers and applying competitive pressure on employers, the trade association came to be seen as a definitive method of emancipation from the wage system.

The *Tribune* and the Rights of Man saw these associations as the beginning of a new organization of labor that could only come to fruition under the republic. Hailing the tailors' shop as the "first emancipation of labor by its own efforts," the *Tribune* predicted it was the "first step toward a new organization of industry in Europe." Denying Republican incitement of the movement, it lauded the "inventive instinct" of the workers:

"Their experience . . . taught them that the masters are only monopolizers of their labor, who appropriate the value of what they themselves have legitimately earned. The political economy of labor is more correct on this point than all the science of our government economists."[48] Still, Republicans could aid the movement by furnishing the credit that was restricted under a regime of privilege.

Similarly, the Rights of Man supported the movement, while insisting that only the republic could provide the definitive solution.[49] In two pamphlets issued during the strikes, Grignon and Efrahem, members of the society and leaders of the tailors and shoemakers, called for a federation of trades to centralize strike assistance, defending strikes as the only way of obtaining immediate relief while awaiting the "wise organization of labor" that would come with the republic.[50] On December 8 after most of the strikes had been crushed by wholesale arrests and prosecutions,[51] the propaganda committee of the society convoked leaders of various trades to draw political lessons from the defeat.[52] Since neither strikes nor associations could survive government repression, workers would have to concentrate on building the political revolution that alone could establish associations on a firm basis.[53] At a public trial two months later, Vignerte renewed the Republican pledge to the working class: "The day when France will be free and the nation sovereign, the essential duty of the Republic will be to furnish the proletarians with the means of forming themselves into cooperative associations and exploiting their own industry themselves."[54]

Thus, the Rights of Man formulated the association program for workers' ownership of industry that later, popularized by Louis Blanc and the Buchezian *L'Atelier,* would become the dominant social policy of the entire Republican movement.[55] Socialist Republicanism did not, as is often supposed,[56] consist of radically new socialist theories masking middle-class reforms. Its main contradiction was precisely the opposite, that between a traditional democratic theory derived from the French Revolution and a radically new working-class and socialist program. Within a theoretical framework that favored capitalist property, class conciliation and middle-class democracy, young Republicans had constructed an essentially working-class organization with a program of workers' associations that would undermine the basis of capitalism and the industrial middle class. Without ever abandoning their traditional proprietary analysis which opposed the people to the bourgeoisie and small to monopolistic property, Republicans developed an organization and program that contained within them the seeds of proletarian dictatorship and theoretical communism.

Notes

[1] *The Origins of Totalitarian Democracy* (London, 1952), esp. pp. 151, 249–260. Research for this article was made possible by a grant from the American Philosophical Society.

[2] The police were often the observers who first perceived the Republican threat to property relations, for example in this period the not always reliable *Mémoires de M. Gisquet*, 4 vols. (Paris, 1840), and Lucien de la Hodde, *Histoire des sociétés secrètes et du parti républicain de 1830 à 1848* (Paris, 1850).

[3] The standard narrative is Georges Weill, *Histoire du parti républicain en France de 1814 à 1870* (Paris, 1900). J. Tchernoff, *Le Parti républicain sous la Monarchie de Juillet: Formation et évolution de la doctrine républicaine* (Paris, 1901), stresses the filiation of ideas among individual Republicans rather than the formation of a collective ideology. Gabriel Perreux, *Au temps des sociétés secrètes: La propagande républicaine au début de la Monarchie de Juillet (1830–1835)* (Paris, 1931), adds the results of archival research, which is not always evaluated critically. The best Marxist analysis is Roger Garaudy, *Les sources françaises du socialisme scientifique* (Paris, 1948). Two articles that attempt to define Republican socialism are V. Volgin, "Leveling and Socialist Tendencies in French Secret Societies, 1830–1834," [in Russian] *Historical Questions*, no. 6 (1947), pp. 26–49, and Leo Loubère, "Intellectual Origins of French Jacobin Socialism," *International Review of Social History*, IX (1959), pp. 413–431.

[4] Paul Gonnet, "Esquisse de la crise économique en France de 1827 à 1832," *Revue d'histoire économique et sociale*, XXXIII (1955), pp. 284–289. Gabriel Vautier, "La misère des ouvriers en 1831," *La Révolution de 1848 et les révolutions du XIX siècle*, XXII, pp. 607–617. Archives de la Chambre de commerce de Paris, *Enquête industriel pour les années 1831–33*.

[5] Edouard Dolléans, *Histoire du mouvement ouvrier, 1830–1871*, 2 vols. (Paris, 1947), I, pp. 42–72. Jean-Pierre Aguet, *Les grèves sous la Monarchie de Juillet (1830–1874)* (Geneva, 1954), pp. 1–25. Octave Festy, *Le Mouvement ouvrier au début de la Monarchie de Juillet, 1830–1834* (Paris, 1908), pp. 34–63.

[6] September 26.

[7] October 17.

[8] Declaration of principles in *Les sociétés populaires de 1830 par un négociant* (Paris, 1830), pp. 30–34.

[9] *Manifeste de la Société des amis du peuple* (Paris, 1830), p. 23. A complete collection of Republican pamphlets in this period is being published by

M. Léon Centner of the *Editions d'histoire sociale*, who kindly furnished the author with several rare pamphlets.

[10] Alan Spitzer, *Old Hatreds and Young Hopes: The French Carbonari against the Bourbon Restoration* (Cambridge, Mass., 1971), tends to downplay the social Republicanism of the Carbonari. At the trial of the Fifteen, several Republicans referred to their Carbonari antecedents, Société des amis du peuple, *Procès des quinze* (Paris, 1832), esp. Trélat, pp. 98–109. For evidence that is not retrospective one must read *Discours et opinions de Voyer d'Argenson*, 2 vols. (Paris, 1846), esp. II, pp. 5–40.

[11] Pierre Leroux, the Saint-Simonian Republican, "De la philosophie et du Christianisme," *Revue encyclopédique*, LV (1832), pp. 281–323, believed that Saint-Simonian theories of property and exploitation were already implicit in Robespierre's Declaration.

[12] *Défense du citoyen Laponneraye, 21 avril 1832* (Paris, 1832), p. 6. Also, *Cours public d'histoire de France depuis 1789 jusqu'en 1830 par le citoyen Laponneraye* (Paris, 1832).

[13] See esp. Auguste Blanqui at the *Procès des quinze*, pp. 77–86, and his report to the society in February 1832, *Blanqui Mss.*, N.A.F. 9592. Blanqui's views were similar to those of other Republicans at the time, cf. Maurice Dommanget, *Auguste Blanqui: Des origines à révolution de 1848* (Paris, 1969), pp. 97–110.

[14] See *Le Globe*, January 20, February 23, 1831, *L'Organisateur*, October 2, 1830. Also, letter of August 30, 1829 in *Buchez Mss.*, Bibliothèque de la Ville de Paris, f. 201.

[15] Cited in the *Procès des quinze*, p. 42.

[16] Cited in *ibid.*, p. 54.

[17] *Société des amis du peuple*, September 15, 1831, p. 5.

[18] *La voix du peuple*, December 1831, p. 4.

[19] Athenée des ouvriers in *Buchez Mss.*, f. 202.

[20] *L'Européen, journal des sciences morales et politiques*, December 17, 1831, March 31, July 14, 21, 1832. François-André Isambert, "Aux origines de l'association buchézien," *Archives internationales de sociologie de coopération*, No. 6, pp. 29–66, and id., *Politique, religion et science de l'homme chez Philippe Buchez* (Paris, 1967), esp. pp. 82–89.

[21] *Discours de Cavaignac sur le droit d'association*, December 15, 1832.

[22] *La Tribune*, January 31, 1833.

[23] F. V. Raspail, *Lettres sur les prisons de Paris*, 2 vols. (Paris, 1839), I, pp. 300–333. Archives Nationales F⁷ 3885, December 29, 1831. Though the society did not itself publish Robespierrist material, its leading propagandists did so in their own names: Georges Desjardins, ed., *Table des droits de l'homme et du citoyen* (Paris, 1832), Eugène Plagniol, *Association des amis de l'égalité* (Paris, n.d.), Richard Ferrat, *Projet de constitution offert à son pays* (Paris, 1831), Henri Bonnias, *Le 9 Thermidor ou la mort de Robespierre* (Paris, 1831), and Aug. Caunes, *Des Moyens d'instituer le gouvernement de tous* (Paris, 1831). One Rousseauist article, "Loi ou religion naturelle," appeared in the *Voix du peuple*, pp. 5–9. Since Jacobin views were already widespread in the society, there is no particular reason to attribute this or other egali-

tarian writings to Buonarroti as does A. Saitta, *Filippo Buonarroti*, 2 vols. (Rome, 1950), I, pp. 142–156.

[24] F. Rittiez, *Histoire du règne de Louis Philippe, 1830 à 1848*, 3 vols. (Paris, 1855), I, pp. 366–370. AN F⁷ 3885, November 5, 21, 24, 1831.

[25] Louis Blanc, *Histoire de dix ans, 1830–1840* (Paris, 1882), pp. 525–546.

[26] For a membership list at this time see below, n. 39.

[27] Nearly all evidence on the internal operation of the society comes from the Cour des Pairs. Affaire du mois d'avril 1834. *Rapport fait à la cour par M. Girod de l'Ain*, 4 vols. (Paris, 1834), esp. I, pp. 42–79; IV, pp. 91–94, 274–430, 506–509. *Réquisitoire de M. le Procureur-Général présenté à la cour le 8 dec. 1834* (Paris, 1834.) III, pp. 56–87, and AN CC 585–619.

[28] *Ibid.*

[29] The first copy of the Declaration was published by Setier in August 1830. From 1832 multiple editions appeared of which perhaps the most popular was the *Declaration des droits de l'homme et du citoyen avec commentaire par Laponneraye, publiée par les Droits de l'homme*, in its twenty-third printing in 1833.

[30] Société des droits de l'homme et du citoyen, *De l'égalité* (Paris, 1833), p. 22.

[31] *Extrait du dossier d'un prevenu de complicité morale dans l'attentat du 28 juillet* (Paris, 1835), p. 6. Also, Rittiez, II, pp. 92–95.

[32] *Petit catéchisme républicain par un membre de la Société des droits de l'homme* (Paris, 1832), pp. 8–10.

[33] Société des droits de l'homme et du citoyen, *Au rédacteur en chef du National par J. J. Vignerte* (Paris, 1833), p. 2.

[34] *Réquisitoire*, III, p. 397.

[35] *Rapport de Girod de l'Ain*, IV, pp. 87–88.

[36] Société des droits de l'homme et du citoyen, *De l'éducation nationale* (Paris, 1833), p. 13.

[37] *Petit catéchisme*, p. 9.

[38] AN CC 611.

[39] A register in AN CC 616 entitled *Loterie patriotique pour 1832* containing 812 names with ages, professions, functions and coded sections given for most is almost certainly the membership list for 1832. Lists of 33 out of 162 sections in 1834, giving also place of birth, were printed in the *Rapport de Girod de l'Ain*, IV, pp. 274–429.

[40] Since the masters appear to be listed as such, one can assume that other professional designations refer to wage-earners.

[41] Student sections appear to have joined after 1832.

[42] Normal trade distribution was calculated on the basis of deaths in 1832 in *Recherches statistiques sur la ville de Paris et le département de la Seine* (Paris, 1844), V, and the *Statistique de l'industrie à Paris résultante de l'enquête faite par la Chambre de commerce pour les années, 1847–48* (Paris, 1851). Information on literacy and residential patterns for Parisian trades is available in the latter census.

[43] Cf. David H. Pinkney, "The Revolutionary Crowd in Paris in the 1830's," *Journal of Social History*, V (1972), pp. 521–527.

Notes

44 *Règlement de la Société de l'union des doreurs* (Paris, 1832), p. 1.

45 Aguet, pp. 66–87. Festy, pp. 202–271. *Fédération de tous les ouvriers de France, Règlement de la corporation des ouvriers cordonniers* (Paris, 1833).

46 Jules Leroux may have been the typographer who signed J. C. L. in the *Artisan*, October 30, 1830. His advocacy of workers' associations appears characteristically incompatible with his Saint-Simonian economic analysis in "Du salaire," *Revue encyclopédique*, LX (1833), pp. 118–150.

47 *Aux ouvriers typographes. De la nécessité de fonder une association ayant pour but de rendre les ouvriers propriétaires des instruments du travail* (Paris, 1833), p. 13.

48 November 7, 18, 20, 1833.

49 A retrospective police report on May 21, 1834, in AN CC 585 attributes the strike movement to a concerted plan introduced by Voyer d'Argenson and executed by the society. Designed for the prosecution of the society in the April insurrection, this report contains too many distorted and false statements to merit the credibility that Perreux, pp. 296–300, gives it.

50 *Réflexions d'un ouvrier tailleur sur la misère des ouvriers en général, etc.*, signé Grignon (Paris, 1833). *De l'association des ouvriers de tous les corps d'état*, signé Efrahem (Paris, 1833).

51 At the trial of twenty-seven leaders of the tailors the prosecution denounced the audacity of their association project: "In their delirium they went so far as to announce that there would be no more masters and that they were going to manufacture suits with association as their only equipment, without credit, without responsibility and with men who would be equal, would not take orders from anyone and who would work as they alone pleased." *Gazette des tribunaux*, December 2–3, 1833.

52 *Ibid.*, April 26–29, 1834. Those present were arrested, tried, and convicted for inciting strikes, though the strike wave had already passed.

53 See Société des droits de l'homme et du citoyen, *Association des travailleurs* signé Marc Dufraisse (Paris, 1833).

54 *Procès des citoyens Vignerte et Pagnerre, membres de la Société des droits de l'homme* (Paris, 1834), p. 8.

55 For a survey of this association movement see the author's *Origins of the French Labor Movement: The Socialism of Skilled Workers* (University of California Press, Berkeley, forthcoming).

56 Cf. Garaudy, pp. 142–145.

BIBLIOGRAPHY

Aguet, Jean-Pierre. *Les Grèves sous la Monarchie de Juillet*. Geneva, 1954.

Agulhon, Maurice. *La République au village*. Paris, 1970.

————. *Une ville ouvrière au temps du socialisme utopique: Toulon de 1815 à 1851*. Paris, 1970.

Artz, Frederick B. *France Under the Bourbon Restoration, 1814–30*. Cambridge, Mass., 1931.

Barrot, Odilon. *Mémoires posthumes*. Paris, 1875–76.

Bastid, Paul *Les Institutions politiques de la monarchie parlementaire française, 1814–88*. Paris, 1954.

————. "Le Procès des ministres de Charles X," *Revue d'histoire moderne et contemporaine*, 4 (1957), pp. 171–211.

Beach, Vincent W. *Charles X of France: His Life and Times*. Boulder, Colo., 1971.

————. "The Fall of Charles X of France: A Case Study of Revolution," *University of Colorado Studies*, Series in History, No. 2 (November 1961), pp. 21–60.

Beau de Lomenie, E. de. *Les Responsabilités des dynasties bourgeoises*. Vol. I. Paris, 1943.

Bérard, Auguste. *Souvenirs historiques sur la Révolution de 1830*. Paris, 1834.

Bertier de Sauvigny, Guillaume de, ed., *La Révolution de 1830 en France*. Paris, 1970.

————. *The Bourbon Restoration*. Philadelphia, 1966.

Bezucha, Robert. "Aspects du conflit des classes à Lyon, 1831–34." *Mouvement Social*, 76 (juillet–septembre, 1871), pp. 5–26.

Blanc, Louis. *Histoire de dix ans, 1830–1840*. Paris, 1877. 5 vols.

Bory, J-L. *La Révolution de juillet, 29 juillet 1830*. Paris, 1972.

Bourgin, Georges. "La crise ouvrière à Paris dans la second moitié de 1830." *Revue historique*, 198 (1947), pp. 203–214.

Charléty, Sébastien. *La Monarchie de juillet, 1830–1848*. Vol. V in *Historie de France contemporaine*, E. Lavisse, ed. Paris, 1921.

Chevalier, Louis. *Classes laborieuses et classes dangereuses à Paris pendant la première moitié du XIXe siècle*. Paris, 1958.

──────. *La Formation de la population parisienne au XIXe siècle*. Paris, 1950.

Cobban, Alfred. "The Middle Class in France, 1815–1848." *French Historical Studies*, V (Spring, 1967), pp. 39–52.

Comité français des sciences historiques. *1830: Etudes sur les mouvements libéraux et nationaux de 1830*. Paris, 1932.

Contamine, Henry. "La Révolution de 1830 à Metz." *Revue d'histoire moderne*, 6 (1931), pp. 115–123.

Daumard, Adeline. *Les Bourgeois de Paris au XIXe siècle*. Paris, 1970.

Demoulin, R. *La Révolution de 1830*. Bruxelles, 1950.

Dupin, André-Marie. *Mémoires de M. Dupin*. Paris, 1855–61. 4 vols.

Durand, Réné. "La Révolution de 1830 en Côte d'Or." *Revue d'histoire moderne*, 6 (1931), pp. 161–175.

Duvergier de Hauranne, Prosper. *Histoire du gouvernement parlementaire en France 1814–1848*. Paris, 1857–1871. 10 vols.

Esler, Anthony. "Youth in Revolt: The French Generation of 1830," in Robert J. Bezucha, ed., *Modern European Social History*. Lexington, Mass., 1972, pp. 301–334.

Festy, Octave. *Le Mouvement ouvrier au début de la Monarchie de Juillet*. Paris, 1908.

Gille, Bertrand. *Recherches sur la formation de la grande entreprise capitaliste, 1815–1848*. Paris, 1959.

Girard, Louis. *Etude comparée des mouvements révolutionnaires en France en 1830, 1848 et 1870–71* (Les Cours de Sorbonne). Paris, 1960. 2 fascicules.

──────. *La Garde Nationale, 1814–1871*. Paris, 1964.

Giraud-Mangin, M. "Nantes en 1830 et les journées de juillet," *Revue d'histoire moderne*, 6 (1931), pp. 445–468.

Gonnet, Paul. "Esquisse de la crise économique en France de 1827 à 1832." *Revue d'histoire économique et sociale*, 33 (1955), pp. 249–292.

Guizot, François-Pierre. *Mémoires pour servir à l'histoire de mon temps, 1807–1848*. Paris, 1872. 8 vols.

Higgs, David. *Ultraroyalism in Toulouse from its origins to the Revolution of 1830*. Baltimore, 1973.

Higonnet, Patrick-Bernard. "La Composition de la Chambre des Députés de 1827 à 1931," *Revue historique*, 239 (1968), pp. 351–379.

Hobsbawm, E.J. *The Age of Revolution*. New York, 1962.

────── and George Rudé. *Captain Swing: A Social History of the Great English Agricultural Uprisings of 1830*. New York, 1968.

Howarth, T. E. B. *Citizen King: The Life of Louis Philippe, King of the French*. London, 1961.

Johnson, Douglas W. *Guizot: Aspects of French History, 1787–1874*. Toronto, 1963.

Kent, Sherman. *Electoral Procedure under Louis-Philippe*. New Haven, 1937.

Labrousse, Ernest. "1848, 1830, 1789: Comment naissent les révolutions," in *Actes du congrès historique du centenaire de la révolution de 1848*. Paris, 1948.

Bibliography

————. *Le Mouvement ouvrier et les idées sociales en France de 1815 à la fin du XIXe siècle* (Les Cours de Sorbonne). Paris 1948. 3 fascicules.

Leuilliot, Paul. *L'Alsace au début du XIXe siècle; essais d'histoire politique, économique et religieuse, 1814–1830.* 3 vols. Paris, 1959–1960.

Lhomme, Jean. *La Grande Bourgeoisie au pouvoir, 1830–1880.* Paris, 1960.

Lucas-Dubreton, Jean. *Le Culte de Napoléon.* Paris, 1960.

Mantoux, Paul. "Patrons et ouvriers en juillet 1830." *Revue d'histoire moderne et contemporaine,* III (1901), pp. 291–296.

Moore, Barrington, Jr. *The Social Origins of Democracy and Dictatorship.* Boston, 1966.

O'Boyle, Lenore. "The Middle Class in Western Europe, 1815–48." *American Historical Review,* 71, 3 (April 1966), pp. 826–845.

Pilbeam, Pamela. "The Emergence of Opposition to the Orleanist Monarchy, August 1830—April 1831," *English Historical Review,* LXXXV (1970), pp. 12–28.

Pinkney, David H. "Laissez-faire or Intervention? Labor Policy in the First Months of the July Monarchy," *French Historical Studies,* 8 (1963), pp. 123–128.

————. "Les Ateliers de secours à Paris (1830–1831); précurseurs des Ateliers nationaux de 1848," *Revue d'histoire moderne et contemporaine,* 21 (1965), pp. 65–70.

————. "The Crowd in the French Revolution of 1830," *American Historical Review,* 70, 1 (October 1964), pp. 1–17.

————. *The French Revolution of 1830.* Princeton, N.J., 1972.

————. "The Myth of the French Revolution of 1830," *A Festschrift for Frederick B. Artz,* David H. Pinkney and Theodore Ropp, eds. Durham, N.C., 1964.

Pouthas, Charles. "La Réorganisation du Ministère de l'Intérieur et la reconstitution de l'administration préfectorale par Guizot en 1830," *Revue d'histoire moderne et contemporaine,* 9 (1962), pp. 241–263.

Prentout, Henri. "Caen en 1830," *Revue d'histoire moderne,* 6 (1931), pp. 101–114.

Price, Roger D. "The French Army and the Revolution of 1830," *European Studies Review,* III, no. 3 (1973).

Rader, Daniel L. "The Breton Association and the Press: Propaganda for 'Legal Resistance' before the July Revolution," *French Historical Studies,* 2 (1961), pp. 64–82.

Rémond, Réné. *The Right Wing in France from 1815 to DeGaulle.* Philadelphia, 1966.

Rémusat, Charles de. *Mémoires de ma vie.* Paris, 1958–67. 5 vols.

Richardson, Nicholas. *The French Prefectoral Corps, 1814–1830.* Cambridge, England, 1966.

Rudé, George. *The Crowd in History, 1750–1848.* New York, 1964.

Rule, James, and Charles Tilly. "1830 and the Un-natural History of Revolution," *Journal of Social Issues,* 28 (1972), pp. 58–74.

Soboul, Albert. "The French Rural Community in the 18th and 19th Centuries," *Past and Present,* 10 (November 1956), pp. 78–95.

Soldani, S. "Il 1830 in Europa: Dinamica e Articolazione di una caisi generale," *Studi Storici*, 13, 1 & 2 (1972), pp. 34–92, 338–372.

Spitzer, Alan. *Old Hatreds and Young Hopes: The French Carbonari Against the Bourbon Restoration.* Cambridge, Mass., 1971.

Thureau-Dangin, Paul. *Histoire de la Monarchie de Juillet.* Paris, 1888–1900. 7 vols.

Tilly, Charles. "The Changing Place of Collective Violence," in Melvin Richter, ed., *Essays in Theory and History.* Cambridge, Mass., 1970, pp. 139–164.

———. "How Protest Modernized in France, 1845–55," in W. O. Aydelotte, A. G. Bogue, and R. W. Fogel, eds., *The Dimensions of Quantitative Research in History.* Princeton, 1972, pp. 210–224.

Tudesa, André-Jean. *Les Grands Notables en France, 1840–49.* Paris, 1964. 2 vols.

Vidalenc, Jean. *Le Département de l'Eure sous la monarchie constitutionnelle, 1814–1848.* Paris, 1952.

———. "Les troubles de l'Ouest au début de la Monarchie de Juillet," *Actes du 89ᵉ Congrès National des Sociétés de Savantes*, 1963. 1, pp. 331–366.

Villat, Louis. "Besançon en 1830," *Revue d'histoire moderne*, 6 (1931), pp. 176–204.

Weill, Georges. *L'Eveil de nationalités et le mouvement libéral, 1815–48.* Paris, 1930.

———. *Histoire du parti républicain en France (1814–1870).* Paris, 1928.

———. "La Révolution de Juillet dans les départements (août-septembre, 1830)," *Revue d'histoire moderne*, 6 (1931), pp. 289–293.

INDEX